VIOLENCE AGAINST W

Violence against women is an enduring problem around the globe, yet very few books look at the full range of men's violences against women – perpetrated in relationships, in the family, in public spaces, and in institutions. While books that look at different types of violence, such as domestic violence, 'honour'-based violence and rape in isolation are useful for depth, it is only by looking across these different spheres that the true extent of men's violences against women becomes clear. This book usefully covers all of the main forms of violence against women, looking at them from a research, policy and practice perspective.

Including discussion of 15 different types of violence against women, this book is original in offering an introduction to such a broad range of topics, and for including chapters on violences that have rarely been written about, as well as those that are more commonly discussed and those that have been sidelined in recent years. By bringing together work on violence against women committed by partners, family members, strangers, acquaintances, institutions and businesses, this book widens the lens through which we view men's violences against women.

Violence against Women is essential reading for criminologists and sociologists who want to be up to date with the latest knowledge on this topic. It is also an invaluable text for those training to enter or become qualified in the specialist domestic and sexual violence sector.

Nicole Westmarland is Professor of Criminology at Durham University and Director of the Durham Centre for Research into Violence and Abuse. She has held a number of policy, practice and activist roles alongside her academic career, including Chair of Rape Crisis (England and Wales) and Special Advisor to the House of Commons Joint Committee on Human Rights for its Inquiry into Violence against Women and Girls.

'Nicole Westmarland's book *Violence Against Women* is clear, systematic, practical and devoted: it comprises the researcher's intensive experience in the field both as an academic and as an activist. Therefore it is able to offer the most recent, detailed research information, as well as descriptions about the policy-relevant "best practices". The book is very suitable both for students in the field of criminology and those interested in the phenomena more generally. Its systematic character also makes it of value to researchers and PhD students.'
Suvi Ronkainen, *Professor in Research Methodology, University of Lapland, Finland*

'*Violence against Women* documents the extent and dynamics of male violences across a broad spectrum of private, family and public life. In 15 chapters, each devoted to a form of male violence, Professor Westmarland makes a convincing case that the same gender analysis that guides our response to physical, psychological and sexual violence by partners applies equally well to child sexual abuse, violence against parents and the elderly and to the abuse cultivated by celebrity culture, in residential care homes and in educational institutions.

Drawing on the latest research, Westmarland documents the oft-noted gap between the extent of male violences and the current policies, laws and programs she describes. Like the best of feminist criminology, the book is as passionate as it is scholarly. Westmarland puts flesh on the barebones data through heart-rending accounts from victims. Meanwhile, her analyses of current events such as the Jimmy Saville crimes and the massive abuse of adult and child residents at Nottingham and Rotherham makes the book as current as the latest headlines. I know no better introduction to violence against women in modern life.'
Evan Stark, *Emeritus Professor of Public Affairs and Public Health, Rutgers University, USA*

'An invaluable resource for those starting work in the sexual violence sector.'
Lee Eggleston OBE, *Chairwoman, Rape Crisis England & Wales, UK*

'Working and thinking with Nicole Westmarland is a challenging pleasure, she is always ready to make a leap outside feminist orthodoxies whilst fiercely maintaining a feminist perspective. This book will help you think about, and possibly re-think, what we know and do not know about violence against women and girls.'
Liz Kelly, *Roddick Chair on Violence Against Women, London Metropolitan University, UK*

'*Violence against Women* offers an excellent, informative overview of the types of gendered forms of violence and the environments in which they occur. The cutting-edge content underscores the importance of understanding the many facets of violence and invites each of us to act on it. Westmarland stresses the point that violence – in all its forms – is damaging not only to individuals but also to many components of the affected systems of support and protection. The didactic exposition of the material will be appreciated by its primary audience – university students and scholars. However, the book's clarity and accessibility will also make it a captivating resource for anyone interested in learning about the disconcerting variety of men's violence against woman, or anyone affected by its existence in their life.'
Aisha K. Gill, *Associate Professor in Criminology, University of Roehampton, UK*

VIOLENCE AGAINST WOMEN

Criminological perspectives on men's violences

Nicole Westmarland

Routledge
Taylor & Francis Group
LONDON AND NEW YORK

First published 2015
by Routledge
2 Park Square, Milton Park, Abingdon, Oxon, OX14 4RN

and by Routledge
711 Third Avenue, New York, NY 10017

Routledge is an imprint of the Taylor & Francis Group, an informa business

© 2015 Nicole Westmarland

The right of Nicole Westmarland to be identified as author of this work has been asserted by her in accordance with sections 77 and 78 of the Copyright, Designs and Patents Act 1988.

All rights reserved. No part of this book may be reprinted or reproduced or utilised in any form or by any electronic, mechanical, or other means, now known or hereafter invented, including photocopying and recording, or in any information storage or retrieval system, without permission in writing from the publishers.

British Library Cataloguing in Publication Data
A catalogue record for this book is available from the British Library

Library of Congress Cataloging-in-Publication Data
Westmarland, Nicole.
Violence against women : criminological perspectives on men's violences / Nicole Westmarland.
pages cm
ISBN 978-1-84392-399-2 (hardback) — ISBN 978-1-84392-398-5 (pbk.) — ISBN 978-1-315-76883-0 (ebook) 1. Abusive men. 2. Women—Violence against. 3. Women—Crimes against. 4. Abused women. 5. Violent crimes. I. Title.
HV6250.4.W65W4654 2015
364.15082—dc23
2014043221

ISBN: 978-1-84392-399-2 (hbk)
ISBN: 978-1-84392-398-5 (pbk)
ISBN: 978-1-315-76883-0 (ebk)

Typeset in Bembo
by FiSH Books Ltd, Enfield
Printed in Great Britain by Ashford Colour Press Ltd.

This book is dedicated to the 148 women in the UK who have been killed through suspected male violence in 2014.

January
Elsie Mowbray, aged 87.
Sameena Zaman, aged 34.
Sarah O'Neill, aged 22.
Jacqueline Oakes, aged 51.
Caroline Finnegan, aged 30.
Elizabeth Thomas, age unknown.
Milena Yuliyanov, aged 27.
Karen Wild, age unknown.
Maria Duque-Tunjano, aged 48.

February
Clara Patterson, aged 82.
Anon. for legal reasons, aged 47.
Karolina Nowikiewicz, aged 25.
Hollie Gazzard, aged 20.
Leanne Meecham, aged 26.
Christine Lee, aged 66.
Lucy Lee, aged 40.
Donna Graham, aged 51.
Georgina Drinkwater, aged 30.
Tracey Snook-Kite, aged 53.
Mairead McCallion, aged 24.
Sheila Wild, aged 49.
Angela Humphrey, aged 48.

March
Patricia Anne Durrant, aged 65.
Sara Al Shourefi, aged 28.
Becky Ayres, aged 24.
Amandeep Kaur Hothi, aged 29.
Kirsty Wright, aged 21.
Rivka Holden, aged 55.
Cherylee Shennan, aged 40.
Naudel Turner, aged 42.
Shereka Marsh, aged 15.
Hazel North, aged 19.
Tracy Walters, aged 48.
Shirley Mercer, aged 43.
Kanwal Azam, aged 35.
Mashael Albasman, aged 25.
Val Forde, aged 45.

April
Doreen Walker, aged 75.
Senga Closs, aged 47.
Kayleigh-Anne Palmer, aged 16.
Sandra Boakes, aged 70.
Yvette Hallsworth, aged 36.
Isabelle Sanders, aged 51.
Judith Nibbs, aged 60.
Edna Fisher, aged 74.
Pauline Butler, aged 61.
Angela Smeaton, aged 50.
Doreen Webb, aged 64.
Elaine Duncan, aged 46.
Malgorzata Dantes, aged 54.
Ann Maguire, aged 61.
Carol Dyson, aged 53.
Susan Ashworth, aged 47.

May
Natsnet Tekle Nahisi, aged 20.
Angela Ward, aged 27.
Jessica Watkins, aged 21.
Tamara Holboll, aged 67.
Hayley Stringer, aged 29.
Emma Siswick, aged 37.
Emma Mansell, aged 37.
Eileen Glassford, aged 60.
Wendy Ambrose, aged 77.
Mary Craig, aged 43.
Dorothy Beattie, aged 51.
Tahira Ahmed, aged 38.
Helen Dillon, aged 42.
Rui Li, aged 44.
Barbara Hobbis, aged 79.

June
Yvonne Fox, aged 87.
Margaret Evans, aged 69.
Rebecca Bamber, aged 42.
Madina Landsberg, aged 31.
Francine Clark, aged 70.
Jane Bartholomew, aged 39.

Denise Dunlop, aged 32.
Nahid Al Manea, aged 31.
Mingzi Yang, aged 29.
Una Dorney, aged 87.
Sheila Crout, aged 65.
Luan Leigh, aged 42.
Cynthia Beamond, aged 80.

July
Sally Campion, aged 45.
Quoi Chang, aged 50.
Sharon Wall, aged 53.
Sharon Winters, aged 39.
Helen Dawson, aged 48.
Susan Lancaster, aged 67.
Michaela Heaton, aged 38.
Bei Carter, aged 49.
Nonita Karajavait, aged 24.
Tia Kounota, age unknown.
Eleanor Whitelaw, aged 85.

August
Carol Bland, aged 62.
Anayat Bibi, aged 39.
Elizabeth Knott, aged 70.
Sandra Talman, aged 62.
Elaine Flanagan, aged 57.
Shana Cover, aged 34.
Rukshana Miah, aged 35.
Lynn Howarth, aged 43.
Alice Gross, aged 14.

September
Meryl Parry, aged 81.
Leighann Duffy, aged 26.
Pennie Davis, aged 47.
Glynis Bensley, aged 48.
Palmira Silva, aged 82.
Serena Hickey, age uknown.
Karen Catherall, aged 45.
Hannah Witheridge, aged 23.
Dorothy Brown, aged 66.
Nicola McKenzie, aged 37.
Davinia Loynton, aged 59.

Lorna McCarthy, aged 50.
Catherine McDonald, aged 57.

October
Mariama Njie-Jallow, aged 37.
Maria Mayes, aged 67.
Melissa Mathieson, aged 18.
Donna Eastwood, aged 26.
Raheela Imran, aged 45.
Daksha Lad, aged 44.
Trisha Lad, aged 19.
Nisha Lad, aged 16.
Magdalena Welna, aged 23.

November
Leann Foley, aged 32.
Ann Cluysenaar (Jackson) aged 78.
Clare Munro, aged 47.
Margaret Tate, aged 63.
Mary Tear, aged 88.
Cerys Yemm, aged 22.
Eni Mevish, aged 20.
Jane Khalaf, aged 19.
Deborah Ruse, age unknown.
Nicola Langtree, aged 44.
Valerie Davison, aged 59.
Lydia Pascale, aged 26.
Gillian Kettyle, aged 54.
Brenda Davidson, aged 72.

December
Sannah Javed, aged 26.
Andrea Carr, aged 23.
Luciana Maurer, aged 23.
Yvonne Tapp, aged 58.
Carol Ruddy, aged 54.
Alison Morrison, aged 45.
Michelle Grey, aged 42.
Carol-Anne Taggart, age unknown.
Julie Mercer, aged 47.
Sameen Imam, aged 34.
Hawa Mohamed Abdullah, aged 40.
Sandra Brotherton, aged 60.
Nadine Aburas, aged 28.

With thanks to Karen Ingala Smith from the Counting Dead Women project for letting me reproduce this from information from her website (kareningalasmith.com/counting-dead-women/2014-2/ – list as updated 14 January 2015).

CONTENTS

List of tables   ix
Acknowledgements   x
Foreword   xi

PART 1
Men's violences in relationships   1

1   Fatal violence – partner homicide   9

2   Physical forms of partner violence   20

3   Sexual violence by partners   29

4   Psychological abuse   39

PART 2
Men's violences in the family   47

5   Violence against mothers and grandmothers   51

6   Forced marriage   61

7   'Honour'-based violence and killings   72

8   Female genital mutilation   81

9   Familial rape and abuse   93

PART 3
Men's violences in public spaces   **103**

10 Sexual violence and harassment in the workplace   107

11 Violence in streets and public spaces   120

12 Stranger and acquaintance rape   131

PART 4
Men's violences in institutions   **143**

13 Sexual violence, celebrity culture and public institutions   147

14 Institutional abuse in residential care   156

15 Violence against women in higher education institutions   164

Afterword – on outrage   *171*
Index   *173*

TABLES

1.1	Women killed by partners/ex-partners per annum 2003–13	11
2.1	Incidents of domestic violence flagged by the police, from Police incident data, Home Office	21
6.1	Summary of consultation arguments	65
6.2	Home Office programme of work	65
12.1	Reasons for not reporting rape	134
15.1	Experience of harassment, stalking, violence and sexual assault by female students	165

ACKNOWLEDGEMENTS

Writing a book as a single parent of a toddler who thinks sleep is for wimps has not been an easy task. I am grateful to those who babysat so that I could write (Amy, Lorraine, the Anderson family), and particularly Louise and Paul who had him for sleepovers. Thanks are also due to staff, postgraduate researchers, students and community members of the Durham Centre for Research into Violence and Abuse for the positive and supportive atmosphere by which they have always surrounded me. Particular thanks go to SJ, Lizzy, Katie, Hannah and Jasmine for background research, proof reading and reference checking. Geetanjali, Aisha and Karen have all kindly checked chapters for me and Nicola has usefully reminded me to take the same advice that I've handed out to others. At the School of Applied Social Sciences my colleagues have been very kind and supportive to me through difficult times. I am grateful to Routledge for bearing with me for so long with this book, especially to Heidi. Thanks also go to Vicki for kindly preparing the index for me. Last but definitely not least, I am grateful to Liz and Clare for being excellent feminist-academic big sisters to me.

When I started this book – too long ago to admit to – my lovely husband Scott was still alive. He was my rock – he stayed home to care for our baby so I could return to work, he cooked my tea for me and he got me un-lost on too many occasions to remember. I wish he were here to see it completed.

FOREWORD

In beginning this book, my intention was to join up some of the dots between different forms of men's violences against women. There are many existing books that deal with different forms of violence against women, but there are few recently published books that explicitly make visible the connections between them. It is only through making these connections that the full extent of men's violences against women becomes clear. This book is based on men's violences against women in England and Wales – if this were extended regionally or globally the connections would be seen even more boldly, and even more connections would emerge.

Invisible connections and the deafening silence

Italian scholar Patrizia Romito has highlighted the invisibility of these connections in her 2008 book *A Deafening Silence*, and this and her theorization of how men's violences can continue to be endemic in modern society act as the foundations to this book. She describes six 'tactics' that are used to support two 'strategies' that operate to hide male violence against women and children. She does acknowledge that talk of 'tactics' and 'strategies' makes male violence sound more 'organized' and less complex than it actually is, and explains that she is not suggesting that these strategies are followed consciously but rather that they are institutionalized in a range of ways.

The six tactics Romito identifies that operate to hide male violence are:

1 *euphemizing* – using language to hide the centrality of male violence against women and refusing to make the male visible in male violence;
2 *dehumanising* – allowing people to distance themselves from acts of cruelty and suffering;

xii Foreword

3   *blaming* – for example the way some forms of therapy shift the blame on to women, the way that women are taught from an early age to mediate their behaviour to prevent men from doing 'stupid things' and the way mothers are blamed for failing to protect their children;
4   *psychologising* – where a political issue is personalized and individualized, for example by saying that a perpetrator is ill and in need of treatment rather than punishment;
5   *naturalizing* – put forward by some socio-biologists and evolutionary psychologists, for example the suggestion that rape is the product of hormones that men cannot suppress; and
6   *separating* – by separating and distinguishing between different forms of men's violences against women the continuity of the acts is hidden; in particular the group of perpetrators is hidden.

The two strategies that these hiding tactics support are *legitimizing* and *denying*. Legitimizing works by not defining an act or behaviour as violence, meaning that it is visible and does not need to be hidden. Romito uses the example of male violence being tolerated when it is against women that are seen as the man's property, including crimes of 'honour' and prostitution. Denying is used when a society no longer allows the legitimizing strategy. Denying can take many forms, but '[t]he most direct form consists simply of not seeing the violence and its consequences' (Romito, 2008: 95). Romito gives the example of attributing another meaning to what has happened – so, it is denied that rape is violence and instead it is seen as 'seduction, passion, hot sex and so on' (p. 95). It is denial that Romito puts forward as the most important, as the 'strategy *par excellence* … the principal social strategy to hide male violence' (p. 122).

The importance of feminism

In the 1970s a series of national conferences were held near the beginning of the resurgence of organized feminism – the 'second wave' women's liberation movement. 'Seven demands' started their development at a conference in Oxford in 1970 and were extended to include violence against women at the National Women's Liberation Conference in 1978 in Birmingham. The 'second wave' asserted women's right to define their own sexuality and demanded:

1   equal pay for equal work;
2   equal education and job opportunities;
3   free contraception and abortion on demand;
4   free 24-hour community-controlled childcare;
5   legal and financial independence for women;
6   an end to discrimination against lesbians; and
7   freedom from intimidation by the threat or use of male violence, and an end to the laws, assumptions and institutions that perpetuate male dominance and men's aggression towards women.

As Fairbairns (2002) points out, these demands did not represent the only feminist activity at the time, and not all feminists necessarily agreed with them all. However, they did provide a useful, coherent list of demands that could be presented to the rest of the world about what the women's liberation movement wanted to achieve. She argues that they serve as a useful reminder of what it meant to be a feminist at the time, and provided structure to what was (and still is) an otherwise unstructured movement.

The seven demands of the women's liberation movement are relevant here for two reasons. The first is perhaps the most obvious – that demand number seven refers to freedom from intimidation by the threat or use of male violence. Four decades on, this demand certainly has not yet been met, as men's violences against women continue to be a serious, life-limiting, global, social problem. However, the demands are also relevant because the previous six overlap the continuing epidemic of men's violences against women. The demands all seek gender equality through an end to discrimination against women – as mothers, as lesbians, as employed workers. Although progress has undoubtedly been made, all of these forms of gender discriminations continue today, and serve to maintain a society in which male violence against women is implicitly condoned and upheld, and sometimes overtly supported and promoted.

The global adoption of feminist analysis of men's violence against women

Feminist theories of violence against women link men's violences to the systematic global discrimination against women and girls, and a world gender order that privileges certain dominant (hegemonic) masculinities (Connell, 2005). Feminist analysis of men's violences against women, as being explicitly linked to the unequal position of women and girls, has now been officially adopted by some of the world's most powerful institutions.

The 1993 United Nations Declaration on Violence Against Women confirmed that violence against women acts as an obstacle to the achievement of equality, development and peace:

> Violence against women is a manifestation of historically unequal power relations between men and women, which have led to domination over and discrimination against women by men and to the prevention of the full advancement of women, and ... violence against women is one of the crucial social mechanisms by which women are forced into a subordinate position compared with men.
>
> *(UN General Assembly, 1993: 2)*

The United Nations Secretary-General Ban Ki-moon has been unwavering in his assertion that violence against women is not inevitable, and that it could be radically reduced and eventually eliminated if the necessary political will and resources were made available (see for example United Nations Secretary-General, 2006).

The United Nations and a range of other global institutions now declare violence against women to be a cause and consequence of gender inequality. ActionAid (2010), for example, names violence against women and girls as 'one of the starkest collective failures of the international community in the 21st century' (p. 1), describing it as a means of social control that maintains unequal gender power relations and reinforces women's subordinate status.

The Istanbul Convention

The Council of Europe Convention on preventing and combating violence against women and domestic violence – known as the Istanbul Convention because of where it was opened for signature – was introduced in 2011. The Istanbul Convention takes as its starting point the link between women's inequalities and the violences committed against them. It recognizes that violence against women is a

> manifestation of historically unequal power relations between women and men, which have led to domination over, and discrimination against, women by men and to the prevention of the full advancement of women.
> *(Council of Europe, 2011: 1)*

Hence, the Convention recognizes violence against women as being structural in nature and as one of the social mechanisms that forces women into a position subordinate to men. It requires parties ratifying the Convention to put in place a broad range of measures to eliminate all forms of discrimination against women, to promote substantive equality, to empower women and to develop a comprehensive framework to protect and provide assistance to all victims of violence against women and domestic violence. At the time of writing, the United Kingdom had signed but not yet ratified the Convention.

Links and overlaps with other systems of oppression

Not all women are equal, and not all women have the same access to safety and freedom, or the resources or ability to leave a context of violence. The United Nations recognizes that some groups of women are especially vulnerable to violence, giving the following examples:

> women belonging to minority groups, indigenous women, refugee women, migrant women, women living in rural or remote communities, destitute women, women in institutions or in detention, female children, women with disabilities, elderly women and women in situations of armed conflict …
> *(UN General Assembly, 1993: 2)*

Where gender-based inequalities intersect with other systems of inequality and/or oppressions, contexts may exist that are more conducive to violence, and empowerment routes may be more restricted. For example, the police might be reluctant to intervene in partner or family violence within an Asian family, believing that such violence is culturally condoned. Women's support organizations might not be accessible to a physically disabled woman, to a woman who does not speak English or to a Black woman who does not want to use an organization that has only white workers. For women with insecure immigration status, accessing resources such as refuge accommodation is particularly difficult.

A note on violences against men

Violence happens to men as well as women. Men mostly experience violence from other men, but women also perpetrate it. Women use violence against men, against children and against other women – within intimate partner relationships, within the family, against strangers and acquaintances, in public spaces and private spaces and within institutions. Women may condone, support or promote the use of violence and abuse within institutions. Nearly all of the violences described in this book can also be committed against men by women or by other men. The fact that this book is about men's violences against women is not to suggest that any of these things do not happen, or are any less traumatic because they happen, to a boy or man.

In England and Wales and across the world, women and girls are killed, raped, attacked, harassed, sexually abused, threatened, mutilated and regulated in their everyday lives at a far higher rate than men and boys. As explained above, this is linked to the systematic global discrimination against women and girls, and a world gender order that privileges certain dominant (hegemonic) masculinities (Connell, 2005). For this reason, it is necessary to join the dots between violences that are linked to women's gender inequalities in order to make visible the connections and to increase understandings. Doing this does not negate men's experiences of violence, nor women's or men's violences that are linked to other systems of power, such as racist hate-crimes, violence against disabled people or the physical chastisement of children. All of these are violences, and are committed and perpetrated by men and women, but they are not the focus of this book. The system of power that is the focus of this book is that based on gender.

Overview of this book

Part 1 is about men's violences against women as (intimate) partners who are in or have been in relationships. Starting with the most extreme – men's fatal violence against women – domestic homicide is discussed in Chapter 1. This is followed by other forms of men's violences against women as partners – physical violence (Chapter 2), sexual violence (Chapter 3) and psychological abuse (Chapter 4).

Men's violences within the family are the focus of Part 2. Although some of the forms discussed in this Part refer to acts of violence and abuse against girls, the acts continue to have an effect into adulthood, which is the rationale for their being included. Some of the forms of violence within this section are supported by, or are even directly perpetrated by, women. For example a woman's female relatives might be involved in forced marriage or in 'honour'-based violence and killings. It is often women who arrange and perform the acts of cutting in female genital mutilation. However, these violences are all part of a system that disadvantages, further oppresses and sometimes kills women and girls. They are largely based on gender discrimination against women that operates in different ways but exists in all cultures. However, rather than 'culture' being to blame, the root is the operation of gender discrimination within different cultures that privileges men as a class and disadvantages women as a class. This is why some acts of female violence are included in a book about men's violences against women – in cases where acts by women are used to uphold men's privilege and support women's inequality. Part 2 contains chapters on men's violence against women as mothers and grandmothers (Chapter 5), forced marriage (Chapter 6), 'honour'-based violence and killings (Chapter 7), female genital mutilation (Chapter 8) and familial rape and abuse (Chapter 9).

Part 3 looks at how men as strangers and acquaintances use violences against women in public and semi-public spaces. Chapter 10 provides an overview of sexual violence and harassment in the workplace – a topic that has become subsumed more recently under headings such as 'workplace bullying' and 'respect at work', obscuring its gendered nature and in doing so erasing the connections with other forms of men's violences against women. Chapter 11 is about violence in the street and in public spaces – a topic that was very much on the agenda of feminist academics such as Liz Kelly and Betsy Stanko in the 1980s but had fallen on fallow ground until recently (in part linked to popular projects such as Everyday Sexism and Hollaback). The final chapter in this Part, Chapter 12, is about stranger and acquaintance rape.

The final part of the book – Part 4 – examines institutions as the space in which men's violences against women are committed, explicitly supported or implicitly condoned. As one of the most prolific sex offenders ever to come to the attention of the police, Chapter 13 is about Jimmy Savile and sexual violence, celebrity culture and public institutions (primarily hospitals). Chapter 14 considers sexual violence within residential care homes – where some girls and women are cared for at different points in (or throughout) their lives. The final chapter (Chapter 15) is about violence against women in higher education institutions – an issue that has been on the US agenda for many years but has only recently started to receive widespread attention in UK universities.

This book therefore contains a brief overview of 15 forms of, or spaces in which, men's violences against women operate. In covering such a wide range, the chapters should be classed as a starting point for further reading. It was impossible to give each form of violence the attention it deserved using this format. A further caveat is that some forms of men's violences against women are missing. Despite covering 15 forms, there are others in England and Wales that have not been covered – such as fatal violence against women by strangers, satanic ritual abuse and prostitution.

The personal is the political. As Liz Kelly (2014) puts it, men's violence is a political act, and our political act as feminists is to speak about it. My quest in this book to join the dots is an academic one, a personal one and a political one.

References

ActionAid (2010) *Destined to Fail? How Violence Against Women is Undoing Development*, London: ActionAid.
Connell, R.W. (2005) *Masculinities* (2nd edition), Oakland, CA: University of California Press.
Council of Europe (2011) *Council of Europe Convention on Preventing and Combating Violence Against Women and Domestic Violence*, Strasbourg: Council of Europe.
Fairbairns, Z. (2002) 'Saying what we want: Women's Liberation and the seven demands', in H. Graham, A. Neilson, E. Robertson and A. Kaloski (eds), *Saying What We Want – Women's Demands in the Feminist Seventies and Now*, University of York: Raw Nerve Books.
Kelly, L. (2014) 'Revisiting the continuum of sexual violence', keynote lecture at North East Feminist Gathering, Newcastle upon Tyne 11–12 October 2014.
Romito, P. (2008) *A Deafening Silence – Hidden Violence against Women and Children*, Bristol: Policy Press.
United Nations General Assembly (1993) Declaration on the Elimination of Violence against Women (A/RES/48/104 of 19 December 1992).
United Nations Secretary-General (2006) *Ending Violence Against Women: From Words to Action. Study of the Secretary-General*, New York: United Nations.

PART 1
Men's violences in relationships

This Part is about violence that is perpetrated against women by their partners – sometimes called intimate partner violence (IPV), domestic violence, domestic abuse or, in the USA, wife battering. For clarity, I prefer the term partner violence here rather than the more commonly used British terms 'domestic violence' and 'domestic abuse'. This is because over the years what the term 'domestic violence' covers has significantly widened, to include for example violence by other family members (this is described later), whereas this Part is specifically about violence and abuse within *intimate partner relationships*. On some occasions however, for example when referring to the work of others, the term 'partner violence' will be used interchangeably with 'domestic violence/abuse'. As in the other Parts, the focus here is on men's violence against women, though this is not to deny or excuse the existence of women's violence against men or other women, or male violence against other men as intimate partners.

The chapters in this Part look at different types of partner violence, starting with partner homicide in Chapter 1. While partner homicide is clearly the most serious, as it results in loss of life for the woman and has devastating life-long consequences for other family members, the other chapters are not ordered by seriousness, in acknowledgement that different forms of violence in different contexts can have different impacts on individual women. In other words, while on the face of it physical violence might appear to be more serious than some forms of psychological abuse such as name-calling and general 'putting down', this is not necessarily the way all women experience it and the context of violence is important. For example, a single incident of physical violence from a dating partner might not have as much an impact on a woman's life as 30 years of emotional abuse and bullying in a marriage.

Physical violence, sexual violence and psychological and financial abuse are considered in the chapters that follow (Chapters 2, 3 and 4). The nature and extent of the forms of violence are discussed, along with key policies, laws, cases and research, followed by a selection of policy and practice responses. Most of the responses described are applicable to different forms of partner violence, so are presented in the chapter they seem to fit best.

Defining domestic violence and partner violence

The term 'domestic violence' started to be used in the mid-1970s (Kelly, 1988) to describe violence and abuse within intimate relationships. By the late 1990s and early 2000s, having a definition of domestic violence that organizations were working from had become important. At first most domestic violence definitions (including the Home Office's) tended to refer only to violence within intimate partner relationships (Hester and Westmarland, 2005). However, from the mid-2000s onwards there was a move towards the inclusion of violence against other family members (e.g. child-to-parent violence), including so-called 'honour' violence, forced marriage, and occasionally female genital mutilation as well. Later, definitions started to include a more explicit recognition that violence and abuse also occur within same-sex relationships. There has also been a move by some (predominantly local authorities) to use the term 'domestic abuse' instead of 'domestic violence' in recognition that many of the behaviours listed within the definitions do not involve physical violence. For others, however, it remains important to name the physical and non-physical ways in which men threaten, abuse and restrict women as 'violence' rather than 'abuse'.

Until recently, Women's Aid defined domestic violence as:

> ... physical, sexual, psychological or financial violence that takes place within an intimate or family-type relationship and that forms a pattern of coercive and controlling behaviour. This can include forced marriage and so-called 'honour crimes'. Domestic violence may include a range of abusive behaviours, not all of which are in themselves inherently 'violent'.
> *(Women's Aid website, accessed January 2014)*

The HM Government 'cross-government definition' (which all departments have agreed on) developed over time and ended up in a place similar to the Women's Aid one for a time. The cross-government definition between 2005 and 2013 was:

> [a]ny incident of threatening behaviour, violence or abuse (psychological, physical, sexual, financial or emotional) between adults who are or have been intimate partners or family members, regardless of gender or sexuality. This includes issues of concern to black and minority ethnic (BME) communities such as so called 'honour based violence', female genital mutilation (FGM) and forced marriage.
> *(Home Office, 2012)*

In March 2013, the government expanded this definition, to include more information about the tactics that underpin partner violence:

> [a]ny incident or pattern of incidents of controlling, coercive or threatening behaviour, violence or abuse between those aged 16 or over who are or have been intimate partners or family members regardless of gender or sexuality. This can encompass, but is not limited to, the following types of abuse:
>
> - psychological
> - physical
> - sexual
> - financial
> - emotional.
>
> - Controlling behaviour is: a range of acts designed to make a person subordinate and/or dependent by isolating them from sources of support, exploiting their resources and capacities for personal gain, depriving them of the means needed for independence, resistance and escape and regulating their everyday behaviour.
> - Coercive behaviour is: an act or a pattern of acts of assault, threats, humiliation and intimidation or other abuse that is used to harm, punish, or frighten their victim. ...
>   - [This] definition, which is not a legal definition, includes so called 'honour' based violence, female genital mutilation (FGM) and forced marriage, and is clear that victims are not confined to one gender or ethnic group.
>
> (Home Office, 2013: 2)

The two key changes in this government definition are (a) reducing the age of responsibility from 18 to 16 and (b) including coercive and controlling behaviour within the definition. In a consultation about the definition of domestic violence there was clear support for making these changes (out of 506 responses 90 per cent thought the definition should change; 85 per cent thought 16–17 year olds should be included and 85 per cent thought coercive control should be included). In February 2014 Women's Aid also adopted this definition.

The origins and significance of the inclusion of the terms coercion and control are explained later in this Part (see Chapter 4). For now, suffice it to note that this is the current definition but, crucially, the behaviours within the definition are not necessarily criminal offences, as stated on page 3 of the official summary of responses to the consultation:

> This definition is not a statutory or legal definition; therefore, any change to the definition would not mean a change in the law. It is used by Government departments to inform policy development and other agencies such as the

police, the Crown Prosecution Service and the UK Border Agency to inform the identification of domestic violence cases.

(Home Office, 2012)

Therefore, only some behaviours that fall under the definitions (both old and new) of domestic violence are actually offences under the criminal law – there is no single crime of 'domestic violence'. Instead, perpetrators are arrested and prosecuted for criminal offences that exist regardless of who commits them. Some offences for which partner violence perpetrators are frequently arrested are criminal damage, common assault, actual bodily harm, harassment, threat to kill and theft (Hester and Westmarland, 2006). In other words, a perpetrator might be arrested, charged and convicted for criminal damage within a domestic violence context, but it would be 'criminal damage' and not 'domestic violence' for which they would be arrested, that would appear on their criminal record and for which they would be sentenced. At the time of writing, a new consultation was under way to consider whether coercive and controlling behaviours within intimate partner relationships should be made a specific criminal offence (Home Office, 2014).

In 2003, the government considered but ultimately decided against introducing a specific offence of 'domestic violence' or including it as an aggravating factor when sentencing, arguing that key to ensuring that violence and abuse within the home are treated as seriously as those outside the home is to treat both contexts the same within the criminal justice system:

> The Government believes that a separate offence of domestic violence would not necessarily help victims. There is a full range of charging options already. To reduce that range – common assault through to grievous bodily harm, and rape – diminishes the offence.
>
> *(HM Government, 2003: 29)*

While this approach does have some advantages – for example it allows for a broad range of offences of different levels of seriousness – it has a number of problems in practice.

First, several studies over the last decade have highlighted that perpetrators reported to the police for domestic violence are very unlikely to be convicted and punished for their offence. In a study in the Northumbria Police area in the early 2000s, it was found that only 4 out of 869 domestic violence incidents resulted in the suspect being convicted and given a custodial sentence (this equates to 0.4 per cent of incidents – fewer than one in two hundred) (Hester et al., 2003; Hester, 2006). In a similar study in Bristol, only 7 out of 784 domestic violence incidents resulted in the suspect being convicted and given a custodial sentence (this equates to 0.9 per cent of incidents – fewer than one in a hundred) (Westmarland and Hester, 2006). Critics of these figures point out that not all of these incidents are crimes, and therefore many could never result in a conviction regardless of the effectiveness of the investigation and prosecution. This is more the case for some forms of financial and psychological abuse than for physical and sexual violence. Behaviours such as 'name-calling' and 'continuously putting the victim down' are common forms of partner violence, covered within the definition of domestic violence, but would be difficult if not impossible to fit within the current criminal justice framework.

Second, a gap between how partner violence is defined in policy and criminal law terms is revealed by contrasting the cumulative nature of domestic violence in the definition and in experience, with the 'single incident' focus of the criminal law framework. As Marianne Hester and I pointed out in 2006:

> Domestic violence involves patterns of violent and abusive behaviour over time rather than individual acts. However, the criminal justice system is primarily concerned with specific incidents and it can therefore be difficult to apply criminal justice approaches in relation to domestic violence.
>
> *(Hester and Westmarland, 2006: 35)*

Similarly, Stark highlights that the term 'domestic violence' is inherently problematic as a criminal framework:

> Viewing woman abuse through the prism of the incident specific and injury-based definition of violence has concealed its major components, dynamics, and effects, including the fact that it is neither 'domestic' nor primarily about 'violence'.
>
> *(Stark, 2007: 10)*

This is a significant limitation, which means that the criminal justice framework fails to account for the 'pattern of coercive and controlling behaviour' that is contained within many definitions of domestic violence. The fact that the definition now refers explicitly to the pattern is a step forward, but is highly limited in an operational sense so long as no changes are made to the criminal law. As mentioned earlier, at the time of writing the Government was considering changing this and introducing a new criminal offence of coercive and controlling behaviour within an intimate partner relationship (Home Office, 2014).

Ethnicity and partner violence

It is important to understand the role that ethnicity plays alongside gender in the perpetration of and responses to male violence against women. Often, ethnicity is only talked about in contexts of family violence and crimes that otherwise disproportionately affect Black, Asian, minority ethnic and refugee women – such as forced marriage and female genital mutilation. Although these forms of violence against women are discussed in Part 2 (on family violence), it is important not to lose sight of how ethnicity intersects with gender for other forms of violence including partner violence. Although across the world Black and Asian women represent majority not minority groups, in England and Wales they are in the minority. Some groups of white women are also ethnic minorities within England and Wales, such as Polish women and traveller women.

Gill and others have argued that Black, Asian, minority ethnic and refugee women are 'doubly victimized' in relation to domestic violence – not only are they victims of the violence that is perpetrated against them, they are also victimized by a society that fails to provide them with support that would be appropriately empowering to them (Gill, 2004; see also Imam, 2002, Gupta, 2003, Hampton et al., 2003). This may take the form of racist responses, e.g. indifference or even hostility when women ask for protection from the state (Patel, 2003). Identified barriers include financial dependence on abusive partners arising from no recourse to public funds, lack of interpretation, previous experiences of poor police responses, community pressure and a lack of accessible information about women's legal entitlements in the UK (McWilliams and Yarnell, 2013).

Having provided an overview of some of the overarching issues relating to partner violence, particularly in how it is defined, the following chapters focus on specific forms of partner violence.

References

Gill, A. (2004) 'Voicing the silent fear: South Asian women's experiences of domestic violence', *The Howard Journal*, 43(5): 465–83.

Gupta, R. (ed.) (2003) *From Homebreakers to Jailbreakers: Southall Black Sisters*, London: Zed Books.

Hampton, R., Oliver, W. and Magarian, L. (2003) 'Domestic violence in the African American community', *Violence Against Women*, 9(5): 533–77.

Hester, M. (2006) 'Making it through the criminal justice system: attrition and domestic violence', *Social Policy and Society*, 5(1): 79–90.

Hester, M. and Westmarland, N. (2005) *Tackling Domestic Violence: Effective Interventions and Approaches*, London: Home Office.

Hester, M. and Westmarland, N. (2006) 'Domestic violence perpetrators', *Criminal Justice Matters*, 66(1): 34–5.

Hester, M., Hanmer, S., Coulson, S., Morahan, M. and Razak, A. (2003) *Domestic Violence – Making it Through the Criminal Justice System*, Bristol: University of Bristol.

HM Government (2003) *Safety and Justice: The Government's Proposals on Domestic Violence*, CM 5847, London: Home Office.

Home Office (2012) *Cross-Government Definition of Domestic Violence – A Consultation – Summary of Responses*, London: Home Office.

Home Office (2014) *Strengthening the Law on Domestic Abuse – A Consultation*, London: Home Office.

Imam, U. (2002) 'Asian children and domestic violence', in C. Humphreys (ed.), *Children's Perspectives on Domestic Violence*, London: Sage.

Kelly, L. (1988) *Surviving Sexual Violence*, Cambridge: Polity Press.

McWilliams, M. and Yarnell, P. (2013) *The Protection and Rights of Black and Minority Ethnic Women Experiencing Domestic Violence in Northern Ireland*, Belfast: Northern Ireland Council for Ethnic Minorities.

Patel, P. (2003) 'The tricky blue line: black women and policing', in R. Gupta (ed.), *From Homebreakers to Jailbreakers: Southall Black Sisters*, London: Zed Books, pp. 160–87.

Stark, E. (2007) *Coercive Control: How Men Entrap Women in Personal Life*, New York: Oxford University Press.

Westmarland, N. and Hester, M. (2006) *Time for Change*, Bristol: University of Bristol.

Women's Aid (2014) 'What is domestic violence? – Women's Aid', [online] available from www.womensaid.org.uk/domestic-violence-articles.asp?section=0001000100220041000 1&itemid=1272&itemTitle=What+is+domestic+violence (accessed January 2014).

1
FATAL VIOLENCE – PARTNER HOMICIDE

Men's fatal violence against women – also known as domestic homicides – consists of the criminal offences of murder, manslaughter and infanticide. In 1992 Jill Radford and Diana Russell edited a collection of essays on 'femicide'. In it, they argue that the term femicide is a useful alternative to the gender-neutral term 'homicide', and that it is important to connect women's homicide to violence against women – indeed, as violence in its ultimate form. They define femicide as the 'misogynistic killing of women by men' (p. xi) and the 'killing of women by men *because* they are women' (p. xiv, their emphasis). The example of Marc Lépine, who committed the mass femicide of 14 female engineering students at the University of Montreal, Canada, in 1989, clearly shows the role of misogyny within femicide. He separated the female students in a lecture theatre from the male, lined them up and shot them, calling them 'fucking feminists' and blaming them for taking the university place that he believed he was entitled to. This chapter uses the terms 'partner homicide' and 'domestic homicide' rather than femicide, partly in recognition that this chapter is not about all killings of women, and partly because these are the terms more commonly used in England and Wales. However, it is important to understand that this is an under-researched and under-theorized area of research into violence against women, and that further research is needed on the links between partner homicide and femicide.

This chapter starts with an overview of official statistics – both internationally and nationally – and then summarizes the academic research on partner homicide. Michael Atherton's triple murder is then used as an example of partner homicide, including excerpts from the Independent Police Complaints Commission inquiry that followed. Two responses are then described, domestic homicide reviews and a call for a national database on men's fatal violence against women.

Official statistics on partner homicide

Based on official statistics and previous studies of intimate partner homicides across the world, the World Health Organization estimates that 38 per cent of all women killed globally were murdered by an intimate partner, and that 6 per cent of men killed were murdered by an intimate partner. They found differences between regions, with intimate partner homicide being highest in the South-East Asia region (55 per cent of all women killed were murdered by an intimate partner) and the high-income region (41 per cent). The African region (40 per cent) and the region of the Americas (38 per cent) were a little below these levels but the authors suggest that, while these regional differences could represent differences in the cultural acceptability of violence against women and thus be 'real' difference, they could also correlate with the quality of data among countries and regions. In other words, care must be taken in accepting any differences as a true picture. The authors also point out that all the prevalence rates are likely to be under-estimations, since the victim–offender relationship was not always recorded in homicide statistics.

The most recent crime statistics for England and Wales cover crimes recorded in 2012/13 (Office for National Statistics, 2014). This data shows that after an increase in all homicides between 1961 and 2002/03, generally the figure for all homicides subsequently reduced until 2010/11, but then rose slightly in 2012/13. In 2012/13 there were, in total, 551 homicides across England and Wales (this includes murder, manslaughter and corporate manslaughter and infanticide). Of these, 69 per cent were male and 31 per cent were female. Therefore, generally speaking, it is men who are most at risk of being killed. For both male and female homicide victims, the most common method of killing was by knife or other sharp instrument such as a broken bottle – this method accounted for 35 per cent of the homicides overall. For female victims, strangulation or asphyxiation was also a common method (16 per cent of female homicide victims were killed in this way).

The data show that men who were murdered were most likely to be killed by a friend or acquaintance (38 per cent of male victims) or a stranger (38 per cent of male victims) whilst women who were murdered were most likely to be killed by a partner or ex-partner (53 per cent of women). In contrast, partners and ex-partners were the least likely group to murder men – accounting for 4 per cent of male victims of homicide. In total in 2012/13, 91 people were recorded as being killed by their partner or ex-partner and, of these, 76 were female and 15 were male.

Table 1.1 shows (using data from data Table 2.5, Office for National Statistics, 2014) the number of homicides per annum where the victim was a woman aged 16 or over who was killed by a partner or ex-partner. The numbers vary between a high of 106 in 2003/4 and a low of 76 in 2012/13.

When considering the scale of deaths of women owing to partner violence, the figures above should be considered a starting point. An unknown number of women die because of partner violence in other ways, for example through suicide

TABLE 1.1 Women killed by partners/ex-partners per annum 2003–13

2003/4	2004/5	2005/6	2006/7	2007/8	2008/9	2009/10	2010/11	2011/12	2012/13
96	106	90	90	80	102	94	96	90	76

or drug or alcohol misuse. Some women die of physical ill health because many years of abuse have left them with various health problems. There are not even any estimates of what this number might look like.

It is not known what proportion of women who were killed by partners/ex-partners had disabilities, and violence against women with disabilities is an under-researched area. However, research both in the UK and in Canada shows that women with disabilities experience high levels of domestic violence (Brownridge, 2006; Hague *et al.*, 2008) and face additional barriers to accessing support (Hague *et al.*, 2008).

Research on men who kill their partners

Dobash *et al.* (2004) conducted research into men who murder an intimate female partner. They used the Murder in Britain Survey to look at different types of murder in detail and compared 424 men who had murdered other men with 106 men who had murdered an intimate partner. Taking an in-depth look at their participants' childhood and adult lives, they found that men who had killed an intimate partner appeared more 'ordinary' or 'conventional' than men who killed other men. Those who murdered partners were significantly more likely than the men who killed other men to have achieved the equivalent of a high school education and to be regularly employed., Again, Dobash *et al.* again found that men who killed partners were more likely to have had a conventional family and childhood background than those who had killed other men. However, the men who murdered their partners were more likely to have had a father who was violent to their mother during their childhood than men who killed other men (23 per cent compared with 11 per cent). While a large proportion of both groups had been involved in persistent criminal activity, this was significantly less likely among men who killed their partners (60 per cent compared with 81 per cent of men who killed other men).

Looking at the context of the murder, and the murder itself, the men who murdered their partners were more likely to have been violent towards the same victim in the past – as would be expected, given the high level of repeat victimization that is inherent in partner violence. Supporting previous research and a body of practice knowledge from refuges and support services, Dobash *et al.* found that the period around separation was a very dangerous time for women. A further similarity they found between the two groups was that 'overkill' – using more violence than necessary to kill – was common in both groups of men (71 per cent of men who murdered other men and 64 per cent of men who killed partners).

This study provides clear support and empirical evidence for theories of partner violence that stress the issue of power and control rather than anger and impulsivity. Rather than a man 'snapping' and *losing* control, the murder was most often part of an ongoing pattern of the *use of* power and control. As the authors conclude, intimate partner murder was not associated with 'the one-off event of high emotion in which the man just "snaps" and acts *out of character* by using violence against his woman partner' but instead such murders 'are more likely to be events in which the man acts *in character* by continuing to use violence against the woman whom he has previously abused' (Dobash *et al.*, 2004: 597–8).

This research provides us with important knowledge of the risk factors associated with partner homicide, and shows that, in many ways, men who murder their partners have more conventional upbringings than men who murder other men.

Risk factors associated with partner homicide

Campbell *et al.* (2003) looked at the risk factors for homicide in abusive relationships from 11 cities across the USA, in the hope such murders could be prevented. They compared the circumstances in which 220 women were killed with those of 343 abused women who had not been killed.

They found that both an abuser's access to a firearm and his use of illicit drugs was strongly associated with intimate partner homicide. The abuser's use of alcohol was not significantly associated with homicide, and neither was alcohol or drug use by the victim. When the authors looked at relationship variables they found, echoing findings from other studies including Dobash *et al.* (2004), that separating from an abusive partner after living together leads to a higher risk of homicide, as does ever leaving or asking the abuser to leave the home. They found that if the victim had a child living at home who was not the biological child of the abuser, the risk that the woman would be murdered was more than doubled. The risk of partner homicide was found to increase where the abuser was highly controlling, and increased nine-fold with the combination of a highly controlling abuser *and* separation after previously living together. When threatening behaviour was considered in addition, previous threats with weapons and threats to kill were both associated with substantially higher homicide risks. Finally, the authors found a link (approaching statistical significance) between abusers' use of forced sex (rape) and partner homicide. Where an abuser had previously used a gun in the worst incident of abuse, the risk of homicide was increased 41 times.

Having access to a gun is less common in the UK than it is in the USA because of more stringent gun control and a different social acceptability and normality of guns. However, this has not prevented debate around the role of guns in the UK, because of their use in some UK-based partner homicides – of particular interest has been whether or not men who are known by the police to use violence against their partners should be granted firearms licences. This question was particularly relevant in the Michael Atherton murders.

The murders by Michael Atherton

In the early hours of New Year's Day 2012, Michael Atherton shot and killed three women – his partner (Susan McGoldrick) and his partner's sister and daughter. He then shot himself. Atherton had a history of domestic abuse, but legally owned six weapons including three shotguns. The case was referred to the Independent Police Complaints Commission (IPCC) to investigate Durham Constabulary's actions in the granting, management and review of Atherton's shotgun certificate and firearms license (IPCC, 2012, Reference: 2012/000063). The IPCC was of the opinion that Durham Constabulary knew of a number of incidents that should have cast doubts upon Atherton's suitability to hold firearms. They noted that this had been discussed within Durham Constabulary following an incident in September 2008, which resulted in the revocation of his certificate and licence – but the decision was subsequently taken to return his weapons.

The domestic violence incidents listed by the IPCC included Atherton being arrested to prevent a breach of the peace (in 2002), and McGoldrick being dragged out of bed by her hair and repeatedly kicked in the ribs (in 2004, for which Atherton was given a police caution for assault). In 2003, when McGoldrick was found at the bottom of the stairs with an injury to her arm, she declined to provide a statement, instead telling the police that she had accidentally fallen down the stairs during an argument. The police officer that attended on that occasion recorded that McGoldrick was displaying 'classic symptoms of emotional abuse' and left details of a women's refuge with her. Despite this catalogue of recorded abuse against McGoldrick, the police officer reviewing Atherton's application for a shotgun certificate decided to recommend the granting of the shotgun licence. However, in the 'general comments' section he acknowledged the history of partner assault and 'domestic incidents', but noted that the partner was present upon interview and that there she appeared to have no concerns (hence failing to recognize the dynamics of domestic violence and the need to speak to her away from the perpetrator).

The application was then sent to the Firearms Licensing Supervisor for review, who questioned whether Atherton should be granted the shotgun licence, attaching a handwritten 'post-it' note to the file that read:

> 4 domestics – last one 24/4/04 – was cautioned for assault. Still resides with partner & [name redacted]. Would like to refuse – have we sufficient info – refuse re public safety.
>
> *(IPCC report, para. 25)*

The Deputy Force Solicitor considered the case and gave legal advice that, if they refused and Atherton appealed, they might 'hit an evidential cul-de-sac' because McGoldrick would be unlikely to be willing to give evidence against her partner. Accordingly, the application for a shotgun licence was granted in 2007, accompanied by a 'warning letter' about further acts of domestic violence.

In 2008, Atherton made a further application, this time for a firearms licence for the purposes of vermin control and target shooting. Again, the licence was granted, accompanied by a warning letter. Later, in September 2008, police were called to Atherton's home following a call from McGoldrick. There had been an 'altercation' involving the two of them and McGoldrick's sister, and Atherton was threatening to 'shoot his head off'. The call handler advised McGoldrick to get herself and her two children out of the house. Atherton was arrested for a Breach of the Peace and, although he had not been armed during the incident, his weapons were removed for safekeeping. An investigation was conducted into whether his guns could be returned, and it was also noted that since the granting of his shotgun licence in 2006, two 'domestic incidents' and one arrest for an incident of affray (though not related to domestic violence) had been logged. It was decided that the guns and the firearms licence be returned (the shotgun licence had not actually been removed at the time of the September 2008 incident) along with a personally served 'final stern and clear warning letter'.

The IPCC concluded that significant information from the Domestic Violence Unit had been overlooked, that no meaningful dialogue had taken place with Atherton or his family to establish the dynamics of the household following the September 2008 incident, that staff in the Firearms Licensing Unit had received little or no formal training by Durham Constabulary, and that decisions had been based on simple paper reviews of previous evidence rather than a review of the circumstances as a whole. They noted that Durham Constabulary had subsequently reviewed their processes and procedures linked to the administration of firearm and shotgun licences. The case has since been influential in national policy discussions.

Responses to partner homicide – Domestic Homicide Reviews

Domestic homicide reviews were first established as part of the 2004 Domestic Violence, Crime and Victims Act, but did not come into force until April 2011. Before then, some areas were already doing them on a voluntary basis. Domestic homicide reviews (DHR) take place following the death of a person aged 16 or over through violence, abuse or neglect and where the alleged perpetrator is related to the victim, is a member of the same household or had been in an intimate personal relationship. They are not intended to replace the work of coroners or criminal courts, which look at how the victim died or who is individually culpable. Rather, the purpose of a DHR is to examine the circumstances around the homicide in order to:

> a) establish what lessons are to be learned from the domestic homicide regarding the way in which local professionals and organisations work individually and together to safeguard victims;
> b) identify clearly what those lessons are both within and between agencies, how and within what timescales they will be acted on, and what is expected to change as a result;

c) apply these lessons to service responses including changes to policies and procedures as appropriate; and

d) prevent domestic violence and abuse homicide and improve service responses for all domestic violence and abuse victims and their children through improved intra and inter-agency working.

(Home Office, 2013a: 6)

Although the guidance for conducting reviews highlights that each homicide will have specific issues that should be explored, they should generally cover the decision-making process and the actions taken or, crucially, not taken. Suggestions of questions that reviews should ask include 'Had the victim disclosed the abuse to anyone and if so, was the response appropriate?', 'Were procedures sensitive to the ethnic, cultural, linguistic and religious identity of the victim, the perpetrator and their families?' and 'To what degree could the homicide have been accurately predicted and prevented?' In one sense, then, by looking at how agencies responded or failed to respond to domestic violence and placing responsibilities on them to act, DHRs can be seen as fitting perfectly into a coordinated community response to domestic violence with agencies having layers of accountability and not being able to ignore or deny violence and abuse.

In 2013 the Home Office analysed the 54 DHRs conducted between their introduction in 2011 and 31 March 2013 in an attempt to draw out some common lessons (Home Office, 2013b). The common themes (which were found in many but not all reviews) were identified as needing more work in the areas of:

- *Raising awareness and communication*: gaps were found in awareness and understanding of domestic violence, in particular that it consists only of physical violence. The analysis found that, despite coercive control being an important risk factor for domestic homicide, there were DHRs in which the power and control aspects were not recognized.
- *Awareness and training for healthcare professionals*: the DHRs highlighted instances of disclosures being made but not followed up by GPs and other healthcare professionals – in some cases reviews stated that the healthcare professional had not known what to do or who to refer to following the disclosure.
- *Information sharing and multi-agency working:* poor information sharing had led to a lack of full understanding of the risks r of a full picture of the situation in some cases. Although on occasion some agencies had not shared information because they felt it would have placed the victim at greater risk, there were cases where sharing was inadequate and the information could have been lawfully shared – preferably with victim consent.
- *Complex needs:* where victims and/or perpetrators had other problems as well as the domestic and sexual abuse, for example alcohol and/or substance misuse or mental illness, the domestic violence and abuse were not always identified. Evidence of 'silo working' was found, meaning poor cooperation or coordination across agencies.

- *Perpetrators and bail:* information sharing was also found to be a problem where a perpetrator had been released on bail or from prison – in some cases existing processes and procedures were not followed. Some examples were found in which perpetrators had returned or attempted to return to the victim's home after release, owing to a lack of suitable accommodation being available.
- *Awareness of the safeguarding needs of children:* in a small number of cases opportunities to make referrals to Children's Services were missed, since the impact of domestic violence and abuse on children had not been considered because the abuse was viewed as solely occurring between adults.

There is no other research yet on DHRs so their ability to create change on a local and national level, and ultimately to reduce the number of domestic homicides, is not yet clear.

However, it is worth pointing out that opinions on whether homicides were preventable or not are highly subjective. Returning to the Atherton case described earlier, in which the IPCC identified a range of failings in the police's actions, the opinion of the DHR overview writer was that it was impossible to say that the deaths were predictable or that, if other actions had been taken, the eventual tragic outcome would have been averted. This contrasts with the view given by the coroner, who was of the opinion that the deaths certainly had been avoidable:

> Whilst it is therefore difficult to state with any certainty that any of the deaths was predictable there were missed opportunities across a range of service providers, where further investigation, intervention and diversion was possible to establish and examine in more detail the violence and alcohol abuse within the home environment. This would have raised overall concerns about both family and possibly the wider matter of public safety. Even if any of the opportunities had in fact been taken and completed in line with what is now regarded as best practice, it cannot be said with absolute conviction that they would have made a difference to the eventual tragic outcome.
> (DHR Overview author, in Safe Durham Partnership Board, *Domestic Homicide Overview Report*)

> In my opinion these deaths were avoidable. The systemic shortcomings highlighted by me today lead me to conclude, that on a balance of probabilities, the four deceased would not have died when they did in the manner they did had there been robust, clear and accountable procedures in place.
> (Coroner, cited in Safe Durham Partnership Board, *Domestic Homicide Overview Report*)

Therefore, as regards domestic homicide and its risk factors, DHRs might be better placed to learn lessons across sites than to act as any form of 'inquiry' into agencies' actions. For 'inquiry' to be realized, there will need to be more openness about the reports, and a larger number of people outside local authorities (academics and voluntary sector organisations) need to be involved for greater transparency in the analysis of lessons.

Responses to partner homicide – calls for a national database

Karen Ingala Smith is a feminist activist in the area of male violence against women. In 2012 she started a blog called 'Counting Dead Women' in which she talks about women and homicide, and makes sure that women's stories and, crucially, men's violence, are made visible. She keeps track of every woman who is known to have been killed by men to make sure they are known about and not forgotten. In her blog, she explains why she set up the 'Counting Dead Women' project.[1] She explains that, while the Home Office does record and publish data on homicide victims, including the relationship status and sex of the victim, this does not provide enough information to tell us about fatal male violence against women. Specifically, she points out that the Home Office data does not mention the sex of the killer, that it does not connect different forms of male violence against women and, finally but crucially, that it dehumanizes women. As she observes, the statement that 'on average two women per week are killed through domestic violence in England and Wales' is trotted out so frequently – in training days, introductions to reports, lectures – that people do not seem to get outraged or upset about it any more. In addition, by only looking at the ways in which women are killed within the domestic violence context, killings of women by men outside this context are rendered invisible and not talked about. She explains that 'through connecting and naming the women killed, I'm trying to make the horror and unacceptability of what is happening feel more real' (Ingala Smith website, accessed October 2014).

Ingala Smith's work therefore not only counts women who have died because of partner violence, but extends the survey to the killing of women by men in a wider range of contexts: as strangers, as family members, as work colleagues, as sons, as brothers, etc. as well as in the role of partner. This results in a larger number than the 'two women per week', or the partner homicide numbers listed earlier in this chapter. According to Ingala Smith's counts, 143 UK women were killed through suspected male violence in 2013 and 126 women in 2012. While this chapter is about partner homicide, not all killings of women, the disparity between the official figures and Ingala Smith's figures does highlight the importance of being specific about what is classed as domestic violence and demanding clarity when the term is used. While Ingala Smith is clear that her figures are of deaths of women at the hands of any men – known or otherwise – the official figures relate only to partner violence; nonetheless the term 'domestic violence' is used in the 'two women per week' statement. In fact, if family violence and 'honour'-based violence were added in, as well as any deaths following female genital mutilation, on the government's own definition the figure would be much higher – and closer to Ingala Smith's findings.

At the time of writing, Ingala Smith, who is also Chief Executive of domestic violence charity Nia, was collaborating with Women's Aid with the support of law firm Freshfields Bruckhaus Deringer to develop a database of all killings of women by men over the last five years in England in order to build a clearer picture.

Summary

We are a probably a long way from being able to stop men from committing acts of fatal violence against their female partners and ex-partners. While Domestic Homicide Reviews are a step forward, lessons learned need to be put into practice. Greater knowledge about men's fatal violence against women is essential to being able to intervene and provide the protection that women need at times of particularly high risk – such as soon after they leave a relationship. It is important to remember the lessons from the research by Dobash et al. (2004) – that on a number of dimensions men who murder partners differ from men who murder other men and that they tend to have fairly conventional lives and childhoods. This means that it is particularly important not to rely on stereotypes of 'murderers' when considering which men might kill their partners. In some cases there might be little that people around the woman could have done to keep her safe from a man determined to kill her. In other cases there are obvious problems – such as allowing a known perpetrator of domestic violence to have a gun licence as in the Atherton case.

Note

1 I am grateful to Karen Ingala Smith for her kind permission to reproduce material in this chapter.

References

Brownridge, D. (2006) 'Partner violence against women with disabilities: prevalence, risk and explanations', *Violence Against Women*, 12(9): 805–22.

Campbell, J.C., Webster, D., Koziol-McLain, J., Block, C., Campbell, D., Curry, M.A., Gary, F., Glass, N., McFarlane, J., Sachs, C., Sharps, P., Ulrich, Y., Wilt, S.A., Manganello, J., Xiao, X., Schollenberger, J., Frye, V. and Laughon, K.. (2003) 'Risk factors for femicide in abusive relationships: results from a multisite case control study', *American Journal of Public Health*, 93(7): 1089–97.

Dobash, R.E., Dobash, R.P., Cavanagh, K. and Lewis, R. (2004) 'Not an ordinary killer – just an ordinary guy. When men murder an intimate woman partner', *Violence Against Women*, 10(6): 577–605.

Domestic Violence, Crime and Victims Act 2004, London: HMSO.

Hague, G., Thiara, R.K., Magowan, P. and Mullender, A. (2008) *Making the Links – Disabled Women and Domestic Violence*, Bristol: Women's Aid Federation of England.

Home Office (2013a) *Multi-agency Statutory Guidance for the Conduct of Domestic Homicide Reviews* (revised 1 August 2013), London: Home Office.

Home Office (2013b) *Domestic Homicide Reviews – Common Themes Identified as Lessons to be Learned*, London: Home Office.

Independent Police Complaints Commission (IPCC) (2012) *Mr Michael Atherton – IPCC Investigation into the Granting, Management and Review of his Shotgun Certificate and Firearm Licence by Durham Constabulary*, Independent Investigation Final Report, IPCC reference 2012/000063, London: IPCC.

Ingala Smith, K. (2014) Counting Dead Women campaign, available at http://kareningalasmith.com/counting-dead-women/.

Office for National Statistics (2014) *Crime Statistics, Focus on Violence Crime and Sexual Offences, 2012/13*, London: Office for National Statistics.

Safe Durham Partnership Board (2013) *Domestic Homicide Overview Report, in Respect of Adult A, Adult B, Adult C, Adult D, Adult E, Adult F*, prepared by independent Overview report author Russell Wate, Durham: Safe Durham Partnership Board [online]. Available from: http://content.durham.gov.uk/PDFRepository/DHR_004_SDP_DHR_Report_FINAL.pdf (accessed 13 January 2015).

2
PHYSICAL FORMS OF PARTNER VIOLENCE

Non-fatal physical forms of partner violence include acts such as pushing, slapping, hitting with a fist or other object, biting, kicking, scratching, burning, strangling, asphyxiating, stabbing, hair pulling, arm or finger twisting and bone breaking. Injuries may be visible, though are often hidden, with physical signs of abuse confined to the torso and lower body that can be hidden by clothing. This type of partner violence can also include throwing and/or breaking objects, commonly items such as food, plates or drinks, and putting fists through doors or windows.

This chapter starts with an overview of official statistics, based on police figures and the government's self-report study. Given that 'domestic violence' is not a standalone criminal offence, as explained in the introduction to this Part, some of the criminal offences that relate to physical violence against women are then listed. A lot of space is given within this chapter to responses to partner violence, though these are equally applicable to physical and non-physical forms of partner violence so also refer to some of the chapters that follow – particularly Chapter 4 on psychological abuse. Domestic violence perpetrator programmes, domestic violence protection orders and the domestic violence disclosure scheme ('Clare's Law') are described in this chapter.

Official statistics

Since partner violence is not a specific crime, it is difficult to know exactly how much domestic violence is recorded within crime statistics. This is because the police must first identify an incident as being domestic abuse. Table 2.1 below shows incidents reported to the police that were flagged up by them as falling under the definition of 'any incidence of threatening behaviour, violence or abuse (psychological, physical, sexual, financial or emotional) between adults, aged 18 and over, who are or have been intimate partners or family members, regardless of gender or sexuality'.

TABLE 2.1 Incidents of domestic violence flagged by the police, from Police incident data, Home Office

England and Wales Police force region	Police incidents 2007/08	2011/12
North East	45,382	55,619
North West	*61,856	120,080
Yorkshire & the Humber	65,620	85,154
East Midlands	41,722	58,161
West Midlands	*65,281	70,922
East of England	58,706	76,368
London	84,142	118,169
South East	95,217	107,917
South West	49,616	*52,715
Wales	*12,696	51,830
Total England and Wales	**580,238**	**796,935**

Note: *These forces have missing data, which makes comparisons difficult.

Police-recorded statistics are widely acknowledged as being only the 'tip of the iceberg' of domestic violence that exists, since it remains so under-reported. Likewise, when looking at numbers of reported incidents, it is increases rather than decreases that are generally acknowledged to be positive in police recording – suggesting that more victims feel able to report violence to the police and that the police are recording incidents properly. The figures for 2007/08 are presented in Table 2.1 alongside those for 2011/12 to show how the recording of incidents increased during this time (around 37 per cent in total, though this does not account for missing data). Every region with complete data saw an increase over this period, which is the direction of travel that would be expected. It is also important to remember that the table shows not only a number of forms of physical and non-physical partner violence, but also a selection of familial violences. Despite these limitations, the figures are useful for getting a general idea of how much violence is reported to and correctly recorded by the police.

Another measure of physical forms of partner violence is the Crime Survey for England and Wales (hereafter Crime Survey – formerly the British Crime Survey). The Crime Survey measures 'intimate violence', which the researchers use as a collective term to refer to physical and non-physical abuse consisting of partner abuse, family abuse, sexual assault and stalking. The non-sexual partner violence element of the Crime Survey asks the following question:

> Thinking about ANY relationships you have had since you were 16, has any PARTNER ever done any of the following things to you? By partner, we mean any boyfriend or girlfriend, as well as a husband, wife or civil partner.

YOU CAN CHOOSE MORE THAN ONE ANSWER TO THIS QUESTION IF YOU WISH

1. Prevented you from having your fair share of the household money
2. Stopped you from seeing friends and relatives
3. Repeatedly belittled you to the extent that you felt worthless
4. Frightened you, by threatening to hurt you or someone close to you
5. Pushed you, held you down or slapped you
6. Kicked, bit, or hit you with a fist or something else, or threw something at you
7. Choked or tried to strangle you
8. Threatened you with a weapon, for example a stick or a knife
9. Threatened to kill you
10. Used a weapon against you, for example a stick or a knife
11. Used some other kind of force against you
12. None of these
13. Have never had a partner/been in a relationship
14. Don't know/can't remember
15. Don't wish to answer

The results of this question reveal that 18.5 per cent of respondents experienced at least one form of non-sexual partner abuse at some point since the age of 16 (24.3 per cent of women and 12.7 per cent of men). The Crime Survey also asks whether these forms of non-sexual partner abuse have happened in the previous 12 months, and the results show that 3.6 per cent experienced this in the last year (4.2 per cent of women and 3 per cent of men) (Office for National Statistics, 2013).

Again, this data refers to a range of types of violence, not just physical violence as per the subject of this part of the book, but it was not possible to divide the 15 points shown in the question box, as the data were not published separately.

Criminal offences – physical forms of partner violence

Some of the criminal offences that offenders can be charged with that constitute physical forms of partner violence are:

- assault occasioning bodily harm – common assault (Offences against the Person Act 1861, s47)
- affray (Public Order Act 1986, s3)
- common assault and battery (Criminal Justice Act 1988, s39)
- shooting or attempting to shoot, or wounding, with intent to do grievous bodily harm (Offences against the Person Act 1861, s18) and
- inflicting bodily injury with or without a weapon (Offences against the Person Act 1861, s20).

Types of physical violence and overlaps with other forms of violence and abuse

In Gill's (2004) study of South Asian women who had experienced partner abuse, examples of the types of violence experienced included being slapped, pushed, physically restrained, choked, hit with a closed hand and hit with an object. While nearly all of the women in her study (17 out of 18) accepted that these acts did constitute physical abuse, she found that many of the women denied this to some extent – arguing that men did not always know that their actions were harmful. Gill argues that this points to a subculture of tolerance of violence against women by some Asian men, in which violence is culturally sanctioned. One of the women interviewed, who had endured physical violence for eight years from her husband, told Gill:

> Just because he slapped me occasionally doesn't mean he really hit me. I didn't consider it as violence ... I don't think he recognises it is wrong.
>
> *(Deep, in Gill, 2004: 473)*

It is also clear from Gill's study how different forms of violence and abuse overlap and often escalate within relationships. Most of the women in her study reported that emotional abuse was used in tandem with physical abuse. One of the women she interviewed – 'Sofia' – explained that at first her partner exerted a little control over her, for example always checking what she was wearing, warning her if she looked at another man and picking her up from places she went. But then it got worse, and he slapped her because she had challenged a decision he had made. The physical violence continued to escalate until it was happening almost every week: 'It seemed like I could not do anything right. I was always doing something wrong' ('Sofia' in Gill, 2004: 470).

Women with disabilities and physical violence from partners

As mentioned in Chapter 1, women with disabilities may be at a greater risk of experiencing partner violence. Where a woman's partner is also her carer, this can increase the net of control that surrounds her. Hague *et al.* (2008) found many examples of this in their research, and also found that this prevented women with disabilities from accessing help and support. Just some of the examples of partner violence in their research included unplugging the battery from a woman's wheelchair, pushing a woman over, placing a phone out of a woman's reach, putting a woman on the stairs where she would be stuck, grabbing a woman's hair, repeatedly raping a woman and a man attempting to suffocate a woman by putting his hand over her mouth. Hague *et al.* (2008) report that some of the women were made to feel that they did not deserve a relationship because of their disability, and that they should be grateful to their partner.

Policy and practice responses to physical forms of partner violence

The policy and practice responses discussed below are relevant to all forms of partner abuse, not just physical abuse.

Responses – perpetrator programmes

A domestic violence perpetrator programme is a groupwork programme for men who want to stop using violence and abuse within intimate partner relationships. They developed in the UK in the late 1980s and early 1990s, and marked a departure from previous domestic violence activism and practice, which had mainly focused on working with women and children (Phillips *et al.*, 2013). There is ongoing debate internationally about the value of domestic violence perpetrator programmes. The question 'but do they work?' is frequently asked, and has only complicated answers. It has not been clear what 'works' means in this context, with many of the early studies using only police reports of physical violence, and/or studying only convicted offenders.

The largest UK study was undertaken by Dobash *et al.* (2000) in Scotland, who compared two groups of men convicted for offences related to domestic violence. The first group were sentenced to attend a domestic violence perpetrator programme and the second received a criminal sentence. The authors found that, during the 12 months after the sentence or programme ended, those attending the perpetrator programme were less likely to use violence in a relationship than those receiving criminal sentences. In the USA, Gondolf (2002) included both court-mandated men and voluntary attendees in his multi-site evaluation of 600 men who had attended well-established perpetrator programmes. He compared those who completed the programme with those who dropped out of it in the early stages and asked their female partners/ex-partners whether violence and abuse had continued or not. He found that men who completed the programme were far more likely to stop using violence than men who dropped out, and that the majority of men who completed the programme were no longer using violence within a relationship at the four-year follow-up point.

The most in-depth study was conducted in the UK by Liz Kelly and myself – called 'Project Mirabal' (after the Mirabal sisters who were assassinated for opposing the dictatorship of Rafael Trujillo). In the early months of Project Mirabal we wanted to see how a range of different groups (men on programmes, female partners/ex-partners, practitioners, funders/commissioners) defined success from their perspective. We found the definitions went far beyond the simplistic 'no more violence' and that success can be broken down into six key measures of success, which apply whether the partners stay together or decide to separate (see Westmarland *et al.*, 2010, Westmarland and Kelly, 2012). The six measures of success are:

1   an improved relationship between men on programmes and their partners/ex-partners, which is underpinned by respect and effective communication;
2   for partners/ex-partners to have an expanded 'space for action' that empowers through restoring their voice and ability to make choices, whilst improving their well being;
3   safety and freedom from violence and abuse for women and children;
4   safe, positive and shared parenting;
5   for men on programmes, enhanced awareness of self and others including an understanding of the impact that domestic violence had on their partner and children; and
6   for children, safer, healthier childhoods in which they feel heard and cared about.

We used a range of research methods – including a longitudinal telephone survey of 100 women whose partners or ex-partners had attended a domestic violence perpetrator programme (covering a 15-month period – from 3 months before the start of the programme until 12 months after the start of the programme), and in-depth interviews with 64 men and 48 female partners or ex-partners near the start and near the end of the man's attendance on a programme (for more information see final report and related publications at www.dur.ac.uk/criva/projectmirabal accessed 16 January 2015).

We found dramatic and significant reductions across the indicators for measure 3 (safety and freedom from violence and abuse for women and children) – particularly in relation to physical and sexual violence (Kelly and Westmarland, 2015). The number of women saying their partner 'made you do something sexual that you did not want to do' reduced from 30 per cent before the programme to zero after it, and the response to 'used a weapon against you' reduced a similar amount (29 per cent to zero). The numbers of women who answered 'Yes' to 'slapped you, pushed you, or thr[ew] something at you' reduced from 87 per cent of the group surveyed before to 7 per cent after. Far fewer women reported being physically injured after the programme (61 per cent before fell to 2 per cent after) and the extent to which children saw/overheard violence also dropped substantially (from 80 per cent to 8 per cent).

However, up to half of the women continued to experience harassment and other abusive acts. These acts did reduce – though not to the same extent as physical and sexual violence. Nonetheless, over half of the women reported feeling 'very safe' after the programme, compared to less than one in ten before it (8 per cent increased to 51 per cent). The qualitative interviews echoed these findings. Overall we found little support for the idea that DVPPs teach men how to be 'better', 'more manipulative' abusers.

For the other measures of success, improvements were found in both the survey and the in-depth interviews. For example, the percentage of women reporting 'he tries to prevent me seeing or contacting my friends/family' reduced from 65 per cent before the programme to 15 per cent after it, and reports that 'he tells me to change the way I dress or my appearance' decreased from 57 per cent of women in the survey to 16 per cent. However, more marginal improvements were seen for other indicators; for example, the percentage reporting 'he tries to use money/finances to control me' improved only marginally.

Responses – Domestic Violence Protection Orders

A Domestic Violence Protection Order (DVPO) can remove a perpetrator from the household and/or prevent contact with victim-survivors (under the Crime and Security Act 2010). DVPOs were piloted in three police force areas (Greater Manchester, West Mercia and Wiltshire) in 2011/12. They were designed to provide some form of protection to victim-survivors where no other enforceable restrictions were available to the police. Senior police officers are able to authorize the issuing of an initial temporary domestic violence protection notice (DVPN) to the perpetrator, and then apply to the magistrates' court for a 14–28 day DVPO.

Kelly *et al.* (2013) evaluated DVPOs using surveys, interviews and focus groups. They considered how the orders are implemented and delivered across the three pilot sites and estimated the impact of the pilot on re-victimization (comparing differences in the numbers of domestic violence incidents occurring before and after a DVPO or another response) and looked at the order's value for money. They found that most DVPOs were granted by the courts after DVPNs had first been authorized by senior police officers – and that more than three-quarters were for the maximum period of 28 days. A very low breach rate was recorded – of just 1 per cent – although this may reflect reporting and recording patterns more than actual breaches. Interviews showed that DVPOs were viewed positively by police, practitioners and victim-survivors. Most victim-survivors reported feeling safer and being glad of the time and space a DVPO gave them to consider their options. The researchers were only able to measure re-victimization by using police records – and they acknowledge the limitations associated with this type of measure. With these caveats, they found that DVPOs had reduced levels of police-recorded re-victimization when compared with cases that had been assigned to 'no further action' following arrest. They found this effect to be heightened in chronic cases (defined here as three or more police call-outs for domestic violence). Kelly *et al.* (2013) conclude that, although their study had limitations including a short follow-up period, a reliance on police re-victimization data and a lack of ability to control for other variables, the research suggests overall that DVPOs have had a positive impact.

On 25 November 2013, to mark the International Day of Action to End Violence Against Women, Home Secretary Theresa May announced that DVPOs would be rolled out across England and Wales from 2014.

Responses – Domestic Violence Disclosure Scheme – right to ask and right to know ('Clare's Law')

As part of the 25 November announcement discussed above, Theresa May also announced that the Domestic Violence Disclosure Scheme would be rolled out nationally. Under certain circumstances, the scheme allows women to be told if their partner had perpetrated partner violence in a previous relationship. This is two-pronged and consists of the *right to ask* (where information is disclosed following a request from a member of the public such as the woman herself or a member of her family) and the *right to know* (where the police make a proactive decision to disclose information in order to protect a potential victim). The Scheme is more commonly known as 'Clare's Law', after Clare Wood who was murdered by George Appleton – her ex-partner – in 2009. She had been unaware of his history of violence against women, and her father – Michael Brown – campaigned for this change as he believed that, had such measures been in place earlier, his daughter might have been saved. In an interview for the BBC News he said – on hearing that the pilot was to be rolled out nationally – 'I'm hoping at the very least there is going to be a substantial drop in death figures'.

Domestic violence practitioners, however, have been sceptical of the usefulness of this change. For example, Karen Ingala Smith points out that in Greater Manchester (which was one of the pilot sites, so was one of the earliest adopters of the scheme) 16 women have been killed by their intimate partner since 2012 (personal correspondence with Ingala Smith, August 2014). In multi-agency meetings I have attended, there seems an almost automatic referral to Children's Services if women with children decide not to leave their partner after being told about his violent past.

Summary

This chapter has described the difficulties involved in discovering how much physical violence exists. Although nearly all police force regions have reported increased rates of reporting over recent years, this is generally considered to be positive rather than negative – suggesting that victims are more likely to make a report to the police, rather than that more incidents are occurring. There exist a range of interventions that can be applied both to physical and other forms of partner violence, but generally their effectiveness is not known or is contested. More resources are needed to develop and pilot new interventions and conduct evaluations.

References

Crime and Security Act 2010, London: HMSO.
Dobash, R.E., Dobash, R.P., Cavanagh, K. and Lewis, R. (2000) *Changing Violent Men*, London: Sage Publications.

Gill, A. (2004) 'Voicing the silent fear: South Asian women's experiences of domestic violence', *The Howard Journal*, 43(5): 465–83.

Gondolf, E.W. (2002) *Batterer Intervention Systems: Issues, Outcomes and Recommendations*, Thousand Oaks, CA: Sage.

Hague, G., Thiara, R.K., Magowan, P. and Mullender, A. (2008) *Making the Links – Disabled Women and Domestic Violence*, Bristol: Women's Aid Federation of England.

Kelly, L. and Westmarland, N. (2015) 'Domestic violence perpetrator programmes: steps towards change. Project Mirabal final report', London and Durham: London Metropolitan University and Durham University. Available at: www.dur.ac.uk/criva/projectmirabal (accessed 16 January 2015).

Kelly, L., Adler, J.R., Horvath, M.A.H., Lovett, J., Coulson, M., Kernohan, D. and Gray, M. (2013) *Evaluation of the Pilot of Domestic Violence Protection Orders*, Home Office Research Report 76, London: Home Office.

Office for National Statistics (2013) *Focus on: Violence and Sexual Offences, 2011/12*, London: Office for National Statistics.

Phillips, R., Kelly, L. and Westmarland, N. (2013) *Domestic Violence Perpetrator Programmes: An Historical Overview*, London and Durham: London Metropolitan University and Durham University.

Westmarland, N., Kelly, L. and Chalder-Mills, J. (2010) *What Counts as Success?* London/Durham: CWASU/CRiVA.

Westmarland, N. and Kelly, L. (2012) 'Why extending measurements of "success" in domestic violence perpetrator programmes matters for social work', *British Journal of Social Work*, 43(6): 1092–110.

3
SEXUAL VIOLENCE BY PARTNERS

The World Health Organization guidelines on violence against women (2013) define sexual violence within the context of intimate partner violence as being:

> [p]hysically forced to have sexual intercourse when you did not want to, having sexual intercourse because you were afraid of what your partner might do, and/or being forced to do something sexual that you found humiliating or degrading.
>
> *(p. 6)*

This chapter considers the range of different forms that sexual violence by partners might take, the associated criminal offences and then some of the myths and problems that women on whom sexual violence is perpetrated by a partner might face. The background to the criminalizing of rape within marriage in the 1990s is then outlined, followed by responses to partner sexual violence including the change in law campaigned for by the family and friends of Jane Clough, who was repeatedly raped, assaulted and then killed by her former partner.

Partner sexual violence is best thought of as an umbrella term that covers a range of acts, including:

- rape – sexual intercourse without consent (including where the woman is too drunk to consent)
- forcing someone to watch pornography and/or act out scenes from pornography against their will
- taking photographs or making videos without consent
- distributing photographs or videos without consent even if they were created consensually
- unwanted sexual touching

- sexualized name-calling (slag, whore, etc.)
- intentionally passing on sexually transmitted diseases including HIV
- forcing someone to watch child rape or other sexual abuse
- forcing someone to have sex in front of a child or another person
- sexual threats ('better behave yourself or you'll get a raping')
- threatening to sexually abuse someone's children/other children in the family
- using someone's past experiences of sexually violent victimization against them
- pressuring someone to do sexual acts that they are not comfortable with
- making someone feel they cannot say no to sexual intercourse or acts
- pressurizing or forcing someone to have group sex
- pressurizing or forcing someone to sell sex for money or other benefit (pimping) and
- reproductive coercion.

Some of the criminal offences that partner sexual violence constitutes are rape, assault by penetration, sexual assault, causing a person to engage in sexual activity without consent, causing or inciting prostitution for gain, controlling prostitution for gain, trespass with intent to commit a sexual offence (all crimes under the Sexual Offences Act 2003) and improper use of a public electronic communications network (Communications Act 2003). However, it is important to understand that not all forms of sexual violence by partners are criminalized – McOrmond-Plummer et al. (2014) point out that calling a partner names such as 'slut' or 'whore' can be forms of sexual violence that are used to degrade or control the victim. Similarly, they argue that reproductive coercion has severe consequences for women whose individual wishes about childbearing are disregarded, but that this is not a criminal act.

Some have argued that partner sexual violence, or intimate partner sexual violence (IPSV) to which it is sometimes abbreviated, has fallen through a gap in terms of the attention it receives as a crime that occurs where the work of domestic violence and sexual violence practitioners intersects. On one hand, it is one form of abuse that happens within intimate partner relationships and is therefore domestic violence, but on the other hand, the nature of such violence and its impacts could be argued to be better understood and dealt with by rape and sexual violence services. Writing from a US perspective Bergen (1996) found that, when the women in her study of battered women who were raped received services from domestic violence services, the trauma left by the sexual violence often went unaddressed. She found that many service providers were uncertain about who should take 'ownership' of partner sexual violence, with the result that women were shunted between agencies (Bergen, 1996). Similarly, Williamson (2014) argues that some issues are addressed while others are marginalized and silenced in service provision, highlighting that 'sexual violence within domestically abusive intimate relationships is often annexed and considered in isolation rather than as part of an ongoing and systematic pattern of abuse' (p. 81). Hague et al. (2008) argue that sexual violence is particularly common against disabled women. In their research they found many examples of women being sexually violated and repeatedly raped – for example, being subjected to demands for sex in return for the provision of care.

McOrmond-Plummer *et al.* begin their book on intimate partner sexual violence with the recollection of what they call professionals' 'horror stories' they had been told over the years. They argue that these are significant and worthy of inclusion because responses to survivors are vitally important. 'Disbelief, minimization, or other responses that deny IPSV and its harms or its criminality service to entrap women further', they write (p. 23). The stories included the following:

- one woman visited her doctor and disclosed that she had woken up to her husband sexually assaulting her; the doctor told her that 'wake-up sex' is 'sexy' and that the woman should appreciate it as such
- another woman reported partner rape to a police unit with specific training in sexual offence cases – but was told it was just 'kinky sex' and not worth reporting and
- when one woman, in tears, told her pastor that she had been raped by her ex-partner, the pastor looked at her 'coldly', his wife got up and left the room and the conversation moved on to how the woman had 'sinned'.

Although these examples are assumed to be from Australia (where the editors are based), responses are unlikely to be any better elsewhere in the world. Matsakis (1992) argues that 'horror stories' such as these are not simply dreadful, uneducated responses to sexual violence but can constitute a 'secondary wounding', defining this as responding to survivors with disbelief, denial, minimization, stigmatization or refusal of help.

Partner rape and the 'real rape' stereotype

In 2011 the Justice Minister, Ken Clarke, appeared to suggest that there were different types of rape and that some types of rape should be treated more seriously than others. In response to the question why the average sentence was five years, Clarke responded on BBC Radio Five Live:

> That includes date rape, 17 year olds having intercourse with 15 year olds … A serious rape, with violence and an unwilling woman, the tariff is much longer than that. I don't think many judges give five years for a forcible rape, frankly.

Despite his later protestations to the contrary, this statement was widely interpreted as him distinguishing between 'date rape' and 'forcible rape', seeing the latter as the more serious, 'real' rape that would warrant a long prison sentence.

While it was easy to dismiss this as political wrangling, or simply a 'mistake' made by Clarke, it is important not to underestimate the problem that the 'real rape' stereotype maintains.

The notion of 'real rape' (Estrich, 1987), or the 'perfect rape' (Adler, 1987), refers to certain characteristics that the general public identify as being what rape 'is'. It is these rapes that will be taken most seriously by the police, prosecutors, juries and judges, and it is these women who will be believed and treated with sympathy. Chennells (2009) combines elements of Estrich's 'real rape' and Adler's 'perfect rape' and describes this as occurring when a 'virginal' woman from a respected background 'is *violently* accosted by *a stranger* either *outside or at home* in the sanctity of her own bedroom. She *resists* but is brutally raped sustaining *multiple, serious, lasting physical injuries*. She runs to *report immediately* (bloodied panties in hand) in a *highly emotive* state to the police' (p. 25, emphasis in original).

To Chennells' example we might add 'who has not been drinking freely or taking drugs (though may have been spiked or forced to drink or take drugs)'.

For survivors of intimate partner sexual violence, rape is rarely a one-off, with some women describing rape as part of their daily married life – part and parcel of an abusive and controlled environment (McOrmond-Plummer, 2009, Parkinson and Reid, 2014). In Parkinson and Reid's (2014) interviews with health professionals, police and women in Australia, they found that professionals used terms such as 'a grey area' to describe intimate partner sexual violence. As girls grow up they are taught to fear strangers and told stories of the 'real rape' stereotype (that is also promoted by large parts of the media). At a university I previously worked at, female students were consistently told to not walk across a stretch of open green fields alone after dark – to buddy up and walk home with a friend or to get a bus or taxi back to their university accommodation. This is despite stranger rape being extremely rare and the greater statistical danger being rape by known men.

According to Glasgow Rape Crisis Centre, it is because of this collective acceptance of the 'stranger rapist' as our greatest threat that we may find it hard to identify a loving husband/partner and father as a rapist (Kerr, 2014). Hecht Schafran (2014), Director of Legal Momentum, the National Judicial Education Programme in New York, gives an example of the dynamics of intimate partner sexual violence not being understood with catastrophic consequences:

> A prime example of what happens when judges do not understand IPSV is the case of Dr Amy Castillo, a pediatrician in Baltimore, Maryland. In 2008, Amy was divorcing her increasingly violent, erratic, and suicidal husband, Mark, who told her that the worst thing he could do to her would be to kill their three children and leave her alive. Amy obtained a Temporary Protective Order against Mark. At the hearing for the Final Protective Order the defense attorney brought out that Amy had sexual relations with Mark shortly before seeking the order. The judge was unable to grasp that this was not a romantic reconciliation but rather a terrified woman acquiescing to a violent man's sexual demand to protect her children and herself from further

harm. The judge denied the Final Protective Order and awarded Mark unsupervised visitation. Shortly after, Mark drowned the three children in a hotel bathtub.

(Hecht Schafran, 2014: 225

Background to the criminalizing of rape within marriage

In England and Wales rape within marriage was only criminalized in 1991 in case law and 1994 in statute (Criminal Justice and Public Order Act 1994). It had previously been judged in common law that married women had no capability or authority to 'not consent':

> The sexual communication between them is by virtue of the irrevocable privilege conferred once for all on the husband at the time of the marriage …
>
> *(R v Clarence, 1888)*

> But the husband cannot be guilty of rape committed by himself upon his lawful wife, for their matrimonial consent and contract the wife hath given up herself in this kind unto her husband, which she cannot retract.
>
> *(Sir Matthew Hale, 1736)*

The criminalization of marital rape was controversial within legal circles. This is because in 1991 it was seen as having been criminalized by judge-made law rather than by an elected government. The case in question was *R v R* in which it was alleged that a husband had attempted to have sexual intercourse with his estranged wife without her consent and physically assaulted her by squeezing her neck with both hands. In this case the issue was not whether he had attempted to force his wife to have sexual intercourse without her consent, but rather whether this fell under the legal definition of 'unlawful' sexual intercourse. Relying upon Hale's now infamous statement (cited above) the defence argued that because the acts were against his wife they could not be classed as unlawful.

In considering this defence, Mr Justice Owen argued that Hale's statement could no longer be seen as valid because it was 'a statement made in general terms at a time when marriage was indissolvable'. However, this dismissal of Hale appeared to relate more to the fact that physical force had been used in the attempted rape than to the lack of consent *per se*:

> I am asked to accept that there is a presumption or an implied consent by the wife to sexual intercourse with her husband; with that, I do not find it difficult to agree. However, I find it hard to believe … that it was ever the common law that a husband was in effect entitled to beat his wife into submission to sexual intercourse … If it was, it is a very sad commentary on the law and a very sad commentary on the judges in whose breasts the law

is said to reside. However, I will nevertheless accept that there is such an implicit consent as to sexual intercourse which requires my consideration as to whether this accused may be convicted for rape.

Mr Justice Owen ruled that the act could be classed as attempted rape and sentenced the defendant to three years' imprisonment. The defendant appealed, arguing that Mr Justice Owen had been wrong to rule that rape within marriage was against the law when the marriage had not been revoked.

The appeal was dismissed unanimously at the Court of Appeal (*R v R* [1991] 2 All English Law Reports 257), where Lord Lane dismissed Sir Matthew Hale's statement as being a 'statement of the common law at that epoch', and stated that 'the common law rule no longer remotely represents what is the true position of a wife in present-day society'. The Court of Appeal concluded:

> [w]e take the view that the time has now arrived when the law should declare a rapist a rapist subject to the criminal law, irrespective of his relationship with his victim.

This judgment was later upheld on appeal to the House of Lords and at the European Court of Human Rights.

Reproductive coercion

The term 'reproductive coercion' was first defined by Miller *et al.* in 2010, as:

> explicit male behaviours to promote pregnancy (unwanted by the woman) … birth control sabotage (interference with contraception) and/or pregnancy coercion, such as telling a woman not to use contraception and threating to leave her if she doesn't get pregnant.
>
> (p. 457)

Williamson (2014) argues that while the discussion of coercion and control is sometimes carried on within domestic and sexual violence literature, it is rarely thought worthwhile to consider them together. She defines reproductive coercion as 'the ways in which decisions about reproduction are made and how the context of VAWG [violence against women and girls] might influence these decisions' (p. 78). In her research, she found that most disclosures of sexual violence within the interviews happened when interviewees were talking about how partner abuse had affected their reproductive choices, and especially about the types of abuse they experienced while pregnant. She argues that women may see sexual coercion as a 'normal' part of heterosexuality, and may 'internalize coercion' and 'give in to demands' from their partners in order to 'keep the peace'.

Policy and practice responses to sexual violence by partners

As highlighted earlier, partner sexual violence is an area that is covered by two usually separate pillars of service delivery – domestic violence and sexual violence services. This means that there is room for several things to happen: for partner sexual violence to be 'owned' by neither and for it to fall through the gaps; for it to be 'owned' by both and a close working partnership to be developed; or for there to be 'turf battles' over who 'owns' partner sexual violence and who, crucially, is given the funding for providing services. MacLeod (2014) argues that, based on available research and statistics, there is likely to be a bigger overlap in the domestic violence arena. This is most clearly explained as 'most domestic violence includes sexual violence, but most sexual violence does not include domestic violence'. I am grateful to Maggie Parks of the Women's Rape and Sexual Abuse Centre in Cornwall for this phrase, as I have found it useful to explain the 'overlap dilemma'. Considering the first part of the phrase first, it is clear that most domestic violence relationships involve some form of sexual violence. Even if rape does not occur, other forms of sexual violence, such as those listed at the beginning of this chapter, are common – for example, being forced to watch and/or act out scenes from pornography. Some mistakenly then regard this as meaning that domestic violence service providers do considerable amounts (or worse, a broad range) of work in the sexual violence area. This can lead to an assumption that standalone sexual violence services – such as Rape Crisis – are no longer needed or that they do not need as much funding. This is why the second part of the phrase above is so important – that '… most sexual violence does not include domestic violence'. This means that while the sexual violence services provide resources for survivors of sexual violence by partners and ex-partners, there are also very large areas of service to adult survivors of child sexual abuse, children and young people who are being raped and abused by family members and women who are raped by strangers and/or acquaintances.

Levy-Peck (2014) highlights that most advocates and advisors working with partner sexual violence will be based within either a domestic violence or a sexual violence service. She points out that there are obvious areas in which they will need to work together – that Rape Crisis advocates may need to work with domestic violence organizations to access safety and financial resources (in the UK context safe housing would also be added to this list), while domestic violence advocates may need to improve understandings of sexual violence and their comfort in discussing these concerns. The bottom line, argues Levy-Peck, is that both sexual and domestic violence organizations need to be 'intentionally welcoming' to survivors of partner violence who might otherwise feel out of place within their organization. MacLeod (2014), writing from the Gold Coast Centre Against Sexual Violence, argues that one way this might be achieved is via training on the duality of the issue of sexual and domestic violence. She argues that this would make the invisible more visible, close gaps in service delivery, increase knowledge and understanding, and acknowledge repeat victimization and potential lethality to, ultimately, achieve better outcomes for survivors.

Responses – changing the law after the repeated partner rapes and murder of Jane Clough

In November 2009, Jonathan Vass was arrested following allegations of months of repeated rape and assault against his former partner Jane Clough, including when she was pregnant. Initially he was remanded in custody, after being charged with nine rapes, a sexual assault and three assaults. However, Judge Simon Newell granted him bail against the advice of the police and the Crown Prosecution Service (CPS), which had warned of the 'extreme likelihood' that Vass would interfere with witnesses. Newspaper reports cite entries from Clough's diary around this time that she was worried that Vass would 'get his revenge' for her reporting the rapes to the police.

In July 2010, in the car park of the hospital where Jane worked as a nurse Vass stabbed Clough, the mother of his 9-month-old baby, 71 times. He briefly walked away after the stabbings, then turned back to slit her throat. When Clough was taken to the hospital accident and emergency department where she had been about to start her shift, her colleagues did not recognize her, so severe were her injuries. Vass was sentenced to life imprisonment for her murder, with a minimum term of 30 years. However, Judge Anthony Russell claimed that the rape charges 'pale[d] into insignificance' next to the murder, and consequently ordered them to be left on file.

Clough's parents set up a campaign called 'Justice for Jane'. They felt that her death had been preventable (if the judge had followed advice and concerns and not bailed Vass) and that it was wholly inappropriate for Vass not to stand trial for the rapes – especially since this was arguably one of the motives for killing Clough.

The campaign was successful and, in 2012, the then Director of Public Prosecutions, Keir Starmer QC, changed the policy. Now, cases of rape linked to murder will be prosecuted rather than being left on file. The campaign was also successful in its second aim, to close a 'bail law loophole' that prevented the bail decision from being challenged. In an amendment to the Bill that became the Legal Aid, Sentencing and Punishment of Offenders Act 2012, sometimes referred to as 'Jane's law', prosecutors are now able to appeal against Crown Court bail rulings. Jane Clough's parents were reported in newspapers to have said that they believed their daughter would still be alive if the CPS had had the right to challenge bail decisions in 2010, with her father saying 'It's time a defendant's right to freedom was superseded by the victim's right to safety. That's all we're asking for' (report available at www.bbc.co.uk/news/uk-england-lancashire-16968088).

Summary

This chapter has shown that partner sexual violence takes a broad range of forms, but there still exists a lack of knowledge about the seriousness of and the damage caused by such violence. Responses can vary, and many have persuasively argued that partner sexual violence does not receive an adequate response from the domestic violence services. The failings of the criminal justice system and the failure of the criminal law to deal with partner violence that includes sexual violence were clearly seen in the murder of Jane Clough, since when the 'Justice for Jane' campaign successfully created a change in the law regarding bail. It is clear from this chapter that significant progress still needs to be made in developing responses to partner sexual violence.

References

Adler, Z. (1987) *Rape on Trial*, London: Routledge and Kegan Paul.
Bergen, R. (1996) *Wife Rape: Understanding the Response of Survivors and Service Providers*, Thousand Oaks, California: Sage.
Chennells, R. (2009) 'Sentencing: the real rape myth', *Agenda*, 23(82): 23–38.
Communications Act 2003, London: HMSO.
Criminal Justice and Public Order Act 1994, London: HMSO.
Estrich, S. (1987) *Real Rape: How the Legal System Victimizes Women Who Say No*, Cambridge, Massachusetts: Harvard University Press.
Hague, G., Thiara, R.K., Magowan, P. and Mullender, A. (2008) *Making the Links – Disabled Women and Domestic Violence*, Bristol: Women's Aid Federation of England.
Hale, Sir Matthew (1736) *History of the Pleas of the Crown*, Vol. 1, Ch. 58.
Hecht Schafran, L. (2014) 'Intimate partner sexual violence and the courts', in McOrmond-Plummer, L., Easteal, P. and Levy-Peck, J.Y. (eds), *Intimate Partner Sexual Violence: A Multidisciplinary Guide to Improving Services and Support for Survivors of Rape and Abuse*, London: Jessica Kingsley Publishers, pp. 221–33.
Kerr, I. (2014) 'Counseling and advocacy perspectives on intimate partner sexual violence', in McOrmond-Plummer, L., Easteal, P. and Levy-Peck, J.Y. (eds), *Intimate Partner Sexual Violence: A Multidisciplinary Guide to Improving Services and Support for Survivors of Rape and Abuse*, London: Jessica Kingsley Publishers, pp. 88–97.
Levy-Peck, J.Y. (2014) 'The role of the advocate in addressing intimate partner sexual violence', in McOrmond-Plummer, L., Easteal, P. and Levy-Peck, J.Y. (eds), *Intimate Partner Sexual Violence: A Multidisciplinary Guide to Improving Services and Support for Survivors of Rape and Abuse*, London: Jessica Kingsley Publishers, pp. 98–109.
Macleod, D. (2014) 'Real not rare: cross-training for sexual assault and domestic violence workers to understand, recognise and respond to intimate partner sexual violence', in McOrmond-Plummer, L., Easteal, P. and Levy-Peck, J.Y. (eds), *Intimate Partner Sexual Violence: A Multidisciplinary Guide to Improving Services and Support for Survivors of Rape and Abuse*, London: Jessica Kingsley Publishers, pp. 110–23.
Matsakis, A.T. (1992) *I Can't Get Over It: A Handbook for Trauma Survivors*, Oakland, California: New Harbinger Publications.
McOrmond-Plummer, L. (2009) 'Considering the differences: intimate partner sexual violence in sexual assault and domestic violence discourse', in Washington Coalition of Sexual Assault Programs, *Intimate Partner Sexual Violence: Sexual Assault in the Context of Domestic Violence*, 2nd edn, Olympia, Washington, WCSAP, pp. 1–4.
McOrmond-Plummer, L. (2014) 'Preventing secondary wounding by misconception: what professionals really need to know about intimate partner sexual violence', in McOrmond-Plummer, L., Easteal, P. and Levy-Peck, J.Y. (eds), *Intimate Partner Sexual Violence: A Multidisciplinary Guide to Improving Services and Support for Survivors of Rape and Abuse*, London: Jessica Kingsley Publishers, pp. 30–40.

Miller, E., Jordan, B., Levenson, R. and Silverman, J.G. (2010) 'Reproductive coercion: connecting the dots between partner violence and unintended pregnancy', *Contraception*, 81(6): 457–9.

Parkinson, D. and Reid, S. (2014) '"Invisible" intimate partner sexual violence: prevention and intervention challenges', in McOrmond-Plummer, L., Easteal, P. and Levy-Peck, J.Y. (eds), *Intimate Partner Sexual Violence: A Multidisciplinary Guide to Improving Services and Support for Survivors of Rape and Abuse*, London: Jessica Kingsley Publishers, pp. 136–46.

R v Clarence [1889] 22 QB 23.

R v R [1991] 3 WLR 767 (House of Lords).

World Health Organization (2013) *Responding to Intimate Partner Violence and Sexual Violence Against Women: WHO Clinical and Policy Guidelines*, New York: WHO.

Williamson, E. (2014) 'Reproductive coercion', in McOrmond-Plummer, L., Easteal, P. and Levy-Peck, J.Y. (eds), *Intimate Partner Sexual Violence: A Multidisciplinary Guide to Improving Services and Support for Survivors of Rape and Abuse*, London, Jessica Kingsley Publishers, pp. 76–87.

4
PSYCHOLOGICAL ABUSE

Psychological abuse – which can include financial abuse, technology-enabled abuse, threats and harassment – is often perpetrated alongside physical and sexual forms of violence. All of these operate to restrict women's lives and narrow what Nordic researcher Eva Lundgren (2004) calls 'life space' and Liz Kelly calls 'space for action'. This chapter starts with a description of how the day-to-day lives of women are restricted and regulated through the forms of abuse listed above. The offence of harassment is then described, followed by some examples of how stalking/harassment operates within a partner violence context. Following this, some responses are discussed that are relevant to all forms of partner violence – specialist domestic violence courts, independent domestic violence advisors/advocates (IDVAs) and restraining orders.

The concepts of 'life space' and 'space for action' being restricted describes how, as fears and threats become more central to a woman's everyday life, she attempts to manage the violence through restraining her own behaviour more and more, while abusive men use this to further restrict her behaviour. I think of it as a bubble, or a net, that surrounds people, and determines how much freedom people have. I then visualize the bubbles/nets of women who experience partner abuse getting smaller and smaller over time. Conversely, research has shown that it is the expansion of this net, or bubble, their space for action, that is crucial for women to regain control over their own lives having had their space previously restrained (Westmarland *et al.*, 2010; Westmarland and Kelly, 2012).

The women in our studies talked about simple, everyday events, but described them as central to their personal and bodily integrity. The phrase 'walking on eggshells' was commonly used to describe how they felt under their partners' web of control. We argued that the emphasis on physical assault in law and policy has resulted in these forms of coercion and control remaining hidden and that when women consequently adapt their behaviour to prevent further physically violent outbursts, this is often misrecognized as individual weakness or personality factors (e.g. 'victim proneness'). Rather, women intentionally and actively narrow their space for action and/or have it narrowed for them by having to live within parameters set by the perpetrator.

This overlaps with Stark's (2007) concept of the 'microregulation of everyday behaviours', which he argues is the primary method men use to establish control. He likens this to a hostage situation, where:

> victims of coercive control are frequently deprived of money, food, access to communication or transportation, and other survival resources even as they are cut off from family, friends and other supports.
>
> *(p. 5)*

Women's entrapment in personal life through this micro-regulation, Stark argues, is inherently gendered, as it is associated with stereotypical female roles (how women clean, dress, care for children, socialize, etc.). Its impact is such *because* of women's vulnerability that in turn stems from sexual inequality. From this perspective partner violence will continue as long as sexual inequality does.

In Gill's (2004) study of South Asian women's experiences of partner violence, she found that psychological abuse typically included verbal attacks that were intended to 'undermine their self-esteem and to exercise control over their presentation of self' (p. 472). She found that name-calling, humiliation, blaming the victim and physical rejection by partners were common. Some of the women in Gill's study reported that psychological abuse took place solely within the home, while others reported that public humiliation was an important tactic – as an 'ultimate display of confidence and power by an abuser' (p. 472). Hence, many acts of psychological abuse are not culturally specific and face women across different ethnicities.

For some women, however, there can be additional oppressions that compound the partner violence and add new opportunities for psychological abuse. For example, for women with insecure immigration status, including asylum seekers and refugees, this status can be used against her by her partner. If a woman tries to leave and go to a women's refuge, her partner may retaliate by contacting immigration authorities and seeking strategies to have her deported (example from Gill, 2004). In her research, Gill (2004) found that partners routinely threatened to call immigration authorities if there is any attempt to report violence. She concluded that immigration status is a coercive tool for abusers who are citizens, and a tactic used to silence women who are not.

Financial abuse

Financial abuse is probably the least researched area of partner violence, with very little academic literature on the topic. Women's Aid define financial abuse as actions that limit and control someone's current and future actions and their freedom of choice, for example interfering with employment, education or training; controlling access to all the household finances; stealing; refusing to contribute to shared household expenses; insisting on loans and credit cards being taken out in the woman's name; and forcing her to take actions that are dishonest, illegal or against her sense of what is right (Women's Aid website).

In a factsheet on domestic violence in Nevada, USA, Powell and Smith (2011) point out that perpetrators may try to cause a victim who is employed to lose her job, for example through harassing behaviour at her work place. They also highlight that 'oppressive accountability' might be used – in which victims who are given access to funds to purchase basic necessities are then required to account for the money in detail. This is a prime example of Stark's (2007) concept of micro-regulation.

Technology-enabled violence and abuse

The intersection between technology and partner violence is an important and growing research area, as men who use violence in relationships increasingly employ technology to extend their net of control over women. Research has found the 'digital age' to have uses and drawbacks in relation to partner violence. Dunlap (2012), for example, highlights that while technology can enable perpetrators to escalate their offending behaviour, technological advances can also enable victims to access support to increase their safety.

In a study on the use of smartphone 'apps' (programmes that are downloadable to mobile devices such as smartphones and tablet computers) in relation to domestic violence, I and a team of researchers found that advances in mobile technology were opening up new weapons of abuse as well as being used to help support victim-survivors (Westmarland et al., 2013). One of the ways that smartphone apps enable men to extend their abuse is through requiring but then controlling social media such as Facebook, and another is the use of sleep apps to monitor their partners' activities while the perpetrator is absent, rather than asleep. However, there also exist a small number of apps that have specifically been designed to support the surveillance of women. The one that we had the most concerns about was called 'Track your wife'. This is a 'discreet' application which means that it covertly runs in the background of the mobile device that it is installed on. The app sends frequent geo-location and time data from Google Maps to a linked website to allow account holders to know the location of the phone and, by extension, of their 'wife'. At the date of the research (July 2013) the app had been installed over 10,000 times.

Harassment

It is useful to consider psychological and financial abuse alongside harassment. This is because they all feature the employment of both non-physical and sexual types of violence and all are intended to narrow the 'life space' and 'space for action' and use the 'microregulation of everyday behaviours' to restrict and limit women's space for action. The psychological and financial abuses perpetrated against a woman by a violent partner seem consistent in many ways with the crime of harassment, and this is even more the case once a relationship has ended or is in the process of ending.

Harassment offences are prosecutable under the Protection from Harassment Act 1997, which states:

> A person must not pursue a course of conduct – which a) amounts to harassment of another, and b) which he knows or ought to know amounts to harassment of the other.
>
> *(Section 1)*

According to a Home Office research study by Harris (2000), the criminal law had two key problems before the 1997 Act was introduced. First, there was little protection for victims who felt frightened by a series of incidents that, while disturbing, fell short of being illegal. Second, it was necessary to prove that there was an intention to cause harassment, alarm or distress under the previous offence options (section 4a of the Public Order Act 1986). While there was another option (section 5 of the same Act – causing harassment, alarm or distress), this had very limited penalties.

The Protection from Harassment Act was implemented primarily to tackle the problem of 'stalking', but it also covered forms of abuse more broadly classed as harassment (unwanted telephone calls, letters, gifts, etc.). Stalking is not actually mentioned in the Act itself, but is discussed in wider government documents around the Act. It is possible that the government, in drafting the Act, were trying to move away from seeing harassment as being linked only to high-profile harassment and 'stalking' of celebrities – tragically and famously resulting in the death of *Crimewatch* presenter Jill Dando.

The following three examples illustrate in different ways how stalking and harassment continue on from and overlap with other forms of partner violence. They are taken from a 2011 report by Napo (the trade union and professional association for Family Court and probation staff), which looked into 80 cases of stalking and harassment selected by Napo members – mainly those working in Probation Victim Liaison Units or probation staff working in prisons. The partner violence cases were not unusual – in 59 of the 80 cases (74 per cent) Napo report a history of domestic violence in previous relationships and that in each case the stalking and harassment occurred when the relationship was ended by the female partner (Napo, 2011).

Example 1

In this case a man was charged with two counts of wounding or inflicting grievous bodily harm with intent. He had a long history of domestic violence and of stalking two previous partners. The domestic violence history included trying to strangle one partner, and using a range of harassing tactics including monitoring women's movements; breaking into their property; and he had even continued to send offensive letters from prison. He made few changes to his attitudes and behaviours while in prison, was said to be 'highly resistant' to attending an offending programme and was described as 'highly manipulative' while in prison. No restraining orders were in place and the police continued to receive multiple complaints from two previous partners.

Example 2

In this case a man was charged with actual bodily harm. He had a history of domestic violence and displayed increasing violence against and attempts to control his partner, although he had no previous criminal convictions. The ways in which he controlled his partner included refusing to let her have contact with her family, controlling her money and refusing her access to medical treatment after the birth of a child. When she left him he continued to keep in touch because of the child, and he used this to maintain contact and control, for example repeatedly texting, calling, turning up at places she went commonly went to and making threats to kill her. He received a 15-month custodial sentence for the physical attack he went on to make on her.

Example 3

A man was charged with breach of a community order and a serious physical assault. He had previously been convicted of a range of offences against an ex-partner. There was evidence of his offending increasing in both frequency and severity. He continued to use violence despite attending a domestic violence programme in the community and undertaking a significant amount of work within the criminal justice system aimed at reducing the risk of his further offending. He had been recalled to prison because he had breached his licence by continuing to harass his ex-partner.

Following the Napo report, and a second report entitled 'The Victim's Voice' that detailed the experiences of 140 stalking victims and their deep dissatisfaction with the criminal justice system, a new consultation was launched in November 2011 to consider legal reform. The new law came into force from November 2012 and includes a new and specific offence of 'stalking', alongside training for professionals, tougher sentencing guidelines, amendments to the Bail Act and new safeguards to prevent vexatious applications for child contact. For an in-depth overview of the campaign for legal reform for stalking see Fletcher and Richards (2013).

Responses – Specialist Domestic Violence Courts

The CPS introduced its Specialist Domestic Violence Court (SDVC) programme in 2005 and has been rolling them out across the country. SDVCs represent a partnership approach to domestic violence in which the police, prosecutors, court staff, the probation service and specialist domestic violence advocates (usually IDVAs) all work together. It is known as a 'whole system' approach rather than being a physical building, or even a courtroom. Practically speaking, this often means that one Magistrate's courtroom is designated the 'domestic violence court' on one or more days of the week. As of 2013, at the end of a major cost-cutting restructure, there are six reported reductions in the number of SDVCs (www.cps.gov.uk/publications/equality/vaw/sdvc.html), leaving a total of 137.

An evaluation of a pilot scheme reported that although three of the five courts evaluated had been running for a year or less, they had resulted in significant changes in practice (Cook et al., 2004). In particular, the evaluators found that SDVCs enhanced the effectiveness of court and support services for victims, that they made advocacy and information sharing easier and that both the participation and the satisfaction of victims were improved, resulting in an increase in public confidence in the criminal justice system (Cook et al., 2004).

Responses – the introduction of Independent Domestic Violence Advisors (IDVAs)

IDVAs are 'trained specialists providing independent advocacy and support to high-risk victims' (HM Government, 2009: 17). The first 100 were trained in 2005/6 and by 2009 there were over 700 across England and Wales (HM Government, 2009). The IDVA role was designed to provide support to ensure a coordinated community response to domestic violence. For example, their role within a Multi-Agency Risk Assessment Conference (MARAC) is a central one. Many have highlighted that although as a job role rather than as an element of a project IDVAs and advocacy represent a relatively new concept, it is not a new practice, since aspects of it have always been integral to services within the women's movement (Coy and Kelly, 2011). Likewise, Robinson (2009) points out that 'the label is newer than the type of work' (p. 11), meaning that while 'IDVAs' and 'advocacy' have not always been the terms used, the forms of support they offer have long been available. In a national evaluation of IDVAs, Robinson (2009) found that 'independence' was acknowledged as one of the key ingredients of an effective IDVA service. Accordingly, the evaluation concluded that IDVAs should be managed by specialist domestic violence projects. Where this was the case, IDVAs were able to prioritize victim safety and provide essential 'institutional advocacy' within a coordinated community response through which they could inform and change practice within multi-agency partnerships.

Responses – restraining orders

There are two types of restraining order – which are also known as injunctions. A non-molestation order can be made to try to stop a partner or ex-partner from using or threatening violence, and prevent intimidation and harassment. An occupation order can restrict a partner or ex-partner from entering a person's house and a specified area around it.

A restraining order can be made under the Family Law Act 1996 or section 5 of the Domestic Violence, Crime and Victims Act 2004. They are made by a court, which has to assess whether it feels a restraining order is necessary to protect a person from harassment or conduct that would put them in fear of violence. Although a restraining order is made under civil rather than criminal law, if someone breaches the order they can face criminal sanctions. The Domestic Violence, Crime and Victims Act 2004 also criminalized the breach of a non-molestation order, with a maximum sentence of five years in prison. It is possible for a victim to apply through the civil law system for a restraining order, or for a court to issue a restraining order on acquittal of any offence – where there has failed to be a conviction but the court feels that it is clear from the evidence presented that the victim is in need of protection from harassment.

Summary

This chapter has described a broad range of interconnected forms of violence and abuse that can all come under a broad heading of psychological abuse. On one hand there is little research directly into some of these forms of abuse, for example financial abuse, but on the other hand many of these forms are inherent in most cases of partner abuse. For this reason, concepts such as Kelly's 'space for action' and Stark's 'microregulation of everyday life' are better descriptors than the division of such partner abuses into separate components.

References

Cook, D., Burton, M., Robinson, A. and Vallely, C. (2004) *Evaluation of Specialist Domestic Violence Courts/Fast Track Systems*, London: CPS/DCA.
Coy, M. and Kelly, E. (2011) *Islands in the Stream: An Evaluation of Four London Independent Domestic Violence Advocacy Schemes*, London: London Metropolitan University.
Domestic Violence, Crime and Victims Act 2004, London: HMSO.
Dunlap, J.A. (2012) 'Intimate terrorism and technology: there's an app for that', *University of Massachusetts Law Review*, 7(10): 10–38.
Fletcher, H. and Richards, L. (2013) 'New advocacy service for victims of stalking', *Criminal Law & Justice Weekly*, 177(20).

Gill, A. (2004) 'Voicing the silent fear: South Asian women's experiences of domestic violence', *The Howard Journal*, 43(5): 465–83.

Harris, J. (2000) *An Evaluation of the Use and Effectiveness of the Protection from Harassment Act 1997*, Home Office Research Study 203, London: Home Office.

Hester, M., Westmarland, N., Pearce, J. and Williamson, E. (2008) *Early Evaluation of the Domestic Violence, Crime and Victims Act 2004*, London: Home Office.

HM Government (2009) *Together We Can End Violence Against Women and Girls: A Strategy*, London: HM Government.

Lundgren E. (2004) *The Process of Normalising Violence*, Stockholm: ROKS.

National Association of Probation Officers (2011) *Stalking and harassment – A Study of Perpetrators*, London: Napo.

Protection from Harassment Act 1997, London: HMSO.

Public Order Act 1986, London: HMSO.

Powell, P. and Smith, M. (2011) *Domestic Violence: An Overview*, Nevada: University of Nevada Cooperative Extension.

Robinson, A.L. (2009) *Independent Domestic Violence Advisors: A Process Evaluation*, Cardiff: Cardiff University.

Stark, E. (2007) *Coercive Control: How Men Entrap Women in Personal Life*, New York: Oxford University Press.

Westmarland, N., Kelly, L. and Chalder-Mills, J. (2010) *What Counts as Success?* London/Durham: CWASU/CRiVA.

Westmarland, N. and Kelly, L. (2012) 'Why extending measurements of "success" in domestic violence perpetrator programmes matters for social work', *British Journal of Social Work*, 43(6): 1092–110.

Westmarland, N., Hardey, M., Bows, H., Branley, D., Chowdhury, K. and Wistow, R. (2013) *Protecting Women's Safety? The Use of Smartphone 'Apps' in Relation to Domestic and Sexual Violence*, SASS Research Briefing no. 12, Durham: Durham University.

Women's Aid Federation of England (2014) *Financial Abuse*, Women's Aid Federation of England website, available at www.womensaid.org.uk/domestic_violence_topic.asp?section=0001000100220049 (accessed October 2014).

PART 2
Men's violences in the family

This Part is about violence against women that happens within the family but that is not exclusively committed by partners or ex-partners. It covers parental abuse as this relates to violence against women as mothers and grandmothers (Chapter 5); forced marriage (Chapter 6); 'honour'-based violence and killings of women (Chapter 7); the genital mutilation of girls (Chapter 8), and familial rape and abuse (Chapter 9).

Although many of the forms of violence against women examined in this Part fall under the Westminster government definition of 'domestic violence' (see Chapter 2), the dynamics that are in play in family violence are different in many ways from those in play in violence against partners. While they all fit under the heading of violence against women, the usefulness of placing them all under a heading of domestic violence is questionable. Liz Kelly and I have previously argued (2014) that, while the current definition assumes that the dynamics are the same, the relevance of coercive control to violence between family members, for example son-to-mother violence or female genital mutilation, is arguably less than its relevance to partner violence. In that article we argued that:

> [c]oercive control is a concept developed to make sense of the many subtle and not so subtle ways in which men impose their will in heterosexual relationships, and it draws on cultural norms about both masculinity and femininity.

We argue that this cannot be simply transferred across into other relationships such as son–mother, and other cross-generational ones, in which the issues of gender and sexuality play out very differently.

The role of culture

Discounting some forms of men's violences against women as being culturally specific, for example linked to particular religions or traditions, is known as 'othering' men's violence – seeing people belonging to cultures other than one's own as the ones with the problematic religions, customs and traditions. The reality is that we live in multi-cultural societies and that different cultures involve different traditions and cultural norms and include some harmful cultural practices. As Gangoli et al. (2011) point out:

> It is difficult to imagine what a community or society without codes of honour would look like or how it would function. Codes of honour stipulate the expected behaviour of members of a community or society, and the sanctions that would be imposed for breaching such codes.
>
> (p. 33)

They observe that in the UK High Court, judges are referred to as 'Your Honour' and Privy Councillors are referred to as 'The Right Honourable', and that when British people describe the honour associated with white British communities it is generally in positive terms, but when the honour is associated with minority communities it often has negative connotations.

Narayan (1997) introduced the phrase 'death by culture' to show how 'culture' was/is used to explain away violence against women from some communities but not from others. Specifically, the word is often used in reference to violence against women from Black and other minority ethnic groups, but not to that arising in white British culture(s). She argues:

> 'cultural explanation[s]' result in pictures of Third World women as 'victims of their culture' in ways that are interestingly different from the way in which victimization of mainstream Western women is understood.
>
> (p. 85)

In the British culture, 'honour' is linked to excusing male violence, for example by excusing violence against a woman perceived to have behaved in ways that are deemed sexually inappropriate, such as being accused of having sex with other men outside her relationship. While crimes committed under these circumstances are not completely excused and do not come under any form of 'honour crime' exception, they do tend to be treated differently to otherwise similar crimes and are not called crimes of 'honour' or 'culture'.

It is linked to these reasons, and the invisibility of the term 'gender' within 'honour crimes' that Aisha Gill (2010) has argued that the term 'honour-based violence' should be abandoned and that violence committed in the name of 'honour' should be squarely identified as violence against women. She argues that because 'honour'-based crimes are culturally mandated, they have been defined as a category of violence distinct from violence against women. Since men who victimize and abuse women in honour-based cultures do so in order to maintain their dominance within society, Gill concludes that such victimization is explicitly gendered and should be classed as one form of violence against women.

As Bradley (2011) argues in *Women, Violence and Tradition*, it is also important to recognize that cultures are not fixed entities; rather, they change, shift and are subject to constant negotiation. Likewise, Thiara and Gill (2010) highlight that, although 'culture' and 'faith' are important in the lives of South Asian women, culture should be thought of as a 'dynamic and contested force rather than a static and unchanging monolith' (p. 33). They argue that it is also important to remember that culture and faith can be sources of support, not just oppression, of women.

Understanding intersectionality

'Intersectionality' is an approach that many argue enables understandings of Black, Asian, minority ethnic and refugee women to be more complex and less prone to the essentializing and stereotyping of their experiences (Bradley, 2011). It was developed by Kimberlé Williams Crenshaw in 1989 to explain how a range of factors intersect in the lives of women in relation to inequality. In 'Mapping the margins: intersectionality, identity politics, and violence against women of color', Crenshaw (1991) pointed out that women have drawn strength from shared experience and have politicized their claims around violence against them. This politicization of the personal, in Crenshaw's words 'recognizing as social and systemic what was formerly perceived as isolated and individual' (pp 1241/2), was important not only in gender politics, but also for other identity-based politics affecting people of colour, African-Americans, and gay men and lesbian women, she highlights. Crenshaw criticizes identity politics as either conflating or ignoring differences within groups – what she calls intragroup differences. She writes:

> Ignoring difference *within* groups contributes to tension *among* groups, another problem of identity politics that bears on efforts to politicize violence against women.
>
> *(p. 1241, emphasis in original)*

She argues that, at that time, both feminist and anti-racist discourses had failed to consider intersectionality – for example the identities of women of colour – and that the experiences of women of colour are frequently the product of racism and sexism intersecting. Crenshaw argues that, although their oppressions intersect, women of colour were adequately represented in neither the feminist nor the anti-racist movement. That is, both groups had marginalized women of colour's experiences of violence.

Having briefly considered some of the issues relating to family violence, including whether or not they fall under the definition of 'domestic violence', '"honour"-based violence', or 'violence against women', the chapters that follow look at different forms of men's violences against women within the family. As mentioned in the Foreword, some of the forms of violence within this section are committed against girls rather than women, but they are included here because of the continuing impact they have in adulthood.

References

Bradley, T. (ed.), (2011) *Women, Violence and Tradition: Taking FGM and Other Practices to a Secular State*, London: Zed Books.

Crenshaw, K. (1991) 'Mapping the margins: intersectionality, identity politics, and violence against women of color', *Stanford Law Review*, 43(6): 1241–99.

Gangoli, G., Chantler, K., Hester, M. and Singleton, A. (2011) 'Understanding forced marriage: definitions and realities', in Gill, A. and Anitha, S. (eds), *Forced Marriage: Introducing a Social Justice and Human Rights Perspective*, London: Zed Books Ltd, pp. 25–45.

Gill, A. (2010) 'Reconfiguring "honour" – based violence as a form of gendered violence', in Idriss, M. and Abbas, T. (eds), *Honour, Violence, Women and Islam*, London and New York: Routledge-Cavendish, pp. 218–31.

Kelly, L. and Westmarland, N. (2014) 'Time for a rethink – why the current government definition of domestic violence is a problem', *Trouble and Strife*, [online] available from: www.troubleandstrife.org/2014/04/time-for-a-rethink-why-the-current-government-definition-of-domestic-violence-is-a-problem/ (accessed October 2014).

Narayan, U. (1997) *Dislocating Cultures: Identities, Traditions, and Third World Feminism*, New York: Routledge.

Thiara, R. and Gill, A.K. (2010) 'Understanding violence against South Asian women: what it means for practice', in Thiara, R. and Gill, A.K. (eds), *Violence Against Women in South Asian Communities. Issues for Policy and Practice*. London: Jessica Kingsley Publishers, pp. 29–54.

5
VIOLENCE AGAINST MOTHERS AND GRANDMOTHERS

The abuse of a parent by their child falls under the government definition of domestic violence. However the term 'parent abuse' has been around in its own right for around the same length of time as the term 'domestic violence' has. Harbin and Madden (1979) are said to have been the first researchers to identify 'parent abuse' as a form of family violence, using the term 'battered parents' for the first time to describe a 'syndrome' that consisted of actual or threatened physical assaults. Over time, the focus on physical violence was expanded to include verbal and psychological forms of abuse (Hunter and Nixon, 2012). This chapter looks at definitions of parent abuse, and describes the reasons why it is an under-researched topic. The nature and prevalence of this type of abuse are discussed, as is fatal violence against female family members, followed by a consideration of the importance of gendering child-to-parent abuse.

Defining parent abuse

Nowadays, the term parent abuse is used to describe a pattern of behaviours such as that outlined by Holt (2013):

> a pattern of behaviour that uses verbal, financial, physical or emotional means to practise power and exert control over a parent. The parent may be a biological parent, step-parent or a parent in a legal capacity, and the son or daughter is still legally a child (i.e. under 18 years) and is usually living in the family home with their parent(s).
>
> *(p. 1)*

This definition looks fairly similar to some definitions of domestic violence – particularly before the new definition was introduced in 2013 to include coercion and control (see Chapter 2 for details). However, there is a notable lack of reference to sexual abuse of parents – an issue that is discussed later in this chapter. The similar definitions reflect some overlaps between parent abuse and partner abuse. Consider, for example, the opening example in Amanda Holt's book on adolescent-to-parent abuse:

> He'll scream and shout at me, awful abuse, absolutely awful abuse. He'll throw things at me, he'll punch holes in doors, he'll threaten to hit me, and this'll be all in front of my three little ones. So when it came to punching holes in the front door, screaming abuse at me at eight o'clock in the morning, I thought, 'No, the time has come to do something about it'. 'Cos one time that he was kicking off, he was throwing things at me and it ricocheted off me and hit my youngest baby, who is 21 months you know, and a shoe ricocheted off me and hit him. Well I can't have that. I didn't do anything about it at the time, but that sort of behaviour I can't have. He's done it in front of his friends, thrown big pieces of hardboard at me and garden toys and everything and I said to his friends, 'Look, I'm not a horrible mum, John is just like this'.
>
> (Sally, mother of John, aged 15, cited in Holt, 2013: 1)

Although the gender-neutral term 'parent abuse' is commonly used in research, policy and practice, and will be used in this chapter where it is impossible to distinguish to what extent different findings relate to mothers and grandmothers as opposed to 'parents' and 'grandparents' more generally, it is clear from most of the literature on the topic that in fact it is a deeply gendered phenomenon. Hunter and Nixon (2012) identify the gendered nature of family violence clearly and unequivocally, explaining that 'scrutiny of the international evidence suggests that parent abuse is both increasingly prevalent and a gendered issue, with mothers more likely to be abused by their (most frequently male) adolescent children' (p. 213). Following the focus of this book, this chapter will therefore concentrate where possible on the abuse of women within the family – usually mothers and grandmothers, but also sisters and aunts.

Adolescent-to-parent/grandparent violence – an under-researched area

The starting point for Condry and Miles (2014) is the fact that adolescent-to-parent violence is virtually invisible to policy and policing – in both related areas of youth justice and domestic violence. This limited knowledge and policy attention is not unique to England and Wales, with some other countries coming to similar conclusions recently (see for example Vink et al., 2014 making similar points about the Netherlands). As a result of the definition of domestic violence now in use in England and Wales widening to include over-16s rather than over-18s, the number of adolescents that are recorded as committing family violence is now higher. That is, by extending the definition, more young people will be labelled as perpetrators of domestic violence, regardless of whether that violence is committed against partners or other family members such as mothers and grandmothers.

Just as partner violence has previously been brushed under the carpet, as something that happens within the family and therefore should not be the concern of the state ('a man's home is his castle'), family violence has been hidden by the same invisibility cloak. This may be even more acute in situations of family violence where the perpetrators can be children and young people. Condry and Miles (2014) point out that the dominant discourse within criminology has been one of youth violence existing *outside* rather than *inside* the home. Added to this, they argue, the public and policy assumption has been that parents are able to assert control over their children, and this does not fit with the idea that they may be victims of their children's actions. Likewise, Hunter and Piper (2012) argue that 'parents are expected, in law and by society, to be in control as the dominant partner in an unequal parent–child relationship makes it more difficult for parents to admit to a lack of control' (p. 218). Holt adds to this that the term 'abuse' usually refers to an abuse of *power*, and therefore is committed by those with more power against those with less. This, she argues, is what makes 'parent abuse' distinctive from other forms of abuse within the family – not just partner abuse but also child abuse, elder abuse and sometimes sibling abuse – and makes it particularly transgressive of conventional notions of power relations (Holt, 2013). In this sense, it may have more in common with female-to-male partner violence than it does with patterns of male violence against women. However, this is to ignore dynamics other than age and, particularly, to downplay the role of gender, and we must also consider intersections with age, class and disability. These are the axes of power that need to be considered in relation to violence against parents.

The nature and prevalence of violence against mothers and grandmothers

Condry and Miles (2014) point out that very little research has taken place in the UK on this topic, and therefore much of what we know has emerged from a small selection of other countries and also from disciplines other than criminology (psychology, psychiatry, etc.). The Crime Survey England and Wales (formerly the British Crime Survey) does not routinely measure child-to-parent violence. The last time it was measured was in the mid-1990s, when the Crime Survey found that around 3 per cent of domestic violence cases were child-to-parent ones (Mirrlees-Black *et al.*, 1996). However, the Crime Survey has always been plagued with problems relating to the way it measures domestic violence. One of the obvious limitations relevant here is its refusal to ask people over the age of 59 about their experiences of domestic violence. It is likely that many or perhaps most grandparents will be over this age. It is also entirely possible that parents who are older (defined here as over 59) may find it more difficult to exert control over their adolescent children than those who are younger when their children reach this age, and therefore might well be more exposed to child-to-parent violence. In this way the Crime Survey ignores two groups of people who are particularly vulnerable to domestic violence. Therefore, even if the Crime Survey did ask about non-partner family violence, it would not move the debate forward without changing its structure and methods.

Smaller-scale studies have suggested that family violence may be more prevalent than the study by Mirrlees-Black *et al.* found. In 2005, a '24-hour snapshot' of domestic abuse was conducted in Bristol (Westmarland *et al.*, 2005). A '24-hour snapshot' collates all domestic violence disclosures over a single 24-hour period reported to a broad range of people and organisations (GPs, solicitors, housing associations, police, social services, etc.). This is designed to be easier for busy organizations to manage than a full prevalence study since it only requires them to coordinate their staff over a single 24-hour period. In our Bristol snapshot, 33 organizations took part; they told us about 175 people who had accessed their service because of domestic violence during that 24-hour period. A unique reference number system was used, which identified that four of these people had accessed two services during the 24-hour period, and both organisations had provided a snapshot return for them, so the data covered 171 people. Using a definition of domestic abuse that included family members where the victim was aged 16 or over, we found that 15 per cent (23 people) had reported experiencing familial domestic abuse. A small proportion (3 per cent, 5 people) had reported experiencing both familial and partner domestic abuse. The snapshot found that where the relationship was familial, most commonly be the victim's child was the offender – accounting for just over half of the cases (52 per cent of familial cases, or 7 per cent of all domestic violence cases reported). In other familial cases, the perpetrator was the victim's parent(s), sibling(s), in-law(s), grandchild(ren), or adoptive parent(s).

As part of a wider study into adolescent-to-parent violence, Condry and Miles (2014) looked at cases reported to the Metropolitan Police between 1 April 2009 and 31 March 2010. A total of 2,336 incidents were recorded, covering a range of offence types. Most frequently, this was violence against the person (51 per cent of cases), criminal damage (30 per cent) or theft and handling (13 per cent of cases). A small proportion of cases were for burglary (2 per cent) and a minority of cases related to sexual offences, drugs, fraud or forgery, and robbery (each accounting for under 1 per cent of cases).

Regardless of whether the victim was the mother or father, the perpetrator was nearly always a son rather than a daughter. The category of son-to-mother offences was the most frequent overall, accounting for two-thirds of the cases. Of course, it is possible that in some incidents both parents were victims, for example burglary or criminal damage cases where the parents were still together/co-habiting.

According to some studies, parent abuse is increasing. Calvete *et al.* (2012) investigated child-to-parent violence in Spain, and argue that available data suggests that increases may be linked to more permissive parenting styles that might be changing family power dynamics. Looking at 1,072 adolescents aged between 13 and 17 from 10 secondary schools in Spain, they found that child-to-parent abuse functioned as a means to obtain positive reinforcements (e.g. money) or to avoid certain tasks. They argue that their findings support the hypothesis that Western 'permissive' parenting styles have seen children increasingly adopting authoritarian roles as they perceive their parents as incapable of exercising control. This, Calvete *et al.* argue, has important implications for interventions and services, which should focus on helping parents exert control over their children's behaviour and re-establish a new pattern of power. However, because of the lack of data in England and Wales, it is impossible to know whether similar increases are occurring here.

Fatal violence against mothers and grandmothers

In Chapter 1 Karen Ingala Smith's blog 'Counting Dead Women' was discussed. This tracks information about men's fatal use of violence against women and gives names and identities to the women killed. In her blog, Ingala Smith has been counting any sexist killings of women, not just those by partners. In one blog, entitled 'Mother Killers: 30 UK men killed – or allegedly killed – their mothers between 2012–2014' (2 February 2014), she writes that when she started her recording exercise she had not expected to find such a high number of women killed by their adult sons. She criticizes the Home Office data for not stating the sex of killers, instead logging both adult sons and daughters together. The data from the Home Office Homicide Index shows that between 2001/2 and 2011/2, 108 women were killed by their adult son or daughter – almost ten each year. It is worth remembering that many of the studies on child-to-parent/grandparent violence are based on adolescents not adults, and thus that the Home Office figures and the Ingala Smith figures below should not be classed as the only instances of fatal violence, since they are based on adult figures.

On Counting Dead Women, Ingala Smith recorded that a minimum of 16 women were killed by their adult sons in 2012, and 12 in 2013. Over the same period, one grandmother was killed by her adult grandson in 2012 and three in 2013 (including one step-grandmother). She notes that the figures are a count in progress and that the 2013 figure in particular is likely to go up as more cases go to court and relationships between victims and alleged killers are made public. In her analysis of the cases, she found that the most common method of killing was stabbing – this was the method of eight of the men who killed their mothers and three of the men who killed their grandmothers. The average (mean) age of the women killed by their sons was found to be 64 (the youngest was 42 and the oldest was 86). The average age of the women killed by their grandsons was 78 (the youngest was 63 and the oldest was 87). Ingala Smith found that the racial distribution was similar to that found in the general UK population.

Ingala Smith argues that these crimes are inherently gendered – and should be classed as sexist crimes. She notes that she found no cases of women killing their fathers during the same period and only two cases of women killing their mothers. Problematic drug use and mental illness were cited in many of the cases where sons killed their mothers (mental illness in 13, drug use in 8, alcohol in 2 and a combination of drugs and alcohol in 2 cases), and drug use was noted in all of the cases of men who killed their grandmothers. However, Ingala Smith warns against drawing *causal* conclusions (while acknowledging them as potential risk factors). She points out that many people with mental health problems or who use drugs and/or alcohol are never violent. In addition, women also experience these problems and rarely go on to kill parents or grandparents. She concludes:

> When looking at men's violence against women – whether their mothers, partners or otherwise – mainstream analyses infrequently ask whether perpetrators are more sexist and misogynistic than men who are not violent to women. Problematic substance use, mental health problems, emotional problems, employment and economic problems, jealousy, 'snapping' and 'rows' are routinely considered, reinforcing the dominant agenda on – the excuses for – what is seen as significant. This must be recast and the role of patriarchy expressed through inequality, sexism, objectification and misogyny needs to be placed at the centre of our analysis of all forms of men's violence against women and our efforts to end it.
>
> *(online – posted 2 February 2014)*

Is parent abuse a form of domestic abuse?

Hunter *et al.* (2010) highlight that although there are similarities between intimate partner and parent abuse, the two should not be treated as congruent. Rather, they argue that there is a more complex set of dynamics at stake in the case of parent abuse. Paula Wilcox approaches this question head on in her 2012 article 'Is parent abuse a form of domestic violence?' She observes that not only is research on parent abuse in short supply, but also that little research looks at the overlap between domestic violence and parent abuse internationally. Wilcox starts by pointing out that children's abusive behaviour towards parents has tended to ignore structural influences such as the social construction of gender, and has instead constructed such abuse as an individual, medical, behavioural or criminal problem. Wilcox uses data from support service Parentline Plus (now called Family Lives), which analysed 30,000 telephone calls, to argue that gendered patterns of violence are evident in parent abuse. Parentline Plus (2008) found that mothers more frequently reported both verbal and physical aggression from their children (66 per cent of long calls from mothers discussed verbal aggression compared with 8 per cent from fathers; 84 per cent of long calls from mothers discussed physical aggressions compared with 8 per cent from fathers).

Responses – legal and policy approaches to parent abuse

As with partner violence and domestic violence more broadly, the approach taken to parent abuse is that of the generic criminal law. There exist no specific offences or policies that relate to the abuse of parents, regardless of gender. Therefore, in policy terms, such abuse falls under the heading of domestic violence but, like partner violence, the actual offences that people will be charged with are contained elsewhere in the legal framework, for example homicide, rape, violence against the person, criminal damage or theft.

Many women have concerns about reporting violent and abusive partners to the police, because they fear further attacks, or because they do not want their partner to get a criminal record that might affect their job prospects. These are also considerations for parents and grandparents considering reporting their child or grandchild to the police. In some cases, depending on the age of the offender, the youth justice rather than the adult criminal justice system might be the relevant framework. According to Hunter and Piper (2012), although the criminal justice system is frequently turned to, arguably it is not well-suited to tackle the issue. They point out that if the offence is too serious for diversion then a Youth Rehabilitation Order (YRO) or even a detention and training order can be made. If a community-based YRO is issued, one possible requirement that could be attached to it is to require a young person to live elsewhere (such as in local authority accommodation) to protect the abused parent. This is just one of the reasons why parents might be reluctant to involve the criminal justice system. In Hunter and Piper's (2012) study one social worker described a situation in which a child had been told not to return to the family home, but the mother was concerned about other options for living arrangements. She had phoned the police because her son had attacked her and smashed her house up. The police had given the son bail on condition that he was not to return to the family home but as he had just turned 16 there was a question mark over where he could go. The social worker found him bed and breakfast accommodation, but the mother was worried about his living alone at age 16, so he was bailed back to the family home again.

In another example they highlight concerns that a mother expressed for her child's welfare should he be removed from the family home:

> [The mother], it appears, is worried that if steps are taken to remove DL from the property he might at worst commit suicide or that, at best, she might lose contact with him.
>
> *(p. 222)*

Accordingly, living accommodation is an additional complicating factor when children and young people are perpetrating the violence and abuse.

Ignoring the gendered nature of adolescent-to-parent violence

Just as 'elder abuse' studies often neglect the role of gender, some parent abuse studies have also been criticized for doing so. Policy makers have been accused of failing to make visible the gendered nature of parent abuse. Hunter and Nixon

(2012) point out that, in the UK, the consultation paper *Together we can end violence against women and girls* (HM Government, 2009), failed to mention the gendered nature of parent abuse – making an argument similar to Ingala Smith's about the invisibility of the gendered nature of such violence.

None of this is to suggest that female children and young people, or indeed adults, are not violent towards their mothers, fathers or grandparents. Nor is it to deny the existence of female violence and abuse. Rather, it seeks to make three points. First, a disservice is being done by subsuming adolescent-to-parent abuse under the heading of domestic violence in definition and policy. This has almost certainly contributed to its invisibility and the relative lack of research attention and therefore theoretical development. Second, organizations that campaign against violence against women should distinguish this form of violence from partner violence in order to make it more visible within their work. Third, organizations working with adolescent-to-parent abuse, for example parenting organizations and those working with elder abuse, should acknowledge that these forms of violence are deeply gendered in nature. As well as the limited England and Wales data already discussed in this chapter, this pattern is replicated elsewhere in the world. For example, in a study of 249 cases in the Netherlands, 87 per cent of perpetrators were boys, and victims were most often their biological mothers (72 per cent). Nearly half the perpetrators lived only with the biological mother (Vink *et al.*, 2014).

Ignoring gender also runs the real risk of marginalizing sexual violence as a form of abuse. If adolescent-to-parent/grandparent violence is seen as one of the last taboos, which many argue to be the case, then incestuous abuse perpetrated by a woman's own children or grandchildren must be extremely difficult to disclose. An example of this form of abuse is described by Ramsey-Klawsnik and Brandl (2009), who argue that professionals supporting victims who experience sexual abuse of this nature need to understand the 'web of forces' that inhibit them from seeking help. They highlight the complex trauma responses faced by E in a case example. E is a widow aged 84 who is having problems with her 53 year old son L. E struggled to cope with L's drinking, depression and sexualized drawings on the walls of his bedroom. L also walked around E's apartment naked, masturbated in her presence and made sexually offensive and threatening comments. She feared he would end up homeless or in prison, and this (alongside her embarrassment) stopped her discussing her problems with others or asking L to leave her apartment. As Ramsey-Klawsnik (2003) had argued earlier, such trauma not only inhibits victims from seeking help but also makes it difficult for them to accept intervention when offered because of concerns that their children would face criminal charges, because of strong mixed emotions towards their abusers, and because they were often dependent on their abusers for care and assistance. Unhelpful or uninformed professional responses to elder sexual abuse can exacerbate the feelings of embarrassment, shame, self-blame or terror that older victims may feel (Ramsey-Klawsnik and Brandl, 2009).

Summary

Little is known about non-partner violence within the family, with some describing the issue of parent abuse as 'one of the most unacknowledged and under-researched forms of family violence' (Hunter and Nixon, 2012: 211). The reliance on a small number of sources in England and Wales in this chapter reflects this limited knowledge base. The conflation of wider family violence within the definition of domestic violence (caused by the lowering from 18 to 16 of the age at which policy regards someone as capable of perpetrating domestic violence) further complicates how and where male violence against mothers and grandmothers is best identified and dealt with. Furthermore, Helen Bonnick (2014) points out that there is hardly any information about how child-to-parent abuse should be understood and responded to within a child protection framework (see also her website www.holesinthewall.co.uk for a good resource on parent abuse generally for parents and practitioners). Although some research in the UK has been started, there is still a long way to go. As Condry and Miles (2014) argue:

> We contend that criminology needs to have a nuanced understanding of family violence in all its forms and cannot continue to have a blank page on violence from adolescents towards their parents.
>
> *(p. 16)*

What is necessary from this point on is that those working with domestic violence and violence against women more widely, and those in the elder abuse field, come together to develop knowledge about male violence against mothers and grandmothers. Working together will reduce the possibility of sexual violence being side-lined, and will hopefully raise the profile of what is currently an under-researched and under-recognized issue in policy terms.

References

Bonnick, H. (2014) 'Understanding parent abuse within a child protection framework', blog post dated October 7 2014, available at www. http://holesinthewall.co.uk/2014/10/07/understanding-parent-abuse-within-a-child-protection-framework/ (accessed 17 December 2014).

Calvete, E., Orue, I. and Gámez-Guadix, M. (2013) 'Child-to-parent violence emotional and behavioral predictors', *Journal of Interpersonal Violence*, 28(4): 755–72.

Condry, R. and Miles, C. (2014) 'Adolescent to parent violence: framing and mapping a hidden problem', *Criminology and Criminal Justice*, 14(3): 257–75.

Harbin, H. and Madden, D. (1979) 'Battered parents: a new syndrome', *American Journal of Psychiatry*, 136: 1288–91.

Holt, A. (2013) *Adolescent-to-Parent Abuse – Current Understandings in Research, Policy and Practice*, Bristol: Policy Press.

HM Government (2009) *Together We Can End Violence Against Women and Girls: A Consultation Paper*, London: HMSO.

Hunter, C., Nixon, J. and Parr, S. (2010) 'Mother abuse: a matter of youth justice, child welfare or domestic violence?', *Journal of Law and Society*, 37(2): 264–84.

Hunter, C. and Nixon, J. (2012) 'Introduction: exploring parent abuse – building knowledge across disciplines', *Social Policy and Society*, 11(2): 211–15.

Hunter, C. and Piper, C. (2012) 'Parent abuse: can law be the answer?', *Social Policy and Society*, 11(2): 217–27.

Ingala Smith, K.I. (2014) 'Mother killers: 30 UK men killed – or allegedly killed – their mothers between 2012–2014', *Karen Ingala Smith*, [online], available from: http://kareningalasmith.com/2014/02/02/mother-killers/ (accessed October 2014).

Mirrlees-Black, C., Mayhew, P. and Percy, A. (1996) *The 1996 British Crime Survey, England and Wales*, Home Office Statistical Bulletin 19/96, London: Research and Statistics Directorate.

Parentline Plus (2008) *'You Can't Say Go and Sit on the Naughty Step Because They Turn Round and Say Make Me.' Aggressive Behaviour in Children: Parents' Experiences and Needs*, available from: http://pelorous.totallyplc.com/public/cms/209/432/256/392/Aggressive%20behaviour%20in%20children%202008.pdf?realName=4XFM9E.pdf (accessed 7 October 2014).

Ramsey-Klawsnik, H. (2003) 'Elder sexual abuse within the family', *Journal of Elder Abuse and Neglect*, 15(1): 43–58.

Ramsey-Klawsnik, H. and Brandl, B. (2009) 'Sexual abuse in later life', Sexual Assault Report, July/August 2009, Kingston, New Jersey: Civic Research Institute.

Vink, R., Pannebakker, F., Goes, A. and Doornink, N. (2014) *Family Violence of Adolescents and Young Adults Against Their Parents. Core Findings from Exploratory Research*, Utrecht, The Netherlands: Movisie/TNO.

Westmarland, N., Hester, M. and Carrozza, A. (2005) *Domestic Violence in Bristol – Findings from a 24-hour Snapshot (Full Report)*, Bristol: University of Bristol.

Wilcox, P. (2012) 'Is parent abuse a form of domestic violence?', *Journal of Social Policy and Society*, 11(2): 277–88.

6
FORCED MARRIAGE

A forced marriage is one where the bride, the groom or both do not freely consent to getting married. It is defined by the government's Forced Marriage Unit as follows:

> A forced marriage is where one or both people do not (or in cases of people with learning disabilities, cannot) consent to the marriage and pressure or abuse is used. It is an appalling and indefensible practice and is recognised in the UK as a form of violence against women and men, domestic/child abuse and a serious abuse of human rights.
>
> The pressure put on people to marry against their will can be physical (including threats, actual physical violence and sexual violence) or emotional and psychological (for example, when someone is made to feel like they're bringing shame on their family). Financial abuse (taking your wages or not giving you any money) can also be a factor.
>
> *(www.gov.uk/forced-marriage, accessed 22 April 2014)*

As Gill and Anitha (2011) highlight, there are a number of international human rights instruments that include the right to *freely consent* to marriage, and that forced marriage therefore violates. This includes the 1948 Universal Declaration of Human Rights, which states that both parties must give their free and full consent to marriage (Article 16(2)).

This chapter looks at the issue of consent in distinguishing between forced and arranged marriages, difficulties in estimating prevalence and the legal framework including the background to the recent creation of a criminal offence of 'forced marriage'. Attempts to use the immigration system in the name of responding to forced marriage are discussed, as are overlaps with men's violences against women under the guise of 'honour'.

Forced or arranged?

The issue of *consent* is therefore central to understanding whether a marriage is forced or not, and this is the case in both international human rights instruments and domestic law and policy (Gangoli et al., 2011). The use of consent as the pivotal factor can be useful in making a clear distinction between marriages that are forced (lack of consent from one or both parties) and those that are arranged (consent from both parties). However, this distinction oversimplifies matters to some extent. As Gangoli *et al.* highlight (2011), although this distinction attempts to accept diverse cultural practices, it renders invisible the more subtle forms of coercion. This, they argue, can result in 'slippage' between forced and arranged marriage. They also observe that scholars have found evidence of degrees of coercion being accepted as the norm within arranged marriages, in a range of contexts (citing the work of Wadley, 1980 and Derné, 2005).

Gangoli *et al.* (2006) researched forced marriage and domestic violence among South Asian communities in the Newcastle, Sunderland and South Tyneside areas of North-East England. They interviewed 37 women and 32 men who had experienced a forced, arranged or love marriage, in order to understand perceptions and experiences of marriage and the impact of their subjects' experiences. The authors found that four of the women defined their marriages as forced, and all had been taken abroad to be married. In addition, all of the forced marriages had involved violence and/or abuse from the woman's extended family before the wedding took place. In one of the cases of forced marriage the woman reported that the marriage had been a good one and that she felt happy in the relationship, although she was keen to stress that this did not mean she was promoting forced marriage:

> [Our relationship now] is ... fantastic, it's taken a lot of hard work ... He's turned out to be a best friend as well as a great husband, he's not your typical Pakistani husband, he's not controlling, he's not violent in any way, I couldn't have chosen a better person for myself to be honest with you. He's absolutely fantastic. I'm certainly not promoting forced marriages, what I'm saying that they do happen but there are choices of what a girl can do, whether a girl is strong enough to make those choices is up to her... I thank Allah everyday for marrying a fantastic husband.
> *(Interviewee quoted in Gangoli et al., 2006: 10–11)*

Arranged marriages in South Asian cultures were seen by the interviewees as both acceptable and important. Arranged marriages were likened to an introduction – an alternative way of meeting a partner and more acceptable than going to a pub or a nightclub. In fact, arranged marriages were seen by some as having advantages over love marriages in terms of being a safe way to find a partner. Many of the interviewees were clear about where the line may be drawn between being forced into marriage and entering an arranged marriage:

Well the difference to me is not having an opinion really. You are marrying him and that's it. You can't say yes and you can't say no. You just have to do it. That to me is being forced into something. Whereas arranged, arrangement is yes or no.

(Interviewee quoted in Gangoli et al., *2006: 12)*

However, in reality Gangoli *et al.* (2006) found that slippage between forced, arranged, and love marriages does exist. Of the 16 women who defined themselves as having an arranged marriage, 11 described some form of coercion having taken place. Sometimes that was through social expectations – one interviewee talked about having it 'drummed into her' that getting married is what she should be working towards and that that is what girls do in life. Another saw her own situation, knowing how much pressure her father was under, as too complex to box off as 'arranged' or 'forced', saying 'Well I was given the choice but if I look at why I said yes then I could say it was forced' (p. 10). This suggests that what is easy to say on paper and hypothetically, often does not have such clear lines in practice. This has led Anitha and Gill (2011) to conclude that coercion and consent are best understood as a continuum.

What is the extent of forced marriage in England and Wales?

In 2005 the Foreign and Commonwealth Office and the Home Office established a new Forced Marriage Unit (FMU) to lead on policy, outreach and people and professionals needing support (via individual casework and a helpline). They work both within the UK (for example offering safety advice) and outside the UK (the FMU website states that in 'extreme circumstances' they will 'rescue' victims being held overseas against their will). They also run training events and campaigns to raise awareness of the issue of forced marriage. Official figures on the extent of forced marriage come from the FMU.

In 2013 the FMU gave advice or support related to a possible forced marriage in 1,302 cases. Of these cases, most involved female victims (82 per cent of cases were female, 18 per cent male) and most (73 per cent) of the victims were aged 21 or under (40 per cent were under the age of 18). The cases involved 74 different countries to which a victim was either at risk of being taken or had already been taken in connection with a forced marriage. Nearly half of the cases (43 per cent) involved Pakistan. India and Bangladesh accounted for around one in ten cases each (India 11 per cent, Bangladesh 10 per cent). The FMU therefore have useful information about patterns of help-seeking behaviour in cases of forced marriage, for example about age and gender of those affected, and countries people were taken to, but does not have any information about the actual numbers of forced marriages in England and Wales. Likewise, as forced marriage was only recently made a specific criminal offence, there is no relevant police or prosecution data to refer to.

In 2009, the Department for Children, Schools and Families commissioned social research company NatCen to conduct research to improve their understanding of the prevalence of forced marriage and to examine responses to cases (Maisey, 2009). They defined a forced marriage for the purposes of their research as 'one conducted without the consent of both parties, and under duress'. Looking at data for 2008, NatCen estimated the number of people who had sought support for forced marriage in England to be between 5,000 and 8,000. Around one-third of cases related to forced marriages that had already taken place, with the other two-thirds relating to threats of marriage. This figure includes only victims who approached agencies for help (for example schools, colleges, youth agencies and voluntary sector organizations) and does not include 'hidden' cases. Amongst this figure, NatCen estimate that most of those seeking help were female (96 per cent), Asian (97 per cent), and that approaching half (41 per cent) were under the age of 18.

Reviewing the criminal justice framework

It is only recently that forced marriage has been a made a specific criminal offence in England and Wales. Previously, it was thought to have been sufficient to prosecute any offences under other existing legislation (e.g. threat to kill, assault, kidnapping, imprisonment). Most other European countries apply existing generic laws to cases of forced marriage, but Austria, Belgium, Cyprus, Denmark and Germany have all specifically criminalized forced marriage (Home Office, 2012). Alongside the generic offences in England and Wales, there was and still is a civil law act on forced marriage – the Forced Marriage (Civil Protection) Act 2007.

In the run up to the criminalizing of forced marriage, a new consultation on the topic was launched by the government in 2011 (a similar consultation had fairly recently taken place in 2005–6: see Forced Marriage Unit, 2006). The new consultation offered the options to a) continue current arrangements under existing criminal law (i.e. prosecute under other offences) or b) create a new criminal offence of forcing someone to marry. The consultation offered the 'for' and 'against' arguments outlined in Table 6.1.

The Home Office (2012) reported that, of the 297 responses to the consultation (175 from members of the public, 40 from statutory agencies, 40 from NGOs/other service providers, 20 from legal experts, 15 from representative bodies, and 7 from people who self-identified as victims), just over half (54 per cent) were in favour of the creation of a new offence. A further 9 per cent were undecided, and 37 per cent were against the creation of a new offence. Importantly, 80 per cent said that they felt the current civil remedies and criminal sanctions were not being used effectively. From these results, alongside other data collected in three workshops they held, the Home Office announced that it had decided to make forcing someone to marry a criminal offence. However, it did recognize that one of the concerns that was raised by many was that new criminal laws might further deter the reporting of forced marriage. Because of this, the government committed itself to a broader programme of work to run alongside the legislative approach. It reported that this programme of work would serve the following functions:

TABLE 6.1 Summary of consultation arguments

For	Against
A new offence could have a deterrent effect and send a clear signal (domestically and abroad) that forcing a person to marry is unacceptable.	Victims may stop asking for help and/or apply for civil remedies due to a fear that their families will be prosecuted and/or because of the repercussions from failed prosecutions.
A new offence could empower young people to challenge their parents or families.	Parents may take their children abroad and force them to marry or hold them there, to avoid prosecution taking place in the UK.
A new offence could make it easier for the police, social services and health services to identify that a person has been forced into marriage as existing legislation may not be easily linked with forced marriages.	An increased risk that prosecution, or threat of prosecution, may make it more difficult for victims to reconcile with their families.
A new offence would provide punishment to the perpetrator.	The behaviour may overlap with existing offences.

Source: (Forced Marriage Unit, Standard Note SN/HA/1003)

TABLE 6.2 Home Office programme of work

To help protect children – We will help those working in education and safeguarding children to know how to spot the earliest signs that a child may be at risk and know what action to take.

To help young people at risk of being taken abroad and forced into marriage – We will run a major summer awareness campaign in summer 2012 aimed at young people between the ages of 15 to 22 who are at risk, or close to someone at risk of being taken abroad and forced into marriage.

To further protect those at risk – We will criminalise the breach of a Forced Marriage Protection Order (FMPO).

To raise awareness across all communities – We will roll out a nation-wide engagement programme focused on prevention and education, delivered through regional road shows and debates and supported by multi-lingual posters.

To ensure victims receive the right support in a joined up way – We will develop and expand current training and guidance for frontline professionals ensuring all the relevant agencies are included – the Crown Prosecution Service (CPS), the police, the judiciary, health agencies, social services, Independent Domestic Violence Advisers and Independent Sexual Violence Advisers – and that [each] local authority nominates a Single Point of Contact to enable a more effective and responsive service for victims.

To help those who have already become victims overseas – We will fund a comprehensive package to provide emotional and practical support over the first six months for victims following their repatriation to the UK by the Forced Marriage Unit.

Source: (Home Office, 2012: 7)

A new criminal offence of forced marriage

Part 10, section 121 of the Anti-social Behaviour, Crime and Policing Act 2014 creates a new criminal offence of forced marriage in England and Wales (section 122 creates an identical offence in Scotland). The new law reads as:

> 121(1) A person commits an offence under the law of England and Wales if he or she –
> a uses violence, threats or any other form of coercion for the purpose of causing another person to enter into a marriage, and
> b believes, or ought reasonably to believe, that the conduct may cause the other person to enter into the marriage without free and full consent.

The maximum sentence on conviction is imprisonment for up to seven years. At the time of writing it is not known when the new law will come into operation, but it is likely to be early in 2015.

Forced Marriage Protection Orders

Forced Marriage Protection Orders (FMPO) are similar to injunctions and were introduced as part of the Forced Marriage (Civil Protection) Act 2007. Applications for the Orders can be made through a Family Court and they contain legally binding conditions to hopefully change the behaviour of people who are trying to force someone into marriage. Emergency orders can be made if necessary to ensure protection is in place immediately. If violence is threatened or used, a power of arrest can be included, enabling police to arrest and return offenders to the court to be tried for contempt of court. Passports may be confiscated as part of an order, and if someone is found in contempt of court for failing to adhere to an order's conditions they may be imprisoned for up to two years. Along with the new criminal offence of forced marriage described in the previous section, the Anti-social Behaviour, Crime and Policing Act 2014 also created a new offence of breaching a FMPO. This means that a person can be arrested and prosecuted for the actual breaching of the Order rather than for contempt of court. The new offence carries with it a maximum sentence of five years' imprisonment.

In the first year of their operation, a government review found that 86 FMPO had been made, and that none had been recorded as being breached (Ministry of Justice, 2009). However, campaign groups such as Karma Nirvana who work directly with people facing forced marriage were critical of the 'no breach' finding. They observed that there was little follow-up or monitoring once the Orders were made, saying that some professionals obtained FMPO and then classed the problem as 'solved' (Karma Nirvana, evidence to Forced Marriage Home Affairs Committee www.publications.parliament.uk/pa/cm201012/cmselect/cmhaff/880/88004.htm #note13, accessed 17 December 2014). It is possible that this has changed since the Orders were introduced, although there are no up-to-date figures on their effectiveness. In addition, changes regarding breaches may be found once the Anti-social Behaviour, Crime and Policing Act 2014 comes into force, since it makes breach of an Order a criminal offence.

Policy and practice responses

Phillips and Dustin argue that there are three broad approaches to state intervention in forced marriage: 1) regulation, 2) working with communities (dialogue) and 3) supporting people under threat of forced marriage (exit). Writing in 2004, they stated that, while all of these approaches were visible in UK policy, interventions tended to be most heavily focused on the third category, exit. They highlight that this approach is the least interventionist and requires people to leave their social group if dissatisfied with their treatment – it does not seek to regulate or criminalize the group's cultural practices. In reality, of course, it is not as straightforward to leave such a social group. Phillips and Dustin highlight that exit from a marriage is a difficult route to take when it entails exit from a family. In the ten years since Phillips and Dustin's analysis, there has been more of a move towards regulation with the creation of one new criminal offence (forced marriage) and one other offence (breach of a FMPO). However, there is a planned programme of work that focuses more heavily on exit. Therefore, today's approach may be best described as focusing on both regulation and exit. However, it remains to be seen to what extent the new offences will be policed and prosecuted.

Immigration-based controls

In 2003 a controversial change was made which the government argued might reduce the number of forced marriages – sometimes referred to by the shorthand 'age policy', because it raised from 16 to 18 the age at which a person could sponsor a partner to enter the UK for marriage. In 2004 the minimum age at which spouses could seek entry to the UK was also raised to 18. In 2006 the Home Office commissioned research from Hester *et al.* (2007) into the impact of these changes and the benefits or risks of further increasing the age – of sponsorship and/or entry – to 21 or even 24. This was part of a European-wide trend, after Denmark raised the age to 24 in 2002.

Hester *et al.* (2007) found no statistical or qualitative evidence that increasing the age to 18 had had any significant impact on the incidence of forced marriage, and this applied equally to changing the sponsorship and entry ages. In considering the question of raising the age further, they found limited support for either suggested age. While some potential benefits were identified (greater maturity, access to education, more likelihood of financial independence), these potential benefits were seen as outweighed by the risks. There were seen to be increased risks to those who were vulnerable or who had experienced forced marriage, in that young British women might be forcibly kept abroad for longer periods of time before they could legally sponsor their spouses. Concerns were also raised that the changes were not primarily linked to the prevention of forced marriage but to the restriction of immigration to the UK, and that this would impact on marriages that had not been forced and hence have a disproportionate effect on minority communities. A further concern was that forced marriage would be pushed further 'underground', with survivors prevented from accessing potential sources of support. Therefore, Hester et al. (2007) concluded that a further increase in the age of sponsorship or entry was unlikely to prevent forced marriage. They recommended that no further change to 21 or 24 should be made. Despite the research findings, the policy was changed further in 2008, barring a partner from outside the EU from entering the UK if they are under 21 years old.

Campaign group Southall Black Sisters has been supporting black and minority ethnic women since 1979. They argued that the 'age policy' is a disproportionate, discriminatory, unfair and unjustifiable response to the problem of forced marriage. They argue that in the vast majority of cases there is no evidence to show a link between forced marriage and gaining entry to the UK:

> The main motivating factors behind forced marriages are complex and it cannot be used to impose immigration controls that have unlawful, discriminatory outcomes for many genuine cases. Forced marriage is largely about the need to control (female) sexuality, protecting cultural and religious norms including family honour, and strengthening family ties.
> *(Southall Black Sisters Press release, 12 October 2011)*

The Supreme Court agreed, in the case of *Quila and Bibi v Secretary of State for the Home Department* [2011] UKSC 45, and stated that the government's ban on non-EU spouses under the age of 21 constituted unlawful interference to a person's right to respect for a private and family life (Article 8 of the Human Rights Act 1998). The Court ruled that, although the Secretary of State was pursuing a 'legitimate and rational aim of seeking to address forced marriage', increasing the minimum visa age from 18 to 21 disproportionately interfered with the rights of those in marriages that have not been forced (Home Office UK Border Agency, 2011). Accordingly, changes to the immigration rules were made to return the minimum marriage visa age to 18 years of age.

Overlaps between 'honour'-based violence and killings

There are overlaps between forced marriage and other forms of men's violences against women. For example, once forced into marriage, partner violence (including sexual violence) may be used against women. However, a more extreme overlap has been highlighted: that with 'honour'-based violence and killings. In some cases, the refusal to marry has led family members to plot to kill because the refusal was seen as bringing dishonour on the family. It is because of the overlaps that many organizations specializing in work with black and other minority ethnic women, such as Imkaan (a national black feminist human rights organization), get involved with violence against women, focusing on all forms of gender-based violence including domestic violence, forced marriage and 'honour'-based violence.

In 2003 Shafilea Ahmed, aged 17, was murdered by her parents – in part for refusing to agree to a marriage they were arranging for her. After being taken to Pakistan, Shafilea drank bleach and was hospitalized for ten weeks on her return to England, and on her release from hospital she was subjected to violence and abuse by her parents. No one intervened to support Shafilea, and she was smothered by her parents, who forced a plastic bag down her throat (it is alleged that her brother passed her mother the bag, who passed it to her father, who killed her). However, it took nearly ten years for her father Iftikar Ahmed and her mother Farzana Ahmed to be convicted and sentenced for her killing.

The Karma Nirvana network provides training and advice for professionals and direct support for those who are at risk of being forced into marriage. They specialize in crimes of violence against women where the issue of 'honour' is at stake – their tag line is 'Supporting victims of honour crimes and forced marriages since 1993'. The network was established by Jasvinder Sanghera, a survivor of forced marriage and 'honour'-based violence. Joining the terms 'karma' (peace) and 'nirvana' (enlightenment), the network aims to achieve both of these things for the victims they support.

Jasvinder Sanghera was born and brought up in Derby in the 1970s and 1980s in a British Sikh family. After seeing two of her sisters taken out of school at 15 and married to strangers, when Sanghera's turn came aged just 14, she refused to marry the man whose photograph she was shown. Regardless of her protestations, flights were booked, a dress ordered and her parents continued to plan the wedding against her will. She ran away to Newcastle with her boyfriend to escape the wedding, and was permanently cut off from the rest of her family. In 1989 one of her sisters killed herself because she felt trapped in an abusive marriage and saw no other way out. This was a pivotal moment in Sanghera's decision to begin campaigning against forced marriage and other forms of 'honour'-based violences against women.

In the summer of 2013, a range of government warnings were put out to teachers, doctors and airport staff to be alert to school-age children who might be taken 'on holiday' to be forced into marriage. The Karma Nirvana network publicized a new intervention known as the 'spoon trick' – if young people call them and are concerned about being taken abroad they are advised to put a spoon or other metal object in their underwear. This way, when they walk through the airport scanners, the metal alarms would go off and there would be the potential to avoid the flight at the last minute.

Summary

The role of coercion and consent in forced marriage is often more complicated in practice than it sounds on paper. Although the UK had previously taken a predominantly 'exit'-based approach to forced marriage, the last ten years has seen this move to a more regulatory approach, with new offences around forced marriage due to come into force – probably in early 2015. Changes around immigration policy in the name of preventing forced marriage – whether genuinely about forced marriage or not – have been struck down as unlawful and were heavily criticized as being disproportionate and unfair by specialist organizations such as Southall Black Sisters. A watching brief should be kept on the operation of the new offences, and the degree to which they are appropriately policed and prosecuted, over the coming years.

References

Anitha, S. and Gill, A. (2011) 'Reconceptualising consent and coercion within an intersectional understanding of forced marriage', in Gill, A. and Anitha, S. (eds), *Forced Marriage – Introducing a Social Justice and Human Rights Perspective*, London: Zed Books, pp. 46–66.

Anti-social Behaviour, Crime and Policing Act 2014, London: HMSO.

Derné, S. (2005) 'The (limited) effect of cultural globalisation in India: implications for culture theory', *Poetics*, 33: 33–47.

Forced Marriage (Civil Protection) Act 2007, London: HMSO.

Forced Marriage Unit (2006) *Forced Marriage: A Wrong Not a Right*, London: Forced Marriage Unit.

Gangoli, G., Razak, A. and McCarry, M. (2006) *Forced Marriage and Domestic Violence among South Asian Communities in North East England*, Bristol: University of Bristol.

Gangoli, G., Chantler, K., Hester, M. and Singleton, A. (2011) 'Understanding forced marriage: definitions and realities', in Gill, A. and Anitha, S. (eds), *Forced Marriage: Introducing a Social Justice and Human Rights Perspective,* London: Zed Books, pp. 25–45.

Gill, A. and Anitha, S. (2011) 'Introduction – framing forced marriage as a form of violence against women', in Gill, A. and Anitha, S. (eds), *Forced Marriage: Introducing a Social Justice and Human Rights Perspective,* London: Zed Books, pp. 1–24.

Hester, M., Chantler, K., Gangoli, G., Devgon, J., Sharma, S. and Singleton, A. (2007) *Forced Marriage: The Risk Factors and the Effect of Raising the Minimum Age for a Sponsor, and of Leave to Enter the UK as a Spouse or Fiancé(e)*, Bristol: University of Bristol.

Home Office (2012) *Forced Marriage – A Consultation. Summary of Responses*, London: Home Office.

Home Office UK Border Agency (2011) *UKBA: New Policy Guidance on the Marriage Visa Age of 21*, London: Home Office.

House of Commons Home Affairs Select Committee (2011) *Forced Marriage*, Eight Report of Session 2010–11, London: The Stationery Office. Available at www.publications.parliament.uk/pa/cm201012/cmselect/cmhaff/880/88004.htm#note13 (accessed 1 October 2014).

Human Rights Act 1998, London: HMSO.

Maisey, R. (2009) *Forced Marriage – Prevalence and Service Response*, London: NatCen.

Ministry of Justice (2009) *One Year On: The Initial Impact of the Forced Marriage (Civil Protection) Act 2007 in its First Year of Operation*, London: Ministry of Justice.

Phillips, A. and Dustin, M. (2004) 'UK initiatives on forced marriage: regulation, dialogue and exit', *Political Studies*, 52(3): 531–51.

Quila and Bibi v Secretary of State for the Home Department [2011] UKSC 45.

Southall Black Sisters (2011) 'Immigration policy on forced marriage is unlawful', *Southall Black Sisters*, available from: www.southallblacksisters.org.uk/immigration-policy-on-forced-marriage-is-unlawful/ (accessed October 2014).

Universal Declaration of Human Rights (adopted 10 December 1948), UNGA Res 217A(III) (UDHR) Art. 16(2).

Wadley, S. (1980) 'Hindu women's family and household rites in a north Indian village', in Falk, N. and Goss, R. (eds), *Unspoken Worlds: Women's Religious Roles*, London: Harper and Row.

7
'HONOUR'-BASED VIOLENCE AND KILLINGS

Violence against women where there is an issue of family 'honour' at stake is known as 'honour'-based violence or 'honour'-based killings. Some people prefer the term 'so called honour'-based violence. The use of the inverted commas and the term 'so called' are there to show that, of course, there is nothing 'honourable' about using violence and fatal violence against women. Rather, the term 'honour' is used to show that the violence or homicide is linked in some part to the role of 'honour' (Welchman and Hossain, 2005).

This chapter describes the role of 'honour' in violence and killing of women by family members. As well as the nature and prevalence of such crimes, it considers how 'honour' is used to excuse men's violence against women and outlines the policing failures that contributed to the death of Banaz Mahmod.

'Honour'-based violence against women

Examples of perceived dishonour recorded by the Iranian and Kurdish Women's Rights Organisation (IKWRO), a London women's organization, include seeking a divorce, refusing an arranged marriage, beginning a relationship that the family does not approve of and even being the victim of a sexual assault.[1] They cite one 15 year old girl who was beaten and placed under house arrest after her father found she had been texting male school friends (IKWRO, 2011b). An 'honour' killing is the fatal arm of 'honour'-based violence. Faqir (2001) defines 'honour' killings as 'the killing of women for suspected deviation from sexual norms imposed by society' (p. 66). Meetoo and Mirza (2007) define 'honour'-based violence as 'extreme acts of violence perpetrated upon a woman when an honour code is believed to have been broken and perceived shame is brought upon the family (p. 187)'.

Both definitions, of killing and of violence in the name of 'honour', are therefore explicitly gendered. However, the definition by IKWRO puts this link to patriarchal ideology more up-front, defining it as:

> So-called family 'honour' is a patriarchal ideology of oppression. Women who make autonomous decisions, particularly relating to their private lives, are believed to have brought 'shame' to their family. 'Honour' crime is performed with the intent of limiting the psychological and physical freedom of women.
> (IKWRO, cited in House of Commons Home Affairs Committee, 2008)

Although 'honour'-based offences are committed by partners as well as family members, this chapter is within the section on family violence to underpin the importance of the wider family systems in this form of violence. Importantly, family members – for example fathers, brothers, sons, and extended family members including in-laws – are often involved in the acts of violence and abuse as well as the woman's husband or partner. Unlike partner violence and homicide, there is often more than one person involved in 'honour'-based killings. Sometimes a woman's female family members are also involved, for example her mother or mother in law. Gill (2010) notes that while cases of 'honour'-based violence against men do occur, they represent a tiny minority of cases – and are mainly associated with the man being seen with women who are considered to be transgressive.

The nature and prevalence of 'honour'-based violence and killings

According to estimates by the United Nations Population Fund (2000), globally around 5,000 women per annum may be killed in the name of 'honour'. In England and Wales it is not known how many cases there are. Home Office figures estimate that there are around twelve per annum – so one per month – but acknowledge that the number may well be much higher because of the probably under-reported nature of the crime. They refer to data on 'honour'-based violence as being 'even patchier' than domestic violence data in terms of judging the extent of the problem (Home Affairs Select Committee, 2008).

In an attempt to fill this knowledge gap, in 2011 IKWRO sent Freedom of Information requests to all 52 police forces across England, Wales, Scotland and Northern Ireland. They asked the forces how many incidents of 'honour'-based violence they had recorded in the previous year. Responses were received from 39 police forces, which had recorded between them a total of 2,823 incidents. From this, IKWRO were able to estimate that the 13 forces that did not respond probably recorded around 500 further incidents. Hence, IKWRO conservatively estimated that there are around 3,000 incidents of 'honour'-based violence every year in the UK (IKWRO, 2011b). The five 'worst' areas (defined as having the most recorded incidents of 'honour'-based violence) were London, West Midlands, West Yorkshire, Lancashire and Manchester. Of the twelve police forces that also provided data for 2009 as well as the requested 2010, nine showed an increase in

74 Men's violences in the family

the number of recorded incidents. IKWRO found that the overall increase across the 12 forces between 2009 and 10 was 57 per cent. Clearly, these figures are likely to underestimate the problem, since most 'honour'-based violence will never be reported to the police, and not all that is reported to the police will necessarily be recognized as such and therefore flagged properly as being 'honour'-related.

The criminal justice system

As with domestic violence, and until recently with forced marriage, there is no specific criminal offence of 'honour-based violence' and incidents are policed and prosecuted using generic offences that already exist such as homicide, rape, assault and harassment. In addition, the Crown Prosecution Service highlights that 'honour'-based crimes could include procuring an abortion, encouraging or assisting suicide, conspiracy to murder and conspiracy to commit a variety of assaults (CPS Legal Guidance, CPS website, no date).

In 2008, the Association of Chief Police Officers developed an 'honour'-based violence strategy, which underlined the need for frontline staff to identify, adequately respond to and protect victims of such violence. This was also emphasized in the Government's 'Call to End Violence Against Women and Girls' strategy. Police training was listed as an action point in both strategies. However, IKWRO (2011a) continue to have concerns about the policing of 'honour'-based violence. While acknowledging that some improvements have been made over recent years, they found that the police were still turning away victims of 'honour'-based violence and were also putting them at increased risk by disclosing victims' details to their abusers on a 'regular basis'. Just some of the examples in an IKWRO (2011a) report of police failings are as follows:

- A woman went to West Drayton police to report threats by her husband to throw acid in her face and to kill her. The police didn't even take a statement and instead went directly to the woman's husband who naturally denied the claims. The police then said that they could not proceed as there was not enough evidence. We had to fight with them just to get them to take the client's statement, and even after this they still didn't press charges.
- A police interpreter in Islington disclosed details of an HBV case to the community. When we raised this, the police dismissed our fears that this posed a risk to the victim's safety.
- A client had to flee her husband and was at high risk of HBV. She received excellent treatment from her local police outside London and was quickly moved to safe accommodation in Haringey. However Haringey Police then phoned the woman's husband alerting him to the fact that the woman was living in Haringey and putting her in danger.
- Another woman was moved to Haringey after death threats from her brothers for resisting a forced marriage and again the police sent a card

detailing numbers that the woman should call in an emergency to her brother, alerting him to the woman's whereabouts.

IKWRO argue that these examples show that training is still needed within the police, and also in other statutory organizations (they also give examples of a mental health worker, social workers, a nurse, a number of housing authorities and a student counsellor guilty of bad practice).

The use of 'honour' to excuse men's violence against women

Meetoo and Mirza (2007) argue that the concept of 'honour' is used to perpetuate violence against women – that it is used by perpetrators as an excusing or mitigating factor when they commit such crimes. In some places this has been enshrined in law. For example, until 1981 in Italy there existed an 'honour crime' status that drastically reduced the criminal penalty for anyone killing their partner, daughter or sister because 'his honour or the honour of the family' had been injured by the victim's sexual conduct (Romito, 2008). In their Shadow Report to the UN Committee on the Elimination of Discrimination against Women (CEDAW), Sen *et al.* (2003) highlighted that many countries around the world still have judicial systems that are lenient to perpetrators of 'honour'-based crimes.

Using the term 'honour' to 'explain' and therefore excuse male violence against women is a victim-blaming approach. It is the female victim who is said to have brought shame upon her family, and she that is said to have acted in a deviant manner. Hence, the woman is often said to have 'brought it on herself'. Gill (2009) describes the case of Rukhsana Naz, a 16 year old from Derby. Naz was forced into marriage at the age of 16, then murdered by her family following an allegation that she had had an affair and become pregnant from this. Gill explains:

> She was effectively judged to have been in contravention of her community's laws and deemed 'sexually deviant'; her behavior represented a violation of fundamental Pakistani norms and values and so brought shame upon her family. Once a family's reputation is thought to have been 'dishonoured' in this way, the 'culpable' woman – whether she be a sister, daughter, or daughter-in-law – is in danger of being killed. The killer will then believe their actions to be a form of 'honour cleansing', i.e. of 'wiping away a stain on the family honour'. Ironically, though perhaps unsurprisingly, this cleansing process is accomplished through the spilling of blood.
>
> *(p. 6)*

An examination of those 'honour' killings that have been prosecuted in the UK shows that almost all of the defendants put forward a cultural defence, according to Gill (2009). This, she argues, allowed them to distance their behaviour from violence against women. Similarly, the judge in the case of the killing of Heshu Yones (described later in this section), cited not gender nor power but culture in his summing-up – describing the case as 'a tragic story arising out of irreconcilable cultural differences between traditional Kurdish values and the values of Western Society' (cited in Gill, 2009: 8).

Misinterpretations of 'honour'-based violence and killings

Meetoo and Mirza (2007) argue that 'honour' killings in the UK have become 'ethnicised' in the British multi-cultural context, by which means they are seen as a specific practice among certain ethnic groups. They argue that, since September 11, the discourse of Islamophobia has worked to further 'other' Muslim women – making them 'visible' yet 'pathologised' as victims.

Gill (2006) analysed media reporting of the killing of Heshu Yones, aged 16, who was killed in 2003 in West London by her father. Her father believed that she had crossed a boundary of acceptable behaviour because she had started a relationship with a boyfriend against his (the father's) wishes; he also believed her to be too 'westernized'. Heshu Yones's father stabbed her 17 times and slit her throat.

Gill found that when the case was reported in the media, terms such as a 'clash of cultures', 'Western ways' and a 'ghastly way of life' were used to describe not only the murder but also the way of life for young Muslim women more generally. Gill recorded some of the questions she was asked while doing media commentary on the topic, which relied heavily on stereotypes and racist attitudes towards minority groups. For example, in one radio phone-in debate Gill was asked 'Are you surprised that he murdered her because of the way she behaved – do minorities treat all their women like this?' Often, the media turned the discussion into one of the 'barbaric ways' of the 'primitive Asian Other', notes Gill (2006: 5). In relation to the killing of Heshu Yones but also those of Rukshana Naz and Sahjda Bibi, Gill concluded that:

> The public discourse in Europe has been simplistic, sensational and essentialist, stigmatizing ethnic and religious groups, and dividing communities between 'us' and 'them' or 'others'. Within this context, the 'others' are criticised as outsiders and as problematic communities, with barbaric and backward cultures.
>
> *(2006: 6)*

This discourse also plays to the idea that Black and Asian men are 'more barbaric' (Meetoo and Mirza, 2007) and therefore inherently use higher levels of violence and abuse against women.

The killing of Banaz Mahmod

Banaz Mahmod was strangled to death in 2006 aged 20 by her father, her uncle and another male relative. By the time she was killed, she had already been subjected to a barrage of serious and repeated acts of physical, sexual and psychological abuse. To date, seven men in total have been convicted and jailed for their roles in her death, including her father and uncle who received life prison sentences. The case has received a great deal of attention, in part because of the continued police failures on the five occasions she attempted to report her fears and actual experiences of rape and other acts of violence to the police. The second reason the case has received such high levels of attention is because of a documentary film – *Banaz – a Love Story* – directed and produced by Deeyah Khan for Fuuse Films. The film premiered at the Raindance Film Festival in London in 2012 and went on to win the 2013 Emmy award for Best International Current Affairs Film. The film was powerful and unique in the way it used actual and devastating footage of Banaz Mahmod attempting to get support and predicting her own death, of the massive police failings evident in the case, but also of the kindness, humility, honesty and dedication to bringing the killers to justice of one Metropolitan Police Chief Inspector – Caroline Goode. The film is available and free to watch online at the Fuuse Films website http://fuuse.net/banaz-a-love-story.

A marriage was arranged for Banaz Mahmod when she was 17 to a man ten years her senior, but she soon reported experiencing violence and abuse from him, including rape. In one police interview she said 'When he raped me it was like I was his shoe that he could wear whenever he wanted to'. She fell in love with someone else, left her husband, requested a divorce and reported his violence and rape against her to the police. However, the police case was plagued by delays, and the family gradually increased the control they exerted over Banaz as they believed she was bringing shame on them by divorcing her husband and starting a new relationship with someone the family did not deem suitable. In one scene in the film, footage is shown of Banaz Mahmod warning police that she was to be killed because of the 'dishonour' she was said to have brought on her family. In the footage in which she was interviewed by West Midlands Police, she says: 'People are following me, still they are following me. At any time, if anything happens to me, it's them'. At the end of one interview recorded on video by the police she asks 'Now I have given my statement, what can you do for me?', but the police did not offer her any assistance and she had no choice but to return home. The IPCC investigation concluded that two officers from West Midlands Police should receive written warnings for conducting a flawed investigation that was poorly supervised and not conducted in a timely manner, and a third officer should receive a 'management development intervention' over his failings to provide adequate supervision (IPCC News, 2 April 2008).

The IPCC also criticized officers from the Metropolitan Police Service for their poor response to Banaz Mahmod when she reported that her family had attempted to kill her. She had been forced to drink alcohol, and believed her father was about to kill her, when she managed to escape by smashing a window and running to a nearby café in distress, with blood on her hands, to ask for help. An ambulance was called and she was taken to hospital. The police in attendance did not log any references to the fact that she feared for her life, and the case was logged on the

Control and Dispatch system as 'female; self harmer; smashed window and bleeding from arms' (IPCC, November 2008). In addition, the female PC that attended the incident recorded Banaz Mahmod as being 'very dramatic', 'drunk' and 'kicking and screaming' according to the IPCC report. She was threatened by the PC with being arrested for criminal damage for the window she broke to escape if she did not 'calm down'. A police search began when Banaz Mahmod was reported missing by her partner just 26 days after this incident. Three months later, on 29 April 2006, her body was found in a suitcase buried in a garden in Birmingham.

At the end of their investigation, the IPCC (2008) made a number of recommendations. After finding a 'lack of awareness' of the trigger factors of domestic violence and the impact of 'cultural issues', they recommended that:

> ... police forces in England and Wales should recognise that so-called 'honour based violence' is more prevalent than previously understood and that this type of crime crosses cultural boundaries. It is therefore important for police forces to raise awareness of these issues by engaging with communities and developing partnerships; review and revise policies and literature in relation to domestic violence and cultural issues; engage with support groups dealing with such issues to develop trust and confidence.

However, the investigation has been criticized for just giving written warnings and words of advice to police officers, something that Gill (2008) argues is both shameful and unjust.

Summary

The Banaz Mahmod case was shocking even to those who had been working in the violence against women sector for some time. To watch in the film a young girl disclosing the repeated rape and abuse by her husband and for the police not to direct her to relevant support organizations is shocking in itself, but that her death threats were not taken seriously leaves the watcher feeling helpless at the scene they know is about to unfold in front of them on the screen. When I have shown the film to staff and student groups, you can almost feel the atmosphere in the room change as they watch the footage of Banaz Mahmod's body being dug up in the suitcase. This film should be part of all police and other orgainzations' training on 'honour'-based violence. It shows both the very best and the very worst of policing today.

Even if the lower estimate of one 'honour'-based killing per month is taken as the starting point, the Banaz Mahmod killing and the work that organizations such as IKWRO are doing show that many of these killings are preventable given appropriate interventions. However, without training, mistakes such as those outlined in this chapter are likely to continue, as are the preventable deaths of women.

Note

1 Thanks to IKWRO for their kind permission to reproduce material in this chapter.

References

Association of Chief Police Officers (2008) *Honour Based Violence Strategy*, London: ACPO. Available at www.acpo.police.uk/documents/crime/2008/200810CRIHBV01.pdf.

Crown Prosecution Service (n.d.) 'Honour based violence and forced marriage: guidance on flagging and identifying cases', *CPS Prosecution Policy and Guidance*, available from: www.cps.gov.uk/legal/h_to_k/forced_marriage_and_honour_based_violence_cases_guidance_on_flagging_and_identifying_cases/ (accessed October 2014).

Faqir, F. (2001) 'Intrafamily femicide in defence of honour: The case of Jordan', *Third World Quarterly*, 22(1): 65–82.

Gill, A. (2006) 'Patriarchal violence in the name of "honour"', *International Journal of Criminal Justice Sciences*, 1(1): 1–12.

Gill, A. (2008) 'MPS "could have done more" to prevent the murder of Banaz Mahmod', *Safe – The Domestic Abuse Quarterly*, Summer, pp. 24–5.

Gill, A. (2009) 'Honour killings and the quest for justice in black and minority ethnic communities in the UK', expert paper prepared for United Nations Expert Group meeting on Good practices in legislation to address harmful practices against women, available at: www.un.org/womenwatch/daw/egm/vaw_legislation_2009/Expert%20Paper%20EGMGPLHP%20_Aisha%20Gill%20revised_.pdf (accessed January 2015).

Gill, A. (2010) 'Reconfiguring "honour" – based violence as a form of gendered violence', in Idriss, M. and Abbas, T. (eds), *Honour, Violence, Women and Islam*, London and New York: Routledge-Cavendish, pp. 218–31.

House of Commons Home Affairs Select Committee (2008) *Domestic Violence, Forced Marriage and 'Honour'-Based Violence*, Sixth Report of Session 2007–09, London: The Stationery Office.

Iranian and Kurdish Women's Rights Organisation (2011a) 'Responses to "honour" based violence in the UK', IKWRO website, available at http://ikwro.org.uk/wp-content/uploads/2012/03/Briefing-on-Government-Reponse-to-HBV-in-the-UK-August-20113.pdf (accessed 1 October 2014).

Iranian and Kurdish Women's Rights Organisation (2011b) 'Nearly 3000 cases of "honour" violence every year in the UK', IKWRO website, 3 December 2011, available at http://ikwro.org.uk/2011/12/nearly-3000-cases-of-honour-violence-every-year-in-the-uk/ (accessed 1 October 2014).

Independent Police Complaints Commission (2008) *Independent Investigation – Executive Summary. Contact between Banaz Mahmod and the Metropolitan Police Service and the West Midlands Police, September 2005–January 2006*, London: IPCC, available from www.ipcc.gov.uk/news/ipcc-concludes-investigation-mps-and-west-midlands-police-dealings-banaz-mahmod (accessed 15 January 2015).

Meetoo, V. and Mirza, H.S. (2007) '"There is nothing 'honourable' about honour killings": Gender, violence and the limits of multiculturalism', *Women's Studies International Forum*, 30: 187–200.

Romito, P. (2008) *A Deafening Silence: Hidden Violence Against Women and Children*, Bristol: Policy Press.

Sen, P., Humphreys, C. and Kelly L. (2003) *CEDAW Thematic Shadow Report: Violence Against Women in the UK*, London: WOMANKIND Worldwide.

UN Population Fund (2000) *The State of World Population 2000*, available from: www.unfpa.org/publications/state-world-population-2000 (accessed October 2014).
Welchman, L. and Hossain, S. (eds). (2005) *'Honour': Crimes, Paradigms and Violence against Women*. London: Zed Books.

8
FEMALE GENITAL MUTILATION

Female genital mutilation, abbreviated to FGM, consists broadly of 'any procedure that's designed to alter or injure a girl's (or woman's) genital organs for non-medical reasons' (www.gov.uk/female-genital-mutilation). It is sometimes referred to by other terms such as 'female cutting' or 'female circumcision'. Although traditionally linked to parts of Africa, the Middle East and Asia, increased migration has led to it being an issue facing England and Wales, and is now a European and indeed a global problem. Although it is usually perpetrated against girls rather than adult women, its physical and psychological effects are lifelong – for example it has particularly severe impacts on women during pregnancy and childbirth – hence its inclusion in this book that is primarily about men's violences against *women*.

This chapter describes the types of FGM that exist, the difficulties involved in knowing exactly how prevalent it is and the physical, psychological and sexual problems it causes. The criminal justice system's response is outlined, as are young people's views on FGM – which are overwhelmingly negative. Finally, the question of whether Western feminists have double standards is considered, given the widespread nature of harmful British cultural practices such as breast implants.

Nature and prevalence

Gaining exact figures on the number of women who have been victim to female genital mutilation or how many are at risk is difficult. However, what is agreed upon is that the practice is widespread. It is thought to be prevalent in 28 countries in Africa and some parts of the Middle East and Asia, with an estimate that between 100 and 140 million women and girl children worldwide have been subjected to it and a further 3 million are at risk (Feldman-Jacobs and Clifton, n.d.). Prevalence rates vary, with countries such as Egypt, Ethiopia, Somalia and Sudan having rates of up to 98 per cent, and other countries such as Nigeria, Kenya, Togo and Senegal having rates of between 20 and 50 per cent (FORWARD website, n.d.). In the UK it is difficult to know exactly how many girls are at risk, but it is estimated to be as many as 6,500 per year (FORWARD website). Research in some countries, for example Eritrea, indicates that the prevalence of FGM might be decreasing, particularly among high-school-educated girls living in non-rural areas (Lbsu, Numbers and Martindale, 2009). Likewise, research suggests that opposition to FGM is increasing amongst younger people in the UK, and that support for FGM on religious grounds is reducing in particular (Options UK, 2013).

Although FGM is usually talked about as a singular form of violence, what it can consist of varies quite substantially. The World Health Organization (2001) breaks FGM down into four major types. Type 1 is 'Clitoridectomy', the partial or total removal of the clitoris. Type 2 is 'Excision', the partial or total removal of the clitoris and the labia minora, with or without excision of the labia majora. Type 3 is 'Infibulation', the narrowing of the vaginal opening through the creation of a covering seal that is formed by cutting and repositioning the inner, or outer, labia (with or without removal of the clitoris). Type 4 is 'Other', which covers all other harmful procedures to the female genitalia for non-medical purposes (e.g. pricking, piercing, incising, scraping and cauterizing the genital area).

The effects of FGM

FGM is usually carried out on young girls and can cause a range of serious health problems including, ultimately, death from severe bleeding or infection. Some cultures perform FGM on babies only a few days old, although later in childhood is more common (Dorkenoo, 1994). Clearly, death is the most severe potential effect of FGM. It is not known what the mortality rate is, since it often takes place in remote locations, which do not always keep death records, and attempts may be made to conceal deaths from authorities (Dorkenoo, 1994). In some cultures death through FGM is seen as the ultimate sacrifice and celebrated, with mothers told that they are 'lucky' to have had their female child taken from them in this way (Mansaray, 2013).

The Foundation for Women's Health Research and Development (FORWARD) is an African Diaspora women's organization that campaigns and supports women in the UK, Europe and Africa to change policies and practices that affect access, dignity and well being in terms of the sexual and reproductive health and rights of African girls and women. They list the short-term health implications as follows, though pointing out that these can vary according to the degree of mutilation:

- severe pain and shock
- infection
- urine retention
- injury to adjacent tissues, and
- immediate fatal haemorrhaging.

Women's individual accounts of their experience of FGM vary quite substantially, and this may influence whether they continue to support the practice and arrange it for their daughters. Abulkadir,, in her 2011 chapter on 'Somali memories of female genital mutilation', presents data from an interview with a Somali woman in London who was cut by a 'proper doctor' who injected her first with anaesthetic; this woman continues to support the practice and intends to have her daughters go through the same experience as she did. Abulkadir contrasts this with an auto-ethnographic account of her own experience, in which she was held down and cut by five women without any anaesthetic. This experience shaped Abulkadir's views on FGM and she now considers it a practice that should be stopped.

In the longer term, FORWARD have identified a range of consequences of FGM, including damage to the external reproductive system, infections of the uterus, vagina, and pelvis, cysts and neuromas, an increased risk of fistula, complications in pregnancy and childbirth, sexual dysfunction, menstrual complications and psychological damage. Hence, for many women, FGM has lifelong health consequences. The ongoing psychosexual problems can make some victims feel suicidal (Dorkenoo, 1994).

For women who have had the infibulation type of FGM (narrowing the vaginal opening through the creation of a covering seal), obstetric problems are inevitable. For childbirth to take place, the vagina must be reopened to allow the baby to be born – this is known as de-infibulation. Sometimes de-infibulation has already occurred in order for sexual intercourse to take place, where the vaginal opening had been significantly reduced – when this practice happens, de-infibulation generally takes place on the night of the woman's wedding (often with a razor blade). It is not surprising therefore that many girls and young women fear their wedding night and develop nightmares (WHO, 2001). Following childbirth, re-infibulation is often undertaken. This pattern of de-infibulation and re-infibulation may take place many times in a woman's lifetime, depending on how many times she gives birth.

Criminal justice approach

In England and Wales, female genital mutilation is illegal under the Female Genital Mutilation Act 2003. This Act covers the direct offence of committing genital mutilation on a woman or girl and two linked offences, of assisting a girl to mutilate her own genitalia, and of assisting a non-UK citizen to mutilate a girl's genitalia while she is in another country. The latter two offences render the aiding and abetting of female genital mutilation unacceptable. The offences all carry a maximum sentence of life imprisonment. Previously, FGM had been a criminal office under the Prohibition of Female Circumcision Act 1985, but this Act did not include the linked offences.

However, despite the illegality of FGM and the related offences, there have not yet been any convictions in England and Wales. In March 2014 the CPS announced that two men were to be charged in the first prosecutions under the Female Genital Mutilation Act. At the time of writing the prosecution was under way. Interestingly, the case concerns FGM committed against a patient at the Whittington Hospital in North London, and one of the men charged is a hospital doctor. Although the media reports did not state the exact nature of the FGM and the victim remains anonymous, the fact that newspaper reports used terms such as 'repaired FGM that had previously been performed on the patient' (*Guardian*, 21 March 2014), and the fact that the act happened after the woman had given birth at the hospital, strongly points to an act of re-infibulation.

The overall usefulness of the legislative approach more generally is evaluated later in this chapter when intervention and campaign approaches towards ending FGM are considered.

Why does it happen?

The children's charity, Plan, is one of the groups that work internationally to end FGM, particularly focusing on working with children in the world's poorest countries. The fact that FGM is often committed against children rather than adult women, at least the first type of FGM, firmly places it as a priority area for many international children's organizations. Plan argues that the overarching reason for FGM practices is the existence of power imbalances between men and women. For example, it is often described as key to a 'good marriage match' because of its perceived links with 'purity' and 'virginity'.

FORWARD point out that many women believe that FGM is necessary and are unaware that FGM is not practised in most of the world (FORWARD website). They agree with Plan, that power inequalities – particularly ensuring compliance of women with the dictates of their communities – are at the heart of justifications given for FGM. However, they also highlight that the roots of FGM are complex and numerous. Despite being linked to 'tradition', they highlight that it has not been possible to determine the precise origins of FGM. FORWARD list the reasons given for FGM as including:

- custom and tradition
- religion – the mistaken belief that it is a religious requirement
- preservation of virginity/chastity
- social acceptance, especially for marriage
- hygiene and cleanliness
- increasing sexual pleasure for the male
- family honour
- a sense of belonging to the group and conversely the fear of social exclusion, and
- enhancing fertility.

Dorkenoo (2001) highlights that a range of enforcement mechanisms exist at a community level to ensure that people conform to FGM practices. These include rejection as a marriage partner of a woman who has not undergone FGM, derogatory songs, public exhibitions, forced FGM and curses being placed upon women. Women who do adhere to FGM are rewarded in a range of ways including celebrations, gifts, being seen as suitable marriage partners and being given respect in the community.

There are therefore a variety of reasons given in response to the question 'Why does it happen?' Often the reasons will vary with the culture and the nature of the FGM being committed.

Young people's views on FGM

As with many forms of violence and abuse, educating young people about FGM and creating new social norms within a whole new generation of men and women is seen as key. Hemmings and Khalifa (2013) found that many of the young people in their study were open to the idea of keeping certain cultural practices but moving away from those that that are harmful. Indeed, many of their interviewees actively wanted to contribute towards ending such practices.

Hemmings and Khalifa used Participatory Ethnographic Evaluation Research (PEER) to look at young people's views on harmful practices – particularly FGM and forced marriage – across the United Kingdom, Portugal and the Netherlands. FGM is illegal in all of these countries; indeed the Netherlands go so far as to include the threat of FGM as a possible reason for seeking asylum. They found that young people, particularly young Guineans in Portugal, had the highest levels of awareness of the practice and that all except two were opposed to FGM. Additionally, many of the Portuguese young people had tried to influence people in their own family to abandon FGM, although often unsuccessfully. In London and the Netherlands they found lower levels of awareness, but that interviewees were unanimously against the practice. The young people in the Netherlands who were interviewed were all of Somali descent, but they felt confident that they themselves were not at risk – that FGM was not an issue that affected them in the Netherlands. They did, however, acknowledge that some new migrants might still support FGM. Amongst all the young people, they found awareness was low about support services and information that were available.

Hemmings and Khalifa found that a number of the interviewees in both the Portuguese and the UK sample recounted a story that they and the researchers were not sure was true or 'urban myth' about how FGM had been performed to curb a young woman's sexual appetite. Whether truth or urban myth, Hemmings and Khalifa point out that it certainly operated as a 'cautionary tale' against women's perceived problematic behaviour, and that in it FGM was seen as the 'cure':

> According to gossip, a young Iraqi girl had her genitals mutilated by family members to curb her libido. She was apparently a highly promiscuous young girl from a fairly successful Iraqi family living in a city in Iraq. She had several boyfriends during her teenage years and engaged in public displays of

affection. When she lost her virginity, her parents could no longer tolerate her premarital affairs and mutilated her genitals. She is believed to have been completely transformed into leading a pure and chaste life.

(Interviewee, cited in Hemmings and Khalifa, 2013: 35)

This echoes research by Brown *et al.* (2013), who found that the control of female sexuality was a major driving force in the continuation of the practice. Amongst the communities they worked with, they found that this motivation was particularly strong for men and for older women such as grandmothers.

Approaches to ending FGM

Brown *et al.* (2013) assessed the approaches of the World Health Organization, the United Nations and specialist FGM organizations in Europe. They found that work concentrated broadly on four main areas: bodily and sexual integrity, human rights, legislation and health.

Bodily and sexual integrity approach

As discussed earlier, the use of FGM as a threat or actual infliction to restrict women's sexual desires is common. This approach takes as its starting point that FGM, particularly those types that include the removal of the clitoris and/or the stitching or narrowing of the vaginal opening (infibulation), removes the potential of sexual pleasure from women. Brown *et al.* (2013) point out that many FGM-affected communities in the EU are concerned about the sexual liberation of women, and what is seen as a liberal attitude towards sex in many European countries. In their research they found that using bodily and sexual integrity as the basis for FGM campaigns and interventions was perceived as threatening the religious and cultural beliefs of such communities. In addition, they found that while many of the women in their study did report physical and psychological pain during sexual intercourse, a minority of women said that they enjoyed sexual intimacy with their husbands. Brown *et al.* also point out that this approach projects the message that all forms of FGM remove sexual enjoyment in the same ways, rather than understanding that different outcomes are linked with different practices. This approach has also been criticized for imposing Western understandings of female sexuality on non-Western communities (Dustin, 2010).

Human rights approach

Brown *et al.* (2013) highlight that the human rights approach has been very influential, both at a national level and at a European and UN level. Labelling FGM as a violation of human rights is the framework that most governments have chosen to adopt. Some of the participants inthe study by Brown *et al.* saw the human rights approach as problematic, for example pointing out that FGM is condemned as a global human rights violation but the circumcision of male children for religious reasons is not seen in the same light. Their participants also highlighted the inconsistency of the approach because it presumes that the right to life, liberty and security of the person (Article 3) has precedence over the right to freedom of thought, conscience and religion (Article 18) under the Universal Declaration of Human Rights. Brown *et al.* conclude that despite some resistance against the framing of FGM as a human rights violation, this has nonetheless been a powerful political approach at a European Union level, with a 'zero tolerance' approach being taken to all forms of FGM.

Legislative approach

As described earlier in this chapter, the legislative approach is one of the approaches taken by England and Wales – with the act of FGM and some related offences punishable on conviction by up to life imprisonment. This is also the approach taken by many other countries. Although at the time of writing a prosecution was under way, as discussed earlier, it remains the case that FGM had already been illegal for nearly thirty years without any criminal prosecution taking place in England and Wales. This has led many to criticize the legislation, questioning the point of having legislation that is not enforced. Phillips (2010) suggests that this means that the Female Genital Mutilation Act is simply 'symbolic'.

A number of other countries have used the legislative approach as one of the strategies towards ending FGM. These include 24 African nations, with the most recent ban being introduced in 2012 in Somalia (Shell-Duncan *et al.*, 2013). While this action in England and Wales has been criticized as being symbolic, this has been the intention behind FGM criminalization in some countries – to communicate a new, state-backed, social norm which, it is hoped, will change behaviour (Shell-Duncan *et al.*, 2013). However, it is clear that while symbolic recognition and the changing of social norms may be important in themselves, the fact that FGM continues to be so widespread suggests that legislation without enforcement is unlikely to be influential in ending FGM. Many have argued that anti-FGM laws are useful in creating an 'enabling environment' in which a support mechanism is available for those who already want or intend to withdraw from or campaign against FGM practices (UNICEF, 2005; Shell-Duncan *et al.*, 2013). However, it is possible that this 'enabling environment' may begin to be diminished if FGM laws are openly and visibly ignored. It will therefore be interesting to see what happens with the first FGM prosecution in England and Wales, and whether prosecutors will take a more proactive approach in the future.

Health approach

The health approach started to be used by campaigners and international organizations in the 1980s. It aims to take the 'politics' out of the practice and instead focus on the short- and long-term health consequences of FGM (Brown *et al.*,

2013). In their research, Brown *et al.* found that one of the problems with using the health approach was that it could result in the assumption that FGM practices that had less severe health risks associated with them were therefore acceptable. They found that while communities accepted the health risks of the most invasive types of FGM such as infibulation, this was not necessarily the case for other types of FGM. Not only were the negative health outcomes not acknowledged for these less invasive types, these types were sometimes seen as having health benefits attached to them, associated with hygiene. The health approach can therefore be seen as contradictory, as potentially inaccurate when dealing with FGM as a whole and therefore as 'watering down' the zero tolerance approach.

Perpetrators of FGM – women abusing women?

It is well established that most of the people who directly perpetrate FGM are women not men. Often the perpetrators are mothers, aunts, grandmothers or neighbours (Hemmings and Khalifa, 2013). In Hemmings and Khalifa's 2013 study, they found that some interviewees even queried how widespread was men's knowledge about the practice.

> I think that the women now see it as a bad thing, because it happens to them. The men, on the other hand, don't really think about it that much because they don't know anything about it (FGM) and the consequences.
> *(Interviewee, cited in Hemmings and Khafila, 2013: 37)*

> I think a lot of girls are against FGM. It has a lot of negative effects on a woman's health. I think a lot of young men find it less bad, because they know very little about it. I think when they know more about it and the consequences for a woman, then they would see it as something that can't be practised anymore.
> *(Interviewee, cited in Hemmings and Khafila, 2013: 37)*

> As a young Somali man I think the practice is unnecessary to practise. The attitude is slowly changing and I can't stress enough that men don't have anything to do with it.
> *(Interviewee, cited in Hemmings and Khafila, 2013: 37)*

Certainly, there is evidence that some groups of young men in particular are beginning to turn their backs on the practice. The Options UK study found that young men saw FGM as an out-dated practice that is not related to what makes a 'good' woman. Indeed, in some cases a woman having experienced FGM was seen as a negative, because it could give a young woman higher levels of anxiety. They also found examples of men openly disapproving of other men who supported FGM, and of older men who had apologized to their daughters for not preventing them from being subjected to FGM.

However, this is a book about male violence against women, and although this is an act directly perpetrated most often, possibly nearly always, by women, it is important to recognize the role that gender and power more widely have in FGM practices. FGM is very much a community rather than an individual issue, with support for the practices very much ingrained in men's views on women's sexuality and linked suitability for marriage. From her research on FGM with Somali men and women, Abulkadir (2011) concluded that it was patriarchal beliefs and values that maintain the continued use of FGM as a 'rite of passage' for many girls. This is why so much of the work is engaged in attempting to create new social norms. As Dorkenoo (1994) highlights:

> …clearly, if in a community sufficient pressure is put on a child to believe that her clitoris or genitals are dirty, dangerous, or a source of irresistible temptation, she will feel relieved … to be made like everyone else.
>
> *(p. 25)*

Feminist double standards?

As will be clear from this chapter so far, for many FGM is a harmful cultural practice with severe health implications including potential fatality. For many it is seen as a violation of women's human rights that marginalizes or denies their sexual and bodily integrity. When first-hand examples are read of the un-anaesthetized cutting of babies, girls and women, it is easy to condemn the acts as barbaric practices that constitute acts of torture.

However, this approach in itself runs the risk, at best, of double standards and, at worst, of racism. A number of painful procedures are performed on Western women's bodies that are considered acceptable in some cultures. Examples such as these, if taken to other cultures and described, may likewise raise concerns. Examples may include women's genital waxing, anal bleaching, labial piercings, and vaginoplasty and labiaplasty for cosmetic reasons – what the media often call the quest for a 'designer vagina'. Just as FGM has long-term health consequences, labiaplasty – surgery on the labia majora (the outer vaginal lips) or labia minora (the inner vaginal lips), generally to make the labia smaller or more symmetrical – can result in permanent scarring, infections, bleeding, irritation and increased or decreased sensitivity depending on nerve damage. As well as Western cultural genital practices – some of which are harmful in that they cause some immediate if not longer-term pain, breast enhancement for non-medical reasons – 'boob jobs' – are common and seen as highly desirable in some Western cultures. Pointing out the contradictions, Gunning (1992) calls this an 'arrogant perception' that typifies Western critiques of other cultures and places on one hand the 'enlightened observer' *versus* the 'ignorant and backward other':

> How bizarre and barbaric must a practice like implanting polyurethane covered silicone into one's breasts be perceived [to be] by one not accustomed to the practice.
>
> *(p. 213)*

Moira Dustin (2010) is another theorist who argues that a double standard is at play when comparing attitudes to FGM/C (some argue the use of the term mutilation/cutting is more appropriate because of these debates) with surgeries carried out in the West such as those described above. She argues that breast enhancement, labial reduction and 'trimming' are all therapeutically unnecessary, and that which if any of these practices are classed as shocking is dependent on the cultural norms of a society.

This is not to suggest that those who point to the contradictions and double standards in relation to discussions of FGM are arguing in favour of FGM, but rather that they wish to increase recognition that 'FGM/C is only one of the many culturally specific ways in which women's bodily and sexual integrity is abused, sometimes with their own participation' (Dustin, 2010: 19). This, and the fact that generally FGM is not consensual and committed against children, has led many UK NGOs to take a pragmatic, child abuse-based approach. This means recognizing the hypocritical aspects of the law but prioritizing the protection of children rather than engaging in academic debates such as that about the similarities between FGM/C and cosmetic surgery in the West. Dustin cites an interview she did with Efua Dorkenoo (former director of FORWARD) who puts it very clearly: 'we don't have time to wait until white women are conscious of their own oppression [in relation to cosmetic surgery]' (Dustin, 2010: 19, Dorkenoo quote from interview with Dustin).

Summary

FGM practices should not be classed as uniform, nor should the arguments against them be presented as incontestable facts (Dustin, 2010). This is one reason why the 'health' approach to intervention is problematic and likely to be ineffective. While the human rights approach has been problematic, it has significant political currency, and has led to some very bold policy moves, for example the zero tolerance approach taken by the European Union. The legislative approach has performed more of a symbolic or enabling role until recently, with critics arguing that (in the UK) the police and the Crown Prosecution Service have been too slow to act despite some FGM clinics openly advertising their cutting 'services'. There are clear contradictions and double standards evident in the way that the international community labels and acts against genital mutilation when it is performed on female children but not when boys are circumcised for religious reasons. Although it is recognized that the circumcision of girls has a much more significant and life-threatening impact throughout their lives than the circumcision of boys, this does not make the circumcision of male children acceptable. Likewise, simply because Western women 'consent', and in most cases pay large sums of money, to have their genitals and breasts surgically altered to fit in with cultural norms, this does not prevent us from classing these acts as harmful cultural practices. The concept of 'harmful cultural practices' is a useful one as it demonstrates both the harm and the cultural aspects of FGM and does not risk the conflation of all types of the practice in the way that the term 'FGM' does. But it must be recognized that those communities within Africa, Asia and the Middle East that practice different types of FGM are not the only cultures with harmful practices.

References

Abulkadir, I. (2011) 'Somali memories of female genital mutilation', in Bradley, T. (ed.), *Women, Violence and Tradition*, London: Zed Books, pp. 51–72.

Brown, K., Beecham, D. and Barrett, H. (2013) 'The applicability of behaviour change in intervention programmes targeted at ending female genital mutilation in the EU: integrating social cognitive and community level approaches', *Obstetrics and Gynecology International*, Article ID 324362, available at www.hindawi.com/journals/ogi/2013/324362/ (accessed 17 December 2014).

Dorkenoo, E. (1994) *Cutting the Rose. Female Genital Mutilation: The Practice and its Prevention*, London: Minority Rights Group.

Dorkenoo, E. (2001) *Female Genital Mutilation: Human Rights and Cultural Relativity*, Culture and Human Rights, Challenges and Opportunities for Human Rights Work Conference, Siem Reap, Cambodia, August 2001.

Dustin, M. (2010) 'Female genital mutilation/cutting in the UK: challenging the inconsistencies', *European Journal of Women's Studies*, 17(1): 7–23.

Feldman-Jacobs, C. and Clifton, D. (n.d.) 'Female genital mutilation/cutting: data and trends update 2010', Population Reference Bureau, available from: www.prb.org/Publications/Datasheets/2010/fgm2010.aspx (accessed 7 October 2014).

Female Genital Mutilation Act 2003, London: HMSO.

Foundation for Women's Health, Research and Development (FORWARD) (n.d.) 'Female genital mutilation (FGM) | FORWARD', available from: www.forwarduk.org.uk/key-issues/fgm (accessed 7 October 2014).

UK Government (n.d.) 'Female genital mutilation (FGM)' – GOV.UK, available from: www.gov.uk/female-genital-mutilation (accessed 7 October 2014).

The Guardian (2014) 'Two men first to be charged in UK under FGM Act', *The Guardian*, 21 March, available from: www.theguardian.com/uk-news/2014/mar/21/fgm-female-genital-mutilation-men-charged (accessed 6 October 2014).

Gunning, I.R. (1992) 'Arrogant perception, world travelling and multicultural feminism: the case of female genital surgeries', *Columbia Human Rights Law Review*, 23(2): 189–248.

Hemmings, J. and Khalifa, S. (2013) *'I Carry the Name of my Parent': Young People's Reflections on FGM and Forced Marriage. Results from PEER Studies in London, Amsterdam and Lisbon*, London: Options UK.

Lbsu, L.A., Numbers, L. and Martindale, L. (2009) 'Female genital mutilation', *Midwives Magazine*, December 2009/January 2010.

Options UK (2013) *The FGM Initiative – Summary of PEER Research*, London: Options UK.

Phillips, A. (2010) *Gender and Culture*, Cambridge: Polity Press.

Mansaray, S. (2013) 'Female genital mutilation', Purple Rose Lecture, Durham University.

Shell-Duncan, B., Wander, K., Hernlund, Y. and Moreau, A. (2013) 'Legislating change? Responses to criminalising female genital cutting in Senegal', *Law & Society Review*, 47(4): 803–35.

UNICEF (2005) *Changing a Harmful Social Convention: Female Genital Mutilation/Cutting*. Florence, Italy: United Nations Children's Fund (UNICEF).

Universal Declaration of Human Rights (adopted 10 December 1948), UNGA Res 217A(III) (UDHR), Arts 3 and 18.

World Health Organization (2001) *Female Genital Mutilation: Integrating the Prevention and the Management of the Health Complications into the Curricula of Nursing and Midwifery*, Geneva: WHO.

9

FAMILIAL RAPE AND ABUSE

The rape and abuse of children within the family environment is defined by Horvath *et al.* (2014) as '… abuse perpetrated by a family member or that takes place within a family context or environment, whether or not by a family member' (p. 9). This definition covers acts that are also variously known as incest or intra-familial child sexual abuse. This is a type of sexual violence that is thought to be vastly under-reported to the police – in the 2011 study by Radford *et al.*, more than one in three children (34 per cent) who had experienced sexual abuse through direct contact by an adult did not tell anyone about it. Even given this limitation, it is difficult to estimate the number of incidents of familial rape and other sexual offences reported to the police. The police do record sex offence crimes against children, but these figures are not broken down by perpetrator type.

This chapter starts by describing the criminal justice framework in relation to familial sex offences, then examines available statistics on familial rape and abuse of children. The long-standing impacts of experiencing this type of abuse are then outlined. I describe the case of Mr X, named by the media as 'the British Fritzl', including the findings from a serious case review into how the abuse could continue for so long within the family, and finally two approaches to preventing or responding to familial rape and abuse are outlined. As with the other chapters in the book, it is not possible to cover familial rape and abuse comprehensively within one chapter, and this should be seen more as a starting point for further reading on the subject.

How much familial rape and abuse of children is there?

As with other forms of violence and abuse, in the absence of a national self-report victimization survey (other than the Crime Survey England and Wales – which only asks about offences since the age of 16) it is difficult to know the true extent of sexual offences against children. Although a special version of the Crime Survey England and Wales has recently been introduced, designed to measure the victimization of children aged 10–15, this does not ask children about any sexual victimization (Millard and Flatley, 2010). Failing to ask children about their experiences of sexual victimization and only asking adults about experiences of sexual violence perpetrated against them after their 16th birthday, is to contribute to the invisibility of sexual violence against children, and to its status of 'something that is not talked about', which is likely to reduce the ability of children and adults to speak out about child sexual abuse.

Despite the lack of self-report statistics, it is generally accepted that a high proportion of the sexual abuse against children happens within the family, and also that there are a high number of adult survivors of familial sexual abuse in childhood. Familial rape and abuse of *adults* within the family is thought to be less common, though as shown in the case of Mr X – described later in this chapter – when it does happen it is no less damaging.

The official statistics show is that the last few years have seen a large increase in the number of sexual offences against children being reported to and recorded by the police (all figures in this paragraph from Office for National Statistics, 2014, Appendix Table A4). This might be because the police have got better at properly recording sexual offences, but it is likely to also represent an increase in willingness to report to the police. For the offence of 'rape of a female child under 16', 3,396 offences were recorded in 2013/14 compared to 2,797 in 2012/13 – an increase of 21 per cent. For 'rape of a female child under 13' there was a similar increase of 19 per cent (up from 2,371 in 2012/13 to 2,833 in 2013/14). Reports of sexual assaults against female children and sexual offences against male children also saw increases over this period. Unusually, given the increases seen in other reports of sexual offences over this period, reported familial sexual offences fell by 4 per cent from 510 in 2012/13 to 491 in 2013/14. This is the lowest number recorded since the Sexual Offences Act 2003 came into force, and is one-third of the number recorded in 2006/07 (1,344). It is unclear why this decline has happened against a general increase for reports of other sexual offences. It is possible that child protection procedures have improved and that fewer offences are being committed, though that is unlikely to describe the massive drop seen from 2006 onwards. It is also possible that there has been a change in police recording techniques for this crime, for example that more familial offences are being recorded under the generic sexual offences such as rape of a female child under 13.

The only self-report study of young people's experiences of abuse in the UK was conducted nearly fifteen years ago by Cawson *et al.* (2000). Although societal attitudes to sexual violence have changed over this period, and the survey pre-dates an overhaul of the sexual offences legislation, it remains the most detailed information available to date. Cawson *et al.* (2000) used a random sample of 2,869 young people aged 18–24 and asked them about their experiences of maltreatment as children. In relation to family members specifically, they found that:

- 3 per cent reported sexual activity in the form of touching or fondling by relatives that were against the reporter's wishes
- 3 per cent reported witnessing relatives exposing themselves.
- 1 per cent experienced oral/penetrative acts or attempts by a relative and
- 1 per cent were exposed to voyeurism or pornography by a relative.

Cawson et al. (2000) concluded that most of the sexual offences experienced by children and young people were not committed by relatives. They found that much larger numbers had experienced sexual abuse by people outside the family – predominantly age peers (boy-/girlfriends, friends of brothers or sisters, fellow pupils/students) or older people outside the family (most commonly neighbours and parents' friends, less commonly strangers and professionals).

Although support organizations do not have any prevalence data, information is available about the nature of the abuse of those contacting them for support. The last statistics available from the NSPCC about callers to ChildLine show sexual abuse was the fourth largest main reason for children calling in 2008/09 (NSPCC, 2009). They also report that 59 per cent of the sexual abuse perpetrators that children called about were family members. This goes against the findings of the research by Cawson et al. (2000), though this difference is probably linked to population difference: those ringing ChildLine were different and probably younger than those participating in the Cawson et al. study. International research suggests that relatives are perpetrators in around a third of child sexual abuse cases (Pineda-Lucatero et al., 2009), though comparisons between studies are difficult because of different definitions of what constitutes 'family'.

Familial offences contained within the Sexual Offences Act 2003

A large number of offences are specifically aimed at sexual violence against children under the criminal law. Most of these are offences regardless of whether the perpetrator is a family member or not: for example, rape of a child under 13, sexual assault of a child under 13, sexual activity with a child, engaging in sexual activity in the presence of a child, paying for sexual services of a child and controlling a child prostitute or a child involved in pornography (N.B. most consider the names of last two offences inappropriate). There is also a list of criminal offences that involve the abuse of a position of trust in connection with the sexual abuse of children; however, these relate to those in a position of power outside the family – for example, perpetrators who are teachers.

In addition to the generic offences, two offences specifically relate to sexual offences against children within the family. A family member is defined as a parent or foster-parent, grandparent, brother, sister, half-brother, half-sister, aunt or uncle. Someone is also considered family within this definition if they live or have lived in the same household or have regularly cared for the child *and* are a step-parent, cousin, stepbrother, stepsister, or have been a foster-parent. For these two offences, there is an exception for spouses and civil partners of those aged 16 and over, and for sexual relationships which pre-date family relationships. The two familial child sex offences contained within the Sexual Offences Act 2003 can be paraphrased as:

1. Section 25. *Sexual activity with a child family member* – where A intentionally touches B, the touching is sexual, the relation of A to B is that of a family member as outlined above, and *either* B is under 18 and A does not reasonably believe that B is 18 or over *or* B is under 13.
2. Section 26. *Inciting a child family member to engage in sexual activity* – where A intentionally incites B to touch, or allow himself to be touched, by A, the touching is sexual, the relation of A to B is that of a family member as outlined above, and *either* B is under 18 and A does not reasonably believe that B is 18 or over *or* B is under 13.

As well as the sex offences against children, there are two offences under the Sexual Offences Act 2003 that relate to sex with an adult relative. It is an offence to have sex with an adult relative either by committing, or consenting to, an act of sexual penetration. These can be paraphrased as:

3. Section 64. *Sex with an adult relative: penetration* – where A is aged 16 or over and he intentionally penetrates B's vagina or anus with a part of his body or anything else, or penetrates B's mouth with his penis, the penetration is sexual, B is aged 18 or over, A is related to B (parent including adoptive parent, grandparent, child, grandchild, brother, sister, half-brother, half-sister, uncle, aunt, nephew or niece), and A knows or could reasonably be expected to know that he is related to B.
4. Section 65. *Sex with an adult relative: consenting to penetration* – As above, but where B consents to the penetration.

Effects of familial child rape and abuse

Most of the literature on the effects of child sexual abuse does not distinguish types of perpetrator. However, where research has distinguished between types of perpetrator, it has tended to find that victims of familial rape and abuse suffer greater physical and emotional symptoms than victims of other types of child sexual abuse as a result of the breach of the relationship of trust with the perpetrator (Horvath *et al.*, 2014). In their review of the impact of familial child sexual abuse, Horvath *et al.* (2014) conclude:

> The impact of child sexual abuse leaves long-term profound psychological damage. The short-term impacts are also extremely damaging but 'hidden'. This makes intervention very difficult and leads to extended suffering.
> *(p. 56)*

Some of the impacts of child sexual abuse generally (not specifically that which takes place within a family environment) include the following:

- Carter *et al.* (2006) found that almost half (48 per cent) of female in-patients with anorexia nervosa had a history of child sexual abuse. Women who were sexually abused as children tended to show more severe symptoms and were more likely to have other, co-occurring, mental health problems.
- Kendler *et al.* (2000) found that women who had been raped as children were at least four times more likely to develop an alcohol misuse disorder than those who had not been sexually abused.
- The Mental Health Foundation and Camelot carried out an inquiry into self-harm amongst 11–25 year olds and found that the risk factors associated with self-harm in younger populations seem to involve a number of common themes, including physical, emotional and sexual abuse (Mental Health Foundation and Camelot, 2006).
- Hayatbakhsh *et al.* (2009) found that, by the age of 21, female survivors of child sexual abuse were almost four times more likely than women who had not been abused to use cannabis frequently.
- Goodwin *et al.* (2005) found that young adults who had experienced childhood sexual abuse were more than four times as likely to experience panic attacks as those who had not been abused.

Child sexual abuse may influence the physical properties of the brain itself. A study by Andersen *et al.* (2008) found that the age at which sexual abuse occurs influences the ways in which the brain is affected. Abuse between the ages 14 and 16 appeared to affect the development of the frontal cortex, a region that is important for decision making, whilst abuse between the ages 3 and 5 affected the development of the hippocampus, a region that lies in the middle of the brain and is important for memory processes.

Mr X – the 'British Fritzl'

In 2008 a man known as Mr X (in order to protect the identity of his daughters) was ordered to spend the rest of his life in jail: he was given 25 life sentences for the repeated rape of his daughters over a 27-year period. Some commentators drew parallels to Josef Fritzl, the Austrian man who repeatedly raped his daughter and kept her locked in a dungeon for 24 years – earning Mr X the nickname 'British Fritzl' in the press.

Press reports estimate that the two sisters were raped over 1,000 times. One was raped from the age of 8, and physical violence was used against them both as well. When they had visible injuries they were kept home from school. Mr X threatened them that they would both be killed if they told anyone what was happening to them, and the prosecutor in the case told of how Mr X would hold the head of his younger daughter next to the flame of their gas fire. As the sisters grew older, the rapes started to result in pregnancies. Between them they had nineteen pregnancies, and nine children were born (though two died at birth).

A serious case review was ordered, after it was found that two social services departments had been in contact with the family, that the school had written off the women's injuries as linked to bullying, and that the family doctor and other medical staff involved in their maternity care had missed opportunities to intervene. Although the women had phoned Childline about the rapes and violent attacks, they had hung up after Childline had told them, in line with the service's policies, that it could not guarantee either their anonymity or that their children would not be taken away from them. This was the same threat that their father had used to deter them from reporting the abuse.

The review found that the family, which contained 12 individuals, had received input from 28 different agencies over a 35-year period. Given some long-term health problems affecting family members, the review highlights that this was not a family that was unknown to agencies – quite the opposite. However, an extreme number of house moves – they moved house 67 times between 1973 and 2008 – made it difficult for practitioners to engage with them effectively. Despite this, the review concluded that during their time in Sheffield (1975–98) enough evidence of escalating violence towards the children had been amassed that they should have been taken into local authority care. For example, seven Child Protection Conferences detailing concern about physical abuse of the children had been held. There was evidence that some professionals were afraid of Mr X, that professionals failed to consider the situation from the child's perspective, that they took the word of the parents without considering the effects on the child, and that they were unrealistically optimistic about the cooperation of the parents.

The family then lived mainly in Lincolnshire between 1988 and 2004. During these years, at least one of the sisters was pregnant every year or on some occasions twice a year, and sometimes they were pregnant at the same time. The sisters were specifically asked about the paternity of their children on 23 separate occasions, and 7 allegations of incest/sexual abuse were reported to professionals during this time by family members and other professionals. Some of the babies died at birth because of genetic disorders that could only occur when both parents carry a particular genetic abnormality, and two of the seven that lived have severe physical disabilities.

The review concluded that opportunities had been missed and that there had been significant misplaced optimism:

> The Serious Case Review identifies that there existed a culture of 'having a quiet word' where informal unwritten information was passed between service[s] sometimes because the professional did not have the understanding or knowledge to escalate the concern, particularly as the belief was that the evidence was either not there to investigate (genetic, DNA) or that the situation had been investigated by the police with no further action required or possible.
>
> *(Cantrill, 2009: 12)*

Responses to familial rape and abuse

Adult survivors of familial child sexual abuse are a group whose support needs are grossly under-served. While adults who experience recent rape are increasingly better served – for example by Sexual Assault Referral Centres and Rape Crisis Centres – Sexual Assault Referral Centres do not usually work with adult survivors and Rape Crisis Centres struggle to find appropriate funding sources to do this work despite high demand. In a survey of Rape Crisis Centres in 2008, only a fifth of survivors who contacted the Centres (21 per cent) were doing so because of sexual violence that had happened in the last 12 months (Women's Resource Centre and Rape Crisis England and Wales, 2008). It is also important to realize that for some women, rape is not a 'one-off' occurrence. An experience as an adult could make childhood memories of sexual abuse more acute, for example.

Horvath et al. (2014) argue that children and young people do not have timely access to interventions after they are abused as children, because the disclosure rate is so low. Even where sexual abuse is known or suspected within the family, research shows that there are still concerns about social workers' and other professionals' abilities to intervene. Horvath et al. (2014) argue that Black and minority ethnic children and disabled children may receive even poorer responses and support. This low disclosure rate means that many interventions are aimed either at the primary prevention level or at the adult survivors' level. Just two possible responses are outlined below, one that is aimed directly at children and one that is controversial but could offer some sense of justice for adult survivors of child sexual abuse.

The NSPCC 'underwear rule'

The NSPCC designed the 'underwear rule' as a simple way for parents to talk to their children at a young age about consent and abuse, that does not require them to talk about sex.[1] The rule spells out the acronym 'PANTS' as a way of remembering it:

- [P]rivates are private – the parts of your body covered by underwear are private and no one should ask to see or touch your private parts. If a doctor, nurse or family member needs to, the adult should explain why and ask if it's OK first.
- [A]lways remember your body belongs to you – no one has the right to make you do anything that makes you feel uncomfortable and you have the right to say no if anyone tries.
- [N]o means no – you have the right to say no to unwanted touch even to someone you know or love such as a family member. You are in control of your body and your feelings should be respected.
- [T]alk about secrets that upset you – there is a difference between 'good' and 'bad' secrets, and you need to feel able to speak up about any secrets that worry you.

- [S]peak up, someone can help – if you feel anxious or frightened you should speak to an adult you trust, such as a family member, teacher, friend's parent, or ChildLine.

Use of restorative justice following a familial sex offence

The use of restorative justice – where the offender and the victim meet in a controlled environment to talk about the impact of the offence on the victim – is highly controversial in relation to sexual and domestic violence. Given the power imbalances that are inherent in abusive relationships, whether in an intimate partner relationship or in a family setting, there is concern that the restorative justice conference would not empower the victim and that the offender might use it to further traumatize her. Given that part of a restorative justice conference involves the victim talking about the impact that the offence has had on her life, it is also of concern that the offender might enjoy hearing about such impacts and feel that he still had a level of control over the victim.

In 2010 we became aware of a restorative justice conference that was going to be held in a rape case. The woman – who is called 'Lucy' in our research – was interested in being involved in research in order to share her experience with a wider audience (McGlynn *et al.*, 2011). We interviewed Lucy, her Rape Crisis counsellor, the conference facilitator and the senior police officer involved in the case. The offender was invited to participate, but declined the invitation.

Lucy is an adult survivor of rape and other forms of sexual abuse that happened when she and the offender, who is a family member, were children. She had made an agreement with the perpetrator that she would not make an official report about the abuse so long as he agreed not to have any close contact with children within the family. In doing this, Lucy made many sacrifices in her life, monitoring from afar the perpetrator's involvement with other family members and staying away from family gatherings at which she might see him.

Restorative justice relies on the offender admitting to the offences they have committed. In Lucy's case, the offender had already admitted that the offences had taken place, as she had contacted the police and made an official report (following the discovery that he had not kept to his word and had been having contact with some children within the family). The offender had been given a police caution, which is only issued if the offender accepts that they have committed the offences and accepts the caution for them. Lucy only found out that a caution had been issued, and that the police had not passed the file to the CPS, via a third party, and she felt let-down and angry about the police 'letting him get away with it'. She recalled feeling 'completely discounted' by this experience and told her Rape Crisis counsellor that she wanted to go to the offender's house and confront him. Concerned about her client doing this on her own, the counsellor suggested a restorative justice conference instead. Lucy agreed to this, saying 'I just wanted him to hear me, without him twisting it really'.

The conference was helpful to Lucy, and when she spoke to us she said she had no regrets. She found it useful that he admitted for the first time that he had 'deliberately created harm and that he knew that having sexual intercourse with me would be harmful'. At the end, the offender apologized, and Lucy told him that she did not accept his apology. The main outcome Lucy requested was for the offender to stop trying to make contact with her through other members of the family and, at the time we interviewed her, the offender had made no attempts to do so. While Lucy found the conference difficult to go through at the time and immediately afterwards, on reflection she felt that it had been the right thing for her to do. She told us 'in retrospect, it was more important to have my say and have him listen than for him to go to prison. It's made me understand my position as victim and see him as the offender, which has enabled me to resolve a lot of conflict' (Lucy, in McGlynn *et al.*, 2011). This was just one woman's experience, and without further research it is impossible to know what the benefits, if any, might be in other cases. However, the lessons that we took from Lucy's experience were that

- preparation is key – in the months leading up to the conference Lucy and her counsellor went through every eventuality, including the likelihood that the offender might not turn up on the day,
- support for victim-survivor is crucial – Lucy received extensive support from her Rape Crisis counsellor before, during and after the conference, and
- never underestimate the strength of victim-survivors – although, in the words of the counsellor, restorative justice could be 'fraught with dangers', both she and the police officer involved in Lucy's case felt that women should be empowered to make their own, informed, decisions about the possibility of restorative justice.

Summary

This chapter has shown that knowledge is lacking about the prevalence of familial rape and abuse; indeed, there is a lack of up-to-date knowledge generally on child sexual abuse, regardless of who perpetrates it. The effects of rape and abuse being perpetrated by a family member may be more extreme because of the additional breach of trust, and this may also result in it being less likely to be reported to the police than abuse by other perpetrators. The case of Mr X shows that, even when sexual abuse is suspected and reported to professionals, there is sometimes still a failure to act. This lack of identification and recognition of sexual abuse might lead to the effects becoming more extreme, as responses from organisations such as Rape Crisis have been forced to focus around primary prevention or support many years or even decades later.

Note

1 Thanks to NSPCC for their kind permission to reproduce material in this chapter.

References

Andersen, S.L., Tomada, A., Vincow, E.S., Valente, E., Polcari, A. and Teicher, M.H. (2008) 'Effect of childhood sexual abuse on regional brain development', *The Journal of Neuropsychiatry and Clinical Neuroscience*, 20(3): 292–301.

Cantrill, P. (2009) *Serious Case Review – Executive Summary – in Respect of: Q Family*, Sheffield: Sheffield Safeguarding Children Board in association with Lincolnshire Safeguarding Children Board.

Carter, J.C., Bewell, C., Blackmore, E. and Woodside, D.B. (2006) 'The impact of childhood sexual abuse in anorexia nervosa', *Child Abuse & Neglect*, 30(3): 257–69.

Cawson, P., Wattam, C., Brooker, S. and Kelly, G. (2000) *Child Maltreatment in the United Kingdom: A Study of the Prevalence of Child Abuse and Neglect*, London: NSPCC.

Goodwin, R.D., Fergusson, D.M. and Horwood, L.J. (2005) 'Childhood abuse and familial violence and the risk of panic attacks and panic disorder in young adulthood', *Psychological Medicine*, 35(6): 881–90.

Hayatbakhsh, M.R., Najman, J.M., Jamrozik, K., Mamun, A.A., O'Callaghan, M.J. and Williams, G.M. (2009) 'Childhood sexual abuse and cannabis use in early adulthood: findings from an Australian birth cohort study', *Archives of Sexual Behavior*, 38(1): 135–42.

Horvath, M.A.H., Davidson, J.C., Grove-Hills, J., Gekoski, A. and Choak, C. (2014) *'It's a Lonely Journey' – A Rapid Evidence Assessment on Intrafamilial Child Sexual Abuse*, London: Office of the Children's Commissioner.

Kendler, K.S., Bulik, C.M., Silberg, J., Hettema, J.M., Myers, J. and Prescott, C. (2000) 'Childhood sexual abuse and adult psychiatric and substance use disorders in women: an epidemiological and co-twin control analysis', *Archives of General Psychiatry*, 57(10): 953–9.

McGlynn, C., Westmarland, N. and Godden, N. (2011) 'Is restorative justice possible in cases of sexual violence?', Durham University Briefing Note, Durham: Durham University.

Mental Health Foundation and Camelot (2006) *Truth Hurts: Report of the National Inquiry into self harm among Young People. Fact or Fiction?* London: Mental Health Foundation.

Millard, B. and Flatley, J. (eds) (2010) *Experimental Statistics on Victimization of Children Aged 10–15: Findings from the British Crime Survey for the Year Ending December 2009* (2nd edition), London: Home Office.

NSPCC (2009) *Children Talking to ChildLine About Sexual Abuse*, ChildLine Casenotes, London: NSPCC.

Office for National Statistics (2014) *Statistical Bulletin: Crime in England and Wales, Year Ending March 2014*, Cardiff: ONS.

Pineda-Lucatero, A.G., Trujillo-Hernández, B., Millán-Guerrero, R.O. and Vásquez, C. (2009) 'Prevalence of childhood sexual abuse among Mexican adolescents', *Child: Care, Health and Development*, 35(2): 184–9.

Radford, L., Corral, S., Bradley, C., Fisher, H., Bassett, C., Howat, N. and Collishaw, S. (2011) *Child Abuse and Neglect in the UK today*, London: NSPCC.

Sexual Offences Act 2003, Chapter 42, London: HMSO.

Women's Resource Centre and Rape Crisis (England and Wales) (2008) *The Crisis in Rape Crisis*, London: Women's Resource Centre.

PART 3
Men's violences in public spaces

There exist a number of prevalence studies that all show the same thing – that young women are the group at the highest risk of experiencing sexual violence, and that this sexual violence is most likely to be perpetrated by known men – such as boyfriends, friends or acquaintances. However, this focus on violence in 'private' life by known men has contributed to some violences, particularly those perpetrated in public spaces, not being asked about in surveys and becoming sidelined in research more generally. This has led, until recently, to an overlooking of violence against women by strangers and acquaintances. This has been particularly the case for those types of violence that are more 'routine' (ironically more prevalent) and normalized.

The chapters that follow look at sexual violence and harassment in the workplace (Chapter 10) – including case studies on the police, the Ministry of Defence, Westminster culture and taxi drivers. Chapter 11 describes violence by strangers in public spaces – the routine, 'everyday' violences that some men commit against women on a daily basis. Finally, the last chapter in this section (Chapter 12) is about rape by strangers and acquaintances.

Violences in public spaces

The UN agency United Nations Women have a Safe Cities initiative that seeks to create safer public spaces for women. They point out that women and girls both fear and experience various forms of sexual violence, ranging from sexual harassment to assaults – including rape and femicide – in public spaces (UN Women website). This fear and reality reduces women's and girls' freedom of movement and also reduces their ability to access services, enjoy cultural and recreational opportunities, and their ability to fully participate in school, work and public life. UN Women highlight that, although violences against women in the private sphere are now widely recognized and often legislated against, violences in public spaces (such as sexual harassment) remain a neglected area with few laws and policies in place to combat them.

Despite knowing that it is 'there', men's everyday violence against women in public spaces/street harassment has been a remarkably under-researched topic over the last two decades. Elvines (2014) suggests that one reason for the relative silence in comparison to the expansion of knowledge of other forms of violence against women is the difficulty in naming this type of violence. While naming the problem is one discussion that has yet to be had in full, or agreed upon, she argues, there is also a lack of agreement about what constitutes men's violence against women in public spaces. Likewise, Kelly (2012) states that it is because the everyday, routine, intimate intrusions have dropped off so many agendas that domestic violence is now seen to be the most common form of violence against women. A connected explanation might be the increasing 'statutorization' of the women's sector, whereby as state funding and interest in *some* men's violences against women increase, the autonomous women's sector has been forced to narrow its focus to correspond with state priorities.

The normalizing of sexual violence

Research with young people reinforces this perception that sexual violence has been normalized, that violence and harassment are a daily, expected, 'normal' occurrence. Hlavka's (2014) research in the USA confirms that girls have very few available safe spaces, and are harassed and assaulted in a range of places including on the playground, on buses and at school. The more it happens, the more indiscriminate and 'normal' it appears to become. As one 13 year old girl said:

> They grab you, touch your butt and try to, like, touch you in the front, and run away, but it's okay, I mean … I never think it's a big thing because they do it to everyone.
>
> *('Patricia', quoted in Hlavka, 2014: 344)*

Hlavka found that the girls talked about male sexuality as being naturally aggressive, and men as unable to control their sexual desires. 'They're boys – that's what they do' was how 'Patricia' put it. Hlavka concluded that the girls understand sexual violence and harassment to be a normal adolescent rite of passage. Within this normalization of harassment, she found that girls seek to downplay even the most serious threats of violence – for example, one girl repeatedly appeared to 'brush off' threats from a young man on the bus that he would go to her house and rape her.

Video games have also been accused of glorifying and rewarding violence against women, adding to its 'normalization'. One of the most frequently quoted examples is the Grand Theft Auto series, in which one of the games (Vice City) rewards the 'hiring' of a prostitute by returning their money to players who kill the prostitute after sex.

Sexualised threats in online public spaces

This section does not include a chapter on sexualized threats in online public spaces because there is not sufficient literature and research on the topic. However, it is important to recognize this as an issue facing women more and more. Men's violences against women in online public spaces reached global news headlines in 2013 when threats against women on Twitter were publicized. The case that received the most publicity was that of feminist campaigner Caroline Criado-Perez, who at the time was headlining a campaign to keep a woman on an English banknote. At the time of the campaign there were moves to remove Elizabeth Fry from £5 notes and to replace her with a man. Criado-Perez started to receive hundreds of sexual and death threats on Twitter, as did women who attempted to intervene, including MP Stella Creasy. I am not going to reproduce the threats here; suffice it to note that they were highly sexualized, explicit, intended to cause fear, and were targeted, personalized and highly specific to women. In January 2014 two people (one man and one woman) were jailed for the threats made to Criado-Perez.

Criado-Perez was neither the first nor unfortunately the last to face sexist abuse on Twitter and other online public spaces. As I have argued elsewhere, although all high-profile figures with an online presence face online abuse to differing extents, the abuse that Criado-Perez, Creasy and others faced and continue to face was of a different nature – it drew explicitly upon the fact that they are women:

> People who speak out publicly about violence against women are frequently objects of gender-based hate speech. And this is what makes it different for women. A man may be abused and threatened with violence if they are in the public eye, but the nature of the threats are different. Rarely would a man be sent threats of the sexualised nature faced by women.
>
> *(Westmarland, 2014, online)*

Men's violences against women in online public spaces are likely to increase as online spaces continue to be places where people spend time. However, at the time of writing there exists a gap in academic research and theory on this topic.

References

Elvines, F. (2014) 'The great problems are in the street – a phenomenology of men's stranger intrusions on women in public space', London: London Metropolitan University unpublished PhD thesis.

Hlavka, H.R. (2014) 'Normalising sexual violence: young women account for harassment and abuse', *Gender & Society*, 28(3): 337–58.

Kelly, L. (2012) Standing the test of time? Reflections on the concept of the continuum of sexual violence', in Brown, J. and Walklate, S. (eds), *Handbook on Sexual Violence*, London: Routledge.

UN Women (n.d.) 'Creating safe public spaces', UN Women, available at www.unwomen.org/en/what-we-do/ending-violence-against-women/creating-safe-public-spaces (accessed October 2014).

Westmarland, N. (2014) 'Court sends the right message in sentencing Criado-Perez trolls', *The Conversation*, 24 January 2014, available from: https://theconversation.com/court-sends-the-right-message-in-sentencing-criado-perez-trolls-22417 (accessed October 2014).

10
SEXUAL VIOLENCE AND HARASSMENT IN THE WORKPLACE

This chapter was originally just going to be named 'sexual harassment' in the workplace – and it still is about this topic. However, the term 'sexual harassment' seems to be used and/or discussed less today than in previous decades, for example when Catherine MacKinnon (1979) introduced it into US legal terminology. This may be because it is unclear what constitutes sexual harassment compared with other terms that could be used to describe the acts involved ('harassment', 'sexualized bullying', 'everyday sexual violence'). It is possible that, rather than naming the acts (as sexual assault, etc.), the term 'sexual harassment' could be seen as downplaying and introducing ambiguity into the acts.

However, there are forms of harassment that would not otherwise be criminal offences, and for this reason the term 'sexual harassment' can be seen as more useful than generic definitions of harassment or bullying frameworks. According to Samuels (2003), it is the strong gender dimension that sets sexual harassment aside from forms of bullying. She cautions feminists to resist the trend towards merging the two, arguing that to do so minimizes the sexual element and removes it from its wider patriarchal environment – thereby downplaying the power relations between men and women. She distinguishes sexual harassment from race and disability harassment, for example, by pointing out that it is unlikely that the other two types of harassing conduct try to be excused as welcome attention, or that the perpetrator would use as a defence that the conduct was welcome. Instead, Samuels agrees that it is most useful to see sexual harassment through the lens of Kelly's (1988) continuum of sexual violence, which regards sexual harassment as a form of violence against women rather than a form of workplace bullying. It is for all of these reasons that I retain in this chapter the term 'sexual harassment' but add 'violence' to it.

This chapter continues to discuss some definitional issues, including the legal framework, and then moves on to look at the extent to which sexual harassment happens in the workplace. Four case studies of sexual harassment in the workplace are then considered – in the police, the Ministry of Defence, in Westminster politics and in the taxi industry. Some of these case studies have parallels with the institutional support for sexual violence that is the focus of Part 4 of this book.

Defining sexual harassment

In a review of sexual harassment literature in the late 1990s, O'Donohue *et al.* (1998) found that there was disagreement about how to define sexual harassment. They summarized the areas of disagreement as: whether a power differential is necessary; whether a location (e.g. the workplace) needs to be specified; how important it is for the victim to perceive the behaviour as problematic; whether only women (or men as well) can be sexually harassed; whether it is enough that an act is harassing in itself or whether there must be further negative consequences; and whether *sexist* as opposed to *sexual* behaviours should be classed as sexual harassment.

Rather than attempting to find a middle ground and come up with a definition that takes these disagreements into account, they instead argued that – at the time of writing – it was too early to establish a 'good' definition of sexual harassment. Instead, they suggested that the important thing was that researchers took these debates into consideration – suggesting also that as further research is conducted some of these issues may become clearer. However, it has arguably got more confusing, as the overlaps between forms of violence against women have become more evident.

O'Donohue *et al.* (1998) argued that although there was disagreement over a general definition (see above), there was clear agreement about subtypes – about what sort of acts were examples of sexual harassment – for example unwanted sexual attention and sexual coercion. And it is this type of description that is usually used now where a definition is needed, along with the purpose or effects of such acts. The European Union, for example, define sexual harassment as present where:

> any form of unwanted verbal, non verbal or physical conduct of a sexual nature occurs, with the purpose or effect of violating the dignity of a person, in particular when creating an intimidating, hostile, degrading, humiliating, or offensive environment.
> *(Equal Treatment Amendment Directive, 2002, Article 1)*

The 1975 Sex Discrimination Act did not actually define sexual harassment; instead, a definition was developed through case law. However, two definitions were included in the 2005 Amendment – unwanted conduct on the grounds of a person's sex (this conduct may or may not be of a sexual nature) and unwanted physical, verbal or non-verbal conduct of a sexual nature (e.g. questions about a person's sex life, or sexual demands).

Rights of Women (2010) give examples of the ways in which might be manifested the first type of harassment – unwanted conduct on the grounds of a person's sex (with the focus on women for the purposes of this book). These include name calling (e.g. calling someone a 'typical woman'), references to women's abilities or work, being rude to women on the team such as ignoring women and only listening to male workers, undervaluing women's contributions and making sexist jokes. They say that these are all forms of harassment if the conduct has either the *purpose* or the *effect* of creating an environment that is intimidating, hostile, degrading, humiliating or offensive.

Rights of Women (2010) also give examples of the actions that the second type of harassment might consist of – unwanted physical, verbal or non-verbal conduct of a sexual nature (again this is classed as sexual harassment if it has either the *purpose* or the *effect* described above):

- direct sexual remarks – comments about a woman's body or looks, sexist jokes
- the display of sexist or pornographic material
- sexual touching, pinching or patting
- sexual innuendo or suggestions and
- demanding that women take clients to a lap-dancing or a burlesque club.

(p. 2)

It is this framework that will be adopted within this chapter, with a particular emphasis on the second type of sexual harassment but with the acknowledgement that much of the first type creates an environment that serves to validate and promote the second type.

Legal framework – the Sex Discrimination Act 1975

Sexual harassment law in the UK has traditionally developed in the context of discrimination law. Samuels (2003) argues that this is problematic because it requires the complainant to demonstrate that she has been treated less favourably than a man – regardless of how bad her treatment was. However, a change at the European level in 2002 required member states to legislate specifically against sexual harassment (The European Equal Treatment Directive, 2002/73/EC). Consequently, an amendment to the Sex Discrimination Act 1975 was made, which applies from 2005.

According to the Sex Discrimination Act 1975, as amended [s4A (relating to acts committed on or after 1 October 2005)]:

1) a person subjects a woman to harassment if,
(a) on the ground of her sex, he engages in unwanted conduct that has the purpose of effect of (i) violating her dignity or (ii) of creating an intimidating, hostile, degrading, humiliating, or offensive environment for her,
(b) he engages in any form of unwanted verbal, non-verbal, or physical conduct of a sexual nature that has the purpose or effect of (i) violating her

dignity or (ii) creating an intimidating, hostile, degrading, humiliating, or offensive environment for her, or

(c) on the ground of her rejection of or submission to unwanted conduct of a kind mentioned in paragraphs (a) or (b), he treats her less favourably than he would treat her had she not rejected, or submitted to, the conduct.

2) Conduct shall be regarded as having the effect mentioned in sub-paragraph (i) or (ii) of subsection (1) (a) or (b) only if, having regard to all the circumstances, including in particular the perception of the woman, it should reasonably be considered as having that effect.

For people employed for over one year, a claim for unfair dismissal or constructive dismissal can be made alongside the sex discrimination case if the person has been dismissed or resigned because of the harassment.

The nature and extent of sexual harassment

Research shows there exist high levels of sexual harassment in the workplace, although it is likely to be a very under-reported issue. Sexual violence and harassment even (or maybe especially) occur in high-profile, 'respectable' workplaces such as the police and in Parliament – examples of both are discussed later in this chapter. However, it is a form of violence against women that might be particularly hard to speak up about. Women may feel it is not 'serious' enough to make a 'fuss' about or that they should be taking it as a 'joke'. As Rights of Women (2010) point out, sexual harassment can be difficult to challenge because women might fear losing their job and therefore their income. They might fear getting a reputation within their industry as a troublemaker, and may prefer to quietly seek a different job rather than to confront the harassment formally. Research by Blackstone et al. (2014) found that as people age, expectations about workplace interactions and themselves as workers change. They found that participants in their research did not always define their early experiences as sexual harassment at the time, but as older workers were more willing to recognize it as such when looking back.

Research on the nature and extent of sexual harassment has tended to focus on case studies of specific occupations, or comparative analyses of two or more types of work. There is no national prevalence figure for the general working population in the UK. In addition, there is a very limited amount of UK research on this topic, meaning that the following section draws more heavily on international research than other parts of this book have. This lack of UK literature was also highlighted in the 2007 working paper for the Equal Opportunities Commission by Hunt et al., who found that most sexual harassment research was conducted in the USA and Australia. Hunt et al. (2007) also highlight that most of the literature specifically on 'sexual harassment' was published in the 1990s, and that since then it tends to have been incorporated more into discussions about 'workplace bullying' (as highlighted also by Samuels and discussed earlier in this chapter). However, they argue that the concept of sexual harassment has a stronger theoretical underpinning, has links to feminist theories and is located within a broader understanding of power relations.

A further issue that many commentators point to is the problems associated with comparing studies on sexual harassment. Findings are often difficult to compare owing to the variety of definitions used – particularly whether respondents were being asked to self-define acts as sexual harassment using their own definitions (which produces lower estimates than acts defined by researchers). For example, in a US meta-analysis by Illies *et al.* (2003), sexual harassment rates using the respondents' own definitions were less than half of those coded as sexual harassment by researchers. However, McDonald (2012) warns that even when looking at longitudinal studies that use the same methods at different time periods, results are inconsistent internationally. This may, of course, mean that rates actually have changed to different extents in different places.

In the USA, a large-scale study covering more than 8,000 Federal employees at three time points (1981, 1988 and 1994) found that, across a range of workplaces, only one form of sexual harassment (pressure for dates) had declined in incidence (US Merit Systems Protection Board, 1994). They found that all of the serious forms of harassment had either stayed the same or increased – including a fourfold increase for 'actual or attempted rape or assault'. However a longitudinal study in Australia found a decrease in levels of sexual harassment – a reduction from 28 per cent in 2003 to 22 per cent in 2008 for women and 7 per cent to 5 per cent for men (Australian Human Rights Commission, 2008). These may be 'true' increases and decreases, explained by changes in different times and different places, or they may result from methodological differences between the two studies.

International studies also find different rates based on different characteristics. In an overview of the literature on the characteristics of harassers and complainants and perceptions of sexual harassment, McDonald (2012) identified the following as being important: gender (most complainants are female and most harassers are male; being divorced or separated; being young; having irregular, contingent or precarious contracts; having non-traditional jobs; having disabilities; being lesbian; coming from ethnic minorities; having 'masculine characteristics' and not meeting feminine ideals (e.g. being assertive); young men and gay men were also targeted for harassment.

Even when official complaints are used as an indicator of sexual harassment rather than self-report studies, it is still difficult to be clear from reported cases about the prevalence of sexual harassment. Hunt *et al.* (2007) point out that in 2005–6 14,250 claims were lodged with employment tribunals on the grounds of sex discrimination in England and Wales, of which 17 per cent were successful at tribunal and a further 13 per cent were conciliated settlements (Employment Tribunals Service, 2006). However, they highlight that this figure covers all sexual discrimination cases, and that sexual harassment cases represent an unknown proportion.

Before moving on to look at the effects and causes of, and possible interventions to prevent, sexual harassment, four case study examples are given in which sexual harassment within specific occupations has been examined in England and Wales – in the police service, in the Ministry of Defence, in the Westminster Parliament and in the taxi industry.

Example – sexual harassment within the Police Service

Alison Halford, at the time Assistant Chief Constable of Merseyside Police, took the service to an industrial tribunal on the grounds of sexual discrimination in 1990. She argued that she had been subject to a culture that was both sexist and racist (the claim was withdrawn following a settlement). This culture of sexism was confirmed by a subsequent Her Majesty's Inspection of Constabulary (HMIC) thematic inspection, which found 'blatant' breaches of equal opportunities policies and a serious problem of sexual harassment (HMIC, 1992).

To provide academic evidence of the nature and extent of the problem, Jennifer Brown designed a survey that looked at the incidence of sexual harassment within the police workplace (Brown, 1998). Women police from six forces were invited to participate, and the study had a very high response rate (70 per cent – total number of female participants was 1,802). A separate sample of civilian women working within two other police forces was also surveyed (53 per cent response rate – 164 women). Both the police and the civilian women were asked about any unwanted/unreciprocated verbal or physical conduct from male police officers that was sexual in nature or had a sexual dimension. Brown listed seven types of potential harassment: suggestive [sexually explicit] jokes; comments about women's appearance; comments on own appearance/physique; sexual insults; persistent requests for unwanted dates; touching/pinching; serious sexual assault. Participants indicated whether they had experienced these often, sometimes, rarely or never, and a 'harassment index' was constructed from the summing of these responses.

Some of the most frequent forms of sexual harassment were non-contact forms, such as 'heard sexually explicit jokes' (99 per cent of policewomen and 87 per cent of civilian women had heard these from policemen in the preceding six months) or 'heard comments about women's physical appearance' (99 per cent of policewomen and 98 per cent of civilian women). However, sexual harassment involving contact – in many if not all cases constituting sexual offences under the criminal law – was also evident: 62 per cent of policewomen and 38 per cent of civilian women said that they had been 'touched, stroked or pinched', and 5 per cent of policewomen and 1 per cent of civilian women said they had been subjected to a 'serious sexual assault'. It is worth remembering that these acts were *perpetrated by policemen* and only in the *six months preceding* the survey being completed. If others within the workplace were also included (prisoners, witnesses, solicitors, general public) and for a longer period (e.g. last 12 months, or ever in working life) then these figures are likely to be substantially higher.

The frequency statistics are shocking enough – and this is also underpinned by examples that some of the women volunteered as additional information on their survey forms. One described police officers as 'the most sexist, homophobic and racist section of society that I have ever encountered' (Brown, 1998: 272). She gave the example of one supervisor who constantly put his arm around her shoulders and made comments about how nice her breasts were. Given that he was a sergeant with more than twenty years' experience, she did not feel able to tell him that she did not like what he was doing. Another described minor sexual assaults such as men 'grabbing her', twanging her bra strap and subtly brushing past her body. Another described a serious sexual assault:

> I was subjected to a sexual assault by my shift where I was held down and my top half stripped. This left me feeling dirty and to an extent vulnerable.
> *(Brown, 1998: 273)*

Brown concluded that, although there had been a range of new policies and legislation to encourage sexual equality, a male-dominated occupational culture continued to exist within the police.

Example – sexual harassment within the Ministry of Defence

In 2006, Rutherford, Schneider and Walmsley sent a questionnaire to all service women (18,178) and gained a 52 per cent response rate (9,384 women). They supplemented this with qualitative data from 29 focus groups and 9 individual interviews. Rather than asking whether service women had experienced 'sexual harassment', they instead provided a breakdown of 'sexualized behaviours directed at them' – in a method similar to that used by Brown in her Police service study. They found that, over the previous 12 months, military personnel and/or civil servants around the respondents had told sexual jokes and stories (98 per cent), used sexually explicit language (94 per cent), displayed, used or distributed sexually explicit materials (67 per cent) and made gestures or used body language of a sexual nature (63 per cent). One in eight (13 per cent, or 182 women) had experienced a sexual assault within the last 12 months. These figures are, not surprisingly, far higher than reported sexual harassment complaints, which a Freedom of Information request shows stood at 35 in 2006–7, 34 in 2007–8 and 34 in 2008–9 (Ministry of Defence, 2010).

In line with other research, the authors found that younger women were most likely to experience sexual harassment – 77 per cent of women under 23 had experienced unwelcome sexual behaviours within the previous 12 months compared to 44 per cent of women in their 40s. Many of the behaviours and harassment were prolonged, with nearly half of the respondents saying that their experiences had lasted more than two months, and nearly a quarter saying they had lasted more than six months.

The qualitative data showed that some men felt that women's involvement in the military should be limited, saying things like 'Females are good at being clerks, chiefs of admin', 'OK there are a few exceptions but on the whole they shouldn't be here', and 'They are emotionally unstable' (men in military quoted in Rutherford *et al.*,

2006). The authors found that some of the sexual objectification described in the focus groups were things that these men thought women should find acceptable, using terms such as '... only grope of an arse' and 'How is that rude? If you tell a girl that she's got nice tits? That's a compliment!'

While the women in the focus groups also gave examples of joining in with things such as sexualized language and jokes, it was clear that these could operate as stress breaking, bonding or fitting in. However, these could also be seen as marginalizing women. Sometimes women pretended to take something as a joke so as not to be accused of not having a sense of humour. However, this in turn could lead to women being accused of inconsistency or being unclear about what behaviours they found offensive. Rutherford et al. found that it was consistently down to the women to define where their individual boundaries lay, and to make the men aware of these in different circumstances. For example, one woman in their study explained:

> Sometimes in a group the banter gets going and one of them will say at the beginning, 'just tell us when it gets too much'. But it's hard to know when to suddenly come in with "It's too much' as it just sort of accumulates. I wonder if they just say that to cover themselves – you know so that if there was a complaint they'd be able to say 'We did say stop if it got too much'
> *(RAF Other Ranks Female, in Rutherford et al. focus group, 2006)*

Rutherford et al. conclude that, although concerns were raised by both women and men around 'political correctness' and the erosion of humour that was seen as vital to the armed forces, it was not sexual language and images *per se* that were the problem. Rather, sexual language and images became problematic when used with the intention of degrading and when used in inappropriate contexts. The authors found that women might prefer just to leave, rather than complain about sexual harassment. By condoning sexual harassment, Rutherford et al. argue, the armed forces perpetuate the view put forward by some of the men that women do not 'belong' in armed service.

Example – the Westminster culture

Most of what we know about sexual violence and harassment within the Westminster Parliament comes from investigative journalism, individual whistleblowers and individual people speaking to journalists about their own experiences. Journalists have dubbed it 'the Palace of Sexminster' as a series of 'scandals' has emerged over recent years. Many of the allegations that have been made relate to older males sexually harassing younger males, and it is clear that this, as well as sexual harassment against women, is a significant problem within Westminster. However, as this book is about violence against women, the example I have chosen to describe here is that of the allegations against Lord Rennard (former Chief Executive of the Liberal Democrats).

In 2013 allegations were made in a Channel 4 documentary that Chris, Lord Rennard had sexually harassed a number of women within the Liberal Democrats. The accusations included taking an intern to his room where he 'propositioned her', 'intimately groping' a female Liberal Democrat while posing for a group photograph and 'groping' two women in his home. The language and euphemisms used in my description here come from media reports, since the reports on the actual review of what happened have not been published. In the Channel Four News report, one woman described how she had been talking to Lord Rennard in the conference bar when he started to touch her legs and knees. She explained that she thought the first time was an accident so she crossed her legs, but that then he did it a second and a third time. In the end she had to physically move away from him. He asked her, nonetheless, whether they should take their coffees upstairs to his room. She described feeling embarrassed, upset and disappointed, and reported the harassment to her line managers the next day.

Another woman on the news report told presenter Cathy Newman that as they were getting a photo taken at a Liberal Democrats event Lord Rennard stood close to her and 'shoved' his hand down the back of her dress. She described feeling humiliated, undermined and ashamed.

Alison Smith, then a Liberal Democrat activist and now an academic, was invited with a friend to Rennard's house. They described on Channel 4 News how he sat on one sofa and they sat on another, then he got up, sat between them and started running his hands down their backs. Smith stood up, said it was not acceptable, and that she was going home. Afterwards she reported the incident to the Chief Whip and also to Jo Swinston, the party spokesperson for women and equality, who agreed to look into the complaint. However, no formal actions were taken at the time against Rennard although a letter leaked to Channel 4 News described someone senior in the party having a conversation in which Rennard was told the behaviour had to stop.

Both the criminal justice system and Alistair Webster QC (who was appointed by the Liberal Democrats to run an internal investigation into whether Lord Rennard had acted in a way that brought the party into disrepute) judged there to be a less than 50 per cent chance that a case could be proven against Lord Rennard in court. However, he was asked to apologize for his behaviour, and Nick Clegg (at the time leader of the Liberal Democrats and Deputy Prime Minister) also issued an apology to the women involved. In it he reports that it is 'clear' that a number of Liberal Democrat women were subjected to behaviour that caused them 'real distress' by someone in a position of 'considerable authority':

> ... I want everyone to be treated with respect in the Liberal Democrats. That is why it is right that Chris Rennard has been asked in this report to apologise, to reflect on his behaviour and why he won't be playing any role in my general election plans for the campaign in 2015.
>
> *(Nick Clegg, on Liberal Democrat Voice website)*

Thus, although on one hand there seemingly was not enough evidence to put Rennard formally on trial for his behaviour, there was an implicit view that the women were telling the truth and that he had acted inappropriately, at the very least.

Example – the gendered victimization of taxi drivers

Transport workers have particularly high levels of violence committed against them, but there is little research into how gender interacts with this victimization. While I was a student my sister and I both had taxis, and we drove these at night to earn money to support ourselves financially through our studies. I used this opportunity as a night-shift taxi driver to study the gendered victimization of taxi drivers, which I submitted as an undergraduate dissertation and subsequently had published in *The Security Journal* (Westmarland and Anderson, 2001). Questionnaire responses were obtained from 74 taxi drivers, of whom 63 were male and 11 were female. The majority had experience of working a night shift (90 per cent of male drivers and 91 per cent of female drivers). My research found that there were no significant differences in the numbers of physical attacks or levels of verbal abuse; attacks on both men and women being high and similar – 45 per cent of women and 46 per cent of men had been physically attacked at work and 73 per cent of women and 87 per cent of men had experienced verbal abuse. However, women were significantly more likely to have been sexually harassed and to consider leaving their jobs owing to violence at work. Female drivers were also significantly more likely than male drivers to report physical attacks to the police. Male customers were the group most likely to be violent towards taxi drivers, regardless of the driver's gender.

However, when the results relating to (self-defined) sexual harassment were analysed a statistically significant difference was found – female taxi drivers were over five times more likely than male drivers to have been sexually harassed at work (73 per cent of women compared to 14 per cent of men). At the time, there was no other research to compare this figure to, as the few other studies of violence and abuse against taxi drivers had not considered sexual harassment (perhaps because it is a predominantly male occupation). While 80 per cent of female taxi drivers who had been physically attacked reported it to the police, none of those who had experienced sexual harassment had made a police report. Female drivers reported experiencing sexual harassment from customers but also from their co-workers (i.e. male taxi drivers).

Effects of sexual harassment

The impacts of sexual harassment include emotional and physical symptoms such as anger, anxiety, depression, tiredness and headaches (O'Donohue *et al.*, 1998). It also contributes to workplace problems, such as decreased performance, low job satisfaction, high levels of absenteeism and ultimately resignation (Hunt *et al.*,

2007). Some research has found symptoms of post-traumatic stress disorder (Willness *et al.*, 2007). Many of the women who have posted their experiences of sexual harassment in the workplace to the Everyday Sexism campaign explain how they cannot help but feel embarrassed about being victimized, although they acknowledge that it should be the harasser that feels this way, not them. Bates (2014) points out that many of the workplace experiences relayed to the project would legally constitute sexual harassment. This is also the case for some of the forms of harassment given in the case studies earlier in this chapter. In this sense, some of the effects of sexual harassment overlap with those of other forms of sexual violence, including sexual assault and rape.

Why does sexual harassment continue?

Pina *et al.* (2009) highlight that, although sexual harassment has been recognized as a serious problem for over 30 years, there is a lack of empirical evidence and a focus on the assessment and treatment of those who do the harassment. They point out that most of what does exist is based on small-scale surveys or on court cases. Reviewing the available literature, they find some contradictory findings: while some studies find harassers to be married, older and hierarchically superior to the women they target, others have found that harassers target co-workers of a similar or even sometimes junior status. For example, the Rutherford *et al.* (2006) study into women in the armed forces discussed earlier in this chapter found that age seemed more important than rank. Pina *et al.* (2009) therefore conclude that, given these inconsistent findings and the very limited amount of evidence available, it would be misleading to model any type of 'typical harasser' – instead concluding that 'sexual harassers appear to permeate all social strata, occupational levels, and age categories' (p. 129).

Research seems to be more consistent on the role of the organizational climate or environment – what Pina *et al.* (2009) call a 'permissive environment'. For example, research by Willness *et al.* (2007) found that a) an organizational climate that tolerates sexual harassment and b) the proportion of women in an occupation and how 'traditional' it is perceived to be both play important roles in explaining the existence and differences in prevalence of sexual harassment. In their meta-analysis, Willness *et al.* (2007) found that having an organizational climate conducive to sexual harassment had the largest effect of any of the variables they considered. Hence, they argue that a permissive organizational climate is central to understanding the conditions under which sexual harassment is more likely to occur. Since we know that this organizational climate is an antecedent it follows, they argue, that we should be able to move towards identifying the organizational policies and procedures that are most critical for prevention.

Willness *et al.* (2007) also found that what they call the 'job gender context' (how many women are in the immediate work environment and whether the job is considered atypical for women) was an antecedent – albeit with a smaller effect than organizational climate. They argue that this should be investigated further in

Summary

Recently, sexual harassment in the workplace has not been considered to be a standalone offence in England and Wales, as often as it was in the 1980s and 1990s. This is likely to be due to two reasons. First, when the New Labour Government started to take some forms of violence against women more seriously (first domestic violence and in their later years rape), the research agenda became very policy-focused, which in turn has guided available research funding. Sexual harassment – indeed, any form of violence against women that is not 'as serious' in policy makers' eyes – was not on the agenda, and neither is it on the current Conservative-Liberal Democrat agenda. Ironically, as described earlier in this chapter, one of the reasons why sexual harassment has re-entered public discussions about violence against women is the allegations against Lord Rennard of the Liberal Democrats. Nonetheless, sexual harassment has not been on the political agenda.

Second, over recent years there has been a groundswell of feminist action, challenging the day-to-day, so-called 'everyday' acts of violence, abuse and sexism. This is linked to the recognition that violence against women is both a cause and a consequence of gender inequalities and therefore sexism. Thus, it may be that sexual violence and harassment in the workplace are being integrated and re-categorized within wider understandings of women, violence, harassment, inequalities and sexism. It is some of these 'everyday' acts of sexism and violence against women that are considered in the following chapter.

References

Australian Human Rights Commission (2008) *Sexual Harassment: Serious Business. Results of the 2008 Sexual Harassment National Telephone Survey,* Sydney: AHRC.

Bates, L. (2014) *Everyday Sexism,* London: Simon & Schuster UK.

Blackstone, A., Houle, J. and Uggen, C. (2014) '"I didn't recognize it as a bad experience until I was much older": age, experience and workers' perceptions of sexual harassment', *Sociological Spectrum: Mid-South Sociological Association,* 34(4): 314–37.

Brown, J. (1998) 'Aspects of discriminatory treatment of women police officers serving in forces in England and Wales', *British Journal of Criminology,* 38(2): 265–82.

Employment Tribunals Service (2006) *Annual Report and Accounts 2005–06,* HC 1303, London: The Stationery Office.

European Parliament and the Council of the European Union, The European Equal Treatment Directive, 2002/73/EC. Available at http://eur-lex.europa.eu/LexUriServ/LexUriServ.do?uri=OJ:L:2002:269:0015:0020:EN:PDF.

Her Majesty's Chief Inspector of Constabulary (HMIC) (1992) *Equal Opportunities in the Police Service,* London: Home Office.

Hunt, C., Davidson, M., Fielden, S. and Hoel, H. (2007) *Sexual Harassment in the Workplace: A Literature Review,* Working Paper No. 59, Manchester: Equal Opportunities Commission.

Illies, R., Hauserman, N., Schwochau, S. and Stibal, J. (2003) 'Reported incidence rates of work-related sexual harassment in the US: using meta-analysis to explain reported rate disparities', *Personnel Psychology*, 56(3): 607–18.

Kelly, L. (1988) *Surviving Sexual Violence*, Cambridge: Polity Press.

Liberal Democrat Voice (2014) 'Internal investigation into allegations against Lord Rennard', *Liberal Democrat Voice*, 15 January 2014, available from: www.libdemvoice.org/internal-investigation-into-allegations-against-lord-rennard-37847.html (accessed October 2014).

MacKinnon, C.A. (1979) *Sexual Harassment of Working Women: A Case of Sex Discrimination*, New Haven, Connecticut: Yale University Press.

McDonald, P. (2012) 'Workplace sexual harassment 30 years on: a review of the literature', *International Journal of Management Reviews*, 14(1): 1–17.

Ministry of Defence (2010) *Sexual Offence and Harassment Complaints 2006 to 2009*, Response to FOI, Ref. FOI 04-09-2009-095251-003.

O'Donohue, W., Downs, K. and Yeater, E.A. (1998) 'Sexual harassment: a review of the literature', *Aggression and Violent Behaviour*, 3(2): 111–28.

Pina, A., Gannon, T.A. and Saunders, B. (2009) 'An overview of the literature on sexual harassment: perpetrator, theory, and treatment issues', *Aggression and Violent Behavior*, 14(2): 126–38.

Rights of Women (2010) *A Guide to Sexual Harassment in the Workplace*, London: Rights of Women.

Rutherford, S., Schneider, R. and Walmsley, A. (2006) *Agreement on Preventing and Dealing Effectively with Sexual Harassment: Quantitative & Qualitative Research into Sexual Harassment in the Armed Forces*, Manchester: Ministry of Defence/Equal Opportunities Commission.

Samuels, H. (2003) 'Sexual harassment in the workplace: a feminist analysis of recent developments in the UK', *Women's Studies International Forum*, 26(5): 467–82.

Sex Discrimination Act 1975, London: HMSO.

US Merit Systems Protection Board (1994) *Working for America: An Update*, Washington, DC: US Government Printing Office.

Westmarland, N. and Anderson, J. (2001) 'Safe at the wheel? Security issues for female taxi drivers', *Security Journal*, 14(2): 29–40.

Willness, C., Steel, P. and Lee, K. (2007) 'A meta-analysis of the antecedents and consequences of workplace sexual harassment', *Personnel Psychology*, 60(1): 127–62.

11
VIOLENCE IN STREETS AND PUBLIC SPACES

The term 'everyday harassment' was coined by Schneider in 1987 to refer to a broad range of seemingly 'banal' behaviours that are actually focused around power and the maintenance of the status quo. In this sense, everyday harassment is predicated on who holds the power, regardless of whether it seems deliberate and conscious or not:

> Only someone who is powerful or believes that they are, will make a joke at someone else's expense or sexualize an interpersonal relationship inappropriately. Consequently, everyday harassment services to maintain the status quo whether or not harassers or their targets are consciously aware of it.
> (Schneider and Phillips, 1997: 670)

Feminists then extended this concept to acts of gendered violence and abuse, and the ways in which violence and harassment intersect in subtle and not so subtle ways in the ways women live their lives. Some of the earliest feminists to explicitly link violence and abuse to the 'everyday' and 'the routine' were Betsy Stanko (1990) and Liz Kelly (1988). This chapter outlines the contributions of Stanko and Kelly to the initial theorization of men's everyday violences against women (with a particular emphasis on violence in streets and public spaces) and then looks at two recent analyses of violence in public spaces – by Bates (2014) and Elvines (2014). Prevalence studies are briefly considered, followed by responses – which have mainly been characterized by informal, 'shouting back'-style activism.

Stanko – *Everyday Violence*

In 1990 Stanko published her book *Everyday Violence: How Women and Men Experience Sexual and Physical Danger*. In this book, she explained that violence can be viewed as an ordinary part of life, and women develop techniques to try to manage this. Her research was based on 51 interviews in the UK and the USA, in which she found that the women in particular recall threats and violent events not in a chronological manner, but rather as a series of situations that are similar in nature. She recounts a time when she was teaching a women's studies class and asked her students to describe the day-to-day actions they take to make themselves feel safer – an hour later the examples were still coming. She found that much of the violence was hidden – both the types of violence they experienced (for example within the family) and in some cases hidden as in not named within their own life stories. Stanko draws attention to one interview, in which a widow in her sixties started by saying that she would not have much to contribute to the research, and by the end of the interview recounted being sexually touched by a shopkeeper when she was 8 years old, feeling physically threatened as an adult by her brother, being attacked while she was working in a hospital as a nurse and being harassed for sex by men after the death of her husband.

At the time, Stanko's feminist approach to researching violence differed from that of 'malestream' criminologists of the time who, she argues, had focused almost entirely on fear of violence from strangers. She outlined in her book the key ways in which her research diverged: first, by viewing violence as an ordinary part of life rather than a disruption to an otherwise calm and violence-free life; second, by focusing not on the acts of violence themselves, but instead on how people negotiate danger – making it a study of how people live their lives in relation to violence; and third, by not focusing only on stranger danger, and not assuming that the home is a safe place.

Stanko's main argument is that women 'manage' danger on a daily and nightly basis. She draws on her own interviews and also on Kelly's continuum of sexual violence (discussed next) to highlight that women experience much of men's violence in the private sphere, yet the public discussion about women and violence only acknowledges women's fear of attack at the hands of strangers (keeping in mind that she was writing this in the late 1980s, before the 'domestic violence revolution'). Rather than viewing violence as one-off 'disruptions' to an otherwise calm life, she argues that it should be viewed as an ordinary part of life. This is not to suggest that people experience violence on a daily basis (though some do), but rather that people take measures to manage danger – for example avoiding certain places, staying alert in the street and resisting arguing with intimate partners. In this sense, violence is always being taken into account as a possible occurrence in people's – particularly women's – lives.

Kelly – harassment within a continuum of sexual violence

Writing at around the same time as Stanko, Kelly (1988) was also shattering the illusion that violence occurs in one-off attacks, and that fear exists only in relation to public spaces and 'stranger danger'. She conducted 60 interviews with women, and found that they experienced different forms of violence and abuse at different points in their lives but that these operated as a 'continuum' rather than as a set of discrete 'attacks'. She called this the 'continuum of sexual violence', and this concept continues to influence academic and practitioners' work on violence against women today (see, e.g., Brown and Walklate's 2011 edited collection). Kelly argued that where violence was acknowledged as existing, it was seen as rare – committed only by deviant men, within dysfunctional families. She sought to connect the 'horrific with the everyday', and to question who decides what is abusive, and what matters. She draws on the work of Herman (1981), who theorized incest as an exaggeration of patriarchal family norms, and Marolla and Scully (1979), who argued that rape represents the end point of a 'socially sanctioned continuum of male sexual aggression'.

Kelly's continuum does not represent a severity scale, with one end of the continuum representing 'severe' and the other end representing 'minor' abuses. Rather, the continuum refers to the many forms of coercion, abuse and assault that are used to control women. She used the term 'continuum' to underline that these forms of violence against women are not discrete – that they represent a 'continuous series of elements or events that pass into one another and cannot be readily distinguished' (p. 76). To this, she has added the notion of a continuum of impacts, meanings and consequences and a continuum of experience in individual women's lives.

Applying the continuum to women of African and Caribbean heritage who have lived for most of their lives in the UK, Kanyeredzi (2014) found that there exists a 'continuum of oppression' which reflects violence and abuse to her body or concept of self. She found that the impacts are indistinguishable and include experiences of racism and the abuse of other family members:

> Women in this study carried narratives of intergenerational trauma faced by their mothers, including how legacies of historical migration formed the sociocultural context to their experiences of violence and abuse.
>
> (p. 186)

Kelly's book is about sexualized violence against women in both the public and the private sphere. She acknowledges that nearly all women recall at least one incident of intimate intrusion during their lifetime and many report multiple experiences – the most common being harassment. However, in the years following Stanko's and Kelly's books, it has not been harassment and the 'everyday' violences that have been focused on, and it was to be over two decades before they were returned to in any significant way.

Bates – *Everyday Sexism*

In 2012 Laura Bates set up a website and Twitter account (@everydaysexism) to document women's experiences of 'everyday sexism'. By this, she means what she refers to as everyday 'pinpricks' of sexist behaviour – those incidents that, viewed individually, seem too difficult to do anything about – the ones that are not 'serious' enough to be worth causing a 'fuss' about – the ones that seem on their own trivial but together document a significant and sustained attack on women. In her book (Bates, 2014), she writes that within two months of the site launching there were over 1,000 posts from across the world. By 2013, 20 months after its launch, the site had received 50,000 posts. Quite quickly, these included not only examples of sexual harassment deemed not serious, but also examples of serious sexual assaults including rape, often ones that women had not been able to report to the police.

Violence against women in public spaces is endemic across the world. However, the less serious (though more frequent) acts are very rarely reported to the police or anyone else, probably because they are thought to be 'not worth the hassle' or for fear that they would not be taken seriously, nothing would be done about them anyway. In her book on everyday sexism, Bates recounts the steps she found herself taking to try to avoid sexual violence in the street – all to no avail. She gives one example of getting dressed in the morning: she put on trousers with a blouse and a chunky jumper on top instead of the pencil skirt that she wanted to wear because of worries about comments being made by strangers in the street about her breasts and bottom. Bates outlines the steps that she takes day in, day out, to try to avoid being harassed by men on the street. Her work reminds me of my time as a night-shift taxi driver, while studying at college and for my undergraduate degree (as discussed in the Chapter 10). In this position the best-case scenario was that you got to the destination before the customer/s realized you were a woman. This was sometimes possible, through saying very little ('where to?') and by dressing in as unisex a way as possible. In my case, this 'working uniform' consisted of jeans, a black bomber jacket (to bulk myself up and disguise breasts) and a baseball cap with hair pushed up underneath.

In Bates's example, however, even after taking these steps – what Kelly (2013) might include under 'safety work' – she was still harassed. Following on from the previous example in which she purposefully got dressed in a way that she hoped would mean she was not subject to sexual comments, she describes a journey to work on her bicycle when some workmen shouted at her 'Look at those tits!' 'I would'. 'Nice view, love!' 'Alright, darling?' She comments that this was the second day in a row that sexual harassment had ruined her journey to work, and the second day in which she had already been sexually harassed before 8.45am.

At the time Bates wrote her book, 8,000 responses to the everyday sexism website/Twitter feed related to everyday sexism on the street. Many of these recounted multiple incidents – and for some women it was a daily occurrence. Women wrote of daily harassment – getting shouted at, followed, stared at – one woman who posted to the site described it as being like a disease. Another talked of her expectation of being harassed or followed after a night out, and another said her 14 year old thinks that getting whistled at and catcalled on her way to school is just part of life.

According to Kelly, it is this manifestation of power through the 'routine use' of violence and aggression against women that connects to the more 'non-routine' assaults such as rape. In this sense, rape and the 'non-routine' assaults become 'extensions of more commonplace intrusions' (Kelly, 1988: 70).

Elvines – men's stranger intrusion in public space

Elvines (2014) extends the term 'intrusions' to 'men's stranger intrusion', which she thinks is a more appropriate and accurate term than 'street harassment'. She argues that the term 'street' describes men's violences in only one part of public space and that the term 'harassment' can decontextualize, degender and imply a limiting framework. Using accounts from 50 women about men's stranger intrusions in public space (her preferred term to street harassment), she categorizes them into 1) ordinary interruptions; 2) verbal intrusions; 3) the gaze; 4) physical intrusions; 5) flashing and public masturbation; and 6) the experience of being followed.

By 'ordinary interruptions', Elvines means a 'mundane extension of current gender orders' (p. 165), such as wolf-whistles, catcalls, beeping car horns or uninvited greetings. All of the women said that they had experienced this form of intrusion, with many of the examples given occurring on public transport. This is one example (which arguably escalated into verbal intrusion – the next category):

> I was just sat on a train. Minding my own business again, and a guy came up to me and sat down and said 'So what line of work are you in?' And I was like 'Excuse me?' And he said, 'What do you do?' And I was like 'I'd rather not talk to you if that's ok' and he said 'Oh whatever line of work you're in it's a waste of your time'. And I'm like 'What the hell? Who are you?' And he said something about me being destined to work in topless modelling … He was sitting a few chairs down and he slowly moved towards me and then he was sitting right next to me and that's when I was like ok this is very threatening, very late at night. It wasn't an empty train but there weren't very many people and I was going to get off at the last stop so I could be possibly the last one off the train. So I think my initial thing was I'm in trouble and secondly I thought 'Why me? Is it something I'm giving off?' So yeah it does go in that cycle … I think it was his stop eventually. Because he tried to get me to get off at his stop. He was going 'Oh c'mon, just let me take a few pictures'.
>
> *(Delilah, interviewed in Elvines, 2014: 168)*[1]

The category of 'verbal intrusions' is also a broad one, making measuring different practices difficult. Elvines categorized them into three types – sexualized comments, comments commanding happiness in women's demeanour and insulting or explicitly threatening comments. Nearly all of the women (48 women – 96 per cent) recalled at least one form of verbal intrusion, with a quarter recalling experiences of all three. 'Sexualized commentary' was found to be the most common, for example evaluations of women's body parts (primarily breasts, bottom or genitals), or graphic comments intimating sexual relations/inviting sex.

Elvines notes that where this category differs from ordinary interruptions is in the explicit sexual motivation:

> (P)eople saying things like 'Alright Blondie, alright sweetheart' doesn't bother me as much as someone coming up to me and saying 'Nice stockings babe', because there's a totally different tone about it. However I don't know if the men who are saying 'Alright gorgeous' are rapists or might assault me or are being sexually predatory, but contextually I don't see those things as being as threatening as someone talking about my appearance in a different way.
>
> *(Alice, interviewed in Elvines, 2014: 173)*

> I was in [city] after my year abroad I'd just been travelling and I was queuing to buy a tube ticket and this man was standing right behind me and he started whispering into my ear 'You're so sexy. I want to have sex with you.'
>
> *(Kirsten, interviewed in Elvines, 2014: 174)*

By 'the gaze', Elvines means being stared at as a form of intrusion in public space. Women exposed to it might feel they are on a catwalk, as if they are performing when they do not want to, that they are being looked at 'like a piece of meat' and being looked at as body parts rather than as a person. The development of new technologies, for example the ability to easily photograph or film women in public spaces – sometimes known as 'creepshots', where men photograph unknown women in public spaces without their consent, often focusing on breasts or bottoms – has extended the gaze, she argues.

Elvines found that three-quarters (76 per cent) of the women in her sample had experienced at least one physical intrusion including rape, sexual assault, physical assault, unknown men blocking their way, being touched in a sexual way but not being clear if it was an intentional sexual assault. In some of the cases, it was a clear case of assault that could be reported to the police as an incident that could be investigated, but in many others there was a degree of doubt over the sexual intent and/or pinpointing the offender that meant offences were unclear, and went unrecognized and unreported:

> I was in a massive crowd of people because it's like a huge station so you're all like getting off the Tube and in the station, and this guy came up behind me and grabbed me between my legs, like properly grabbed me and I was wearing a skirt and he was right behind me so I couldn't see him and I just felt this person grabbing and it was that thing again of shock, I can't believe someone just did that to me in this crowd of people. Like, how did that happen? And then I turned around and there was this guy behind me, quite short old guy who looked a bit weird. I wasn't even sure it was him because … how do you know?
>
> *(Rosalyn, interviewed in Elvines, 2014: 191)*

> I've had lots of men press themselves into me, loads of times, on the Tube. It's really difficult to tell though. If they get too close I tell them don't do that and they back off but you know some men are really clever, they do that as you're getting on and then they move away.
>
> (New Mum, interviewed in Elvines, 2014: 191).

The physical blocking of women's space, included under Elvines's definition of physical intrusions, is something that was recollected by 32 per cent of the women (note that all of these frequencies could be higher if women had been explicitly asked whether these things had happened – instead Elvines's method relied on their mentioning the subject). Elvines argues that the practice of blocking women's space is something that may be missed if research uses a 'harassment' framing – yet for her, this is where the restriction of women's movements in public space can most literally be seen.

Being flashed and sometimes masturbated/ejaculated at in public was also experienced within Elvines's study – particularly by girls and younger women. For some who were flashed at as girls or young women, this was the first time they had seen a penis. Often this happened in open public spaces or on public transport. However, it also happened on the street, in a swimming pool and, in one woman's case, in Morrison's supermarket on a Sunday morning.

Elvines's sixth and final category is 'being followed'. In some cases women were certain that they had been followed, for example because the man went on to approach them, but in other cases women described the feeling of being followed but could not be sure whether this was an intentional behaviour by the man. This 'maybe he was, maybe he wasn't, you'll never know' situation, as exemplified by the following example, Elvines argues, contributes to the difficulties that women have in making sense and meaning of their experiences:

> [M]e and my sister were getting the night bus home one night and we think quite similarly, and I was convinced this guy was looking over at us and he was and then he happened to get off at the same bus stop as us and so we started walking, we hold hands and stand closer and that kind of stuff and I think I was more panicked than she was but she was like 'Yep ok let's walk faster', and he walked faster. I was convinced he was following us, so I said 'Let's just run, let's run home it'll take five minutes', so we started running and I was wearing these strange shoes and I slipped over in the middle of the road. And this happened like two years ago but I really hurt my hip, I slipped over, went into like the half-splits, ripped this ligament, had to call my dad, and the guy just walked straight on past so he wasn't, maybe he was, maybe he wasn't, you'll never know.
>
> (Bea, interviewed in Elvines, 2014: 201)

Elvines's study adds a great amount of depth to what we know about men's intrusions and uses of violence in public space. Although her work was not set up or sufficient to confirm prevalence, the categorizing, recognizing, naming and reframing of intrusions in public life fills an important theoretical and empirical gap in the knowledge base.

The nature and extent of violence in public spaces

As Elvines (2014) points out, the lack of agreement on naming, defining and measuring street harassment means that it is difficult to make meaningful comparisons across surveys. However, in those studies that do exist, the findings are remarkably consistent – with nearly all women experiencing some form of street harassment and most seeing this as a problem. In this section two surveys are picked as indicative of violence and harassment in public spaces, albeit they suffer from many of the methodological problems already acknowledged.

The study on the largest scale is that conducted by the European Union Agency for Fundamental Rights (FRA), which recently completed an EU-wide survey of violence against women. They interviewed 42,000 women across the 28 member states and describe the overall picture as one of 'extensive abuse that affects many women's lives, but is systematically under-reported to the authorities' (FRA, 2014: 3).

It is difficult to unpick the survey findings that are relevant to violence in public spaces, as the interviewers did not ask a question specifically about it. However, the results from two sections – on non-partner physical and sexual violence and on sexual harassment – can be pieced together to provide some indication of prevalence across the EU. These figures show that:

Of those who had experienced non-partner violence, when asked to think about where the most serious incident took place, 20 per cent of physical violence and 12 per cent of sexual violence happened in the street, a square, a car park or some other public space. A further 1 per cent of physical violence and 6 per cent of sexual violence happened in a park or forest, and a further 4 per cent of physical violence and 8 per cent of sexual violence took place elsewhere outdoors. When added to other public spaces such as cafés, shops, schools, work, public transport, etc. the figures reveal that a significant proportion of non-partner violence – 61 per cent of physical violence and 59 per cent of sexual violence – took place outside the victim's home or someone else's home.

Across all forms of sexual harassment (the FRA measured 11 types), it was found that 55 per cent of women had experienced some form of sexual harassment since the age of 15, and 21 per cent had experienced some form in the last 12 months. Very few women – just 4 per cent – reported the harassment to the police. It is worth noting that these figures do not refer only to violence by strangers in public spaces but also to other forms of sexual harassment including that perpetrated by friends and acquaintances and in the workplace. However, when thinking about the most serious case of sexual harassment the women had experienced, most cited one by someone they did not know (68 per cent).

Considering some of the individual forms of harassment, it is perhaps not surprising to find that some forms of harassment are more closely linked to strangers than others. For example, 83 per cent of indecent exposure (flashing) was perpetrated by a stranger, as was 69 per cent of inappropriate staring or leering and 73 per cent of inappropriate advances on social networking websites. Other categories were more evenly divided across different perpetrator groups. For example, although unwelcome touching, hugging or kissing were most likely to be perpetrated by a stranger, at 33 per cent this was not a marked difference from some other perpetrator types (particularly someone in the employment context or some other known person).

These figures, combined, show that physical and sexual violence and sexual harassment are all common experiences for women – albeit not to the same extent as found in non-survey research such as that by Elvines discussed above. However, what is particularly interesting from the EU study how responses differ, both across the 28 countries and across the entire survey, by educational status and occupational grouping. The survey found that sexual harassment was more prevalent in the occupational groups 'general management, director or top management' and 'professional (lawyer, doctor, accountant, architect, etc.)' – with 75 per cent and 74 per cent (respectively) of these groups reporting having experienced sexual harassment since the age of 15. This contrasts with those who were skilled manual workers, or who had never done paid work (44 per cent and 41 per cent of whom, respectively, had experienced sexual harassment since the age of 15). The FRA interpret this as perhaps owing to the first group of professions' greater exposure to situations where harassment may occur – not just being at work, but related contexts such as travelling to work. Alternatively, they argue that the different prevalences could be linked to level of education and to the varying and subjective meanings of what constitutes harassment and what is unwanted and not tolerated. Also of interest is the finding that the highest levels of sexual harassment were found in Western Europe – including the Nordic countries, which otherwise tend to score highly on some measures of gender equality. Sweden (at 81 per cent experiencing sexual harassment since age 15), Denmark (80 per cent), France (75 per cent), the Netherlands (73 per cent), Finland (71 per cent) and the UK (68 per cent), for example, were all higher than the EU average of 55 per cent. In contrast, Bulgaria had the lowest level (at 24 per cent experiencing sexual harassment since age 15), followed by Romania and Poland (each at 32 per cent). This may be because of true differences in prevalence, or may be attributable to different cultural norms around acceptability, bodily integrity and women in public life, or tolerance levels around terms such as 'offensive', 'unwelcome' or 'intrusive'.

Resistance and shouting back – how can violence in public spaces and harassment of women be ended?

In the UK, policy documents have not tended to organize their discussions around violence in public spaces, instead focusing on what are seen as the most serious forms of violence against women and those that are criminal offences. Hence, rapes that occur in public spaces, harassment that meets the legal definition and acts such as flashing and voyeurism, which are criminal offences, have all had policy attention. However, other forms of violence – those that are seen as more routine and less serious – have received rather less attention. Interventions have therefore been limited to feminist activism – particularly 'shouting back' via online media.

Probably the best example of this is Hollaback (www.ihollaback.org). This is an international, non-profit-making organization and a movement to end street harassment. At the time of writing (July, 2014) it had activist groups operating in 79 cities in 26 countries. On an international level, Hollaback argues that street harassment is simultaneously one of the most pervasive but least legislated-against forms of gender-based violence. It links street harassment to gender – being female – but also to LGBTQ communities. Hollaback argues that it is culturally accepted and rarely reported as it is seen as 'the price you pay' for being a woman and/or gay. Interestingly, the movement also refers to sexual harassment as a 'gateway crime', because it creates a cultural environment that supports the acceptability of gender-based violence. Hollaback challenges this by crowd-sourcing incidents of gender-based street harassment – sharing stories and compiling 'hotspots'. This information is then used to document and name street harassment, to present findings to policy makers, and to create new cultural norms, to show that people are not alone in experiencing street harassment and to 'hollaback' (shout back). Their overall vision is 'a world where street harassment is not tolerated and where we all enjoy equal access to public spaces' (Hollaback website).

Summary

Recent years have seen a resurgence in feminist research and activism around men's violence and harassment of women in public spaces. Recent work has linked these everyday forms of violence and harassment to everyday instances of sexism – demonstrating in practice the UN assertion that violence against women is both a cause and a consequence of gender inequality. As Kelly noted in 1988, and as is still the case today, it is the public, everyday harassment of women that is the most commonly experienced form of violence against women. Although surveys differ in methods and definitions, most show that the majority of women – especially though not exclusively young women – face harassment in their everyday public lives. This makes women change the way they live their lives, with many going out of their way to avoid violence and harassment from men in public spaces. Despite this unequal access to public spaces, there has been minimal legislative and policy intervention on violence and harassment in public spaces. Attention has tended to focus on the most serious offences rather than the most frequent. Instead, creating change on the streets has been mainly landed on the shoulders of feminist activists, through campaigns such as 'Hollaback'.

Note

1   Thanks to Fiona Elvines for her kind permission to reproduce material from her PhD thesis in this chapter.

References

Bates, L. (2014) *Everyday Sexism*, London: Simon & Schuster UK.
Brown, J.M. and Walklate, S.L. (eds) (2011) *Handbook on Sexual Violence*, Abingdon: Routledge.
Elvines, F. (2014) 'The great problems are in the street – a phenomenology of men's stranger intrusions on women in public space', London: London Metropolitan University, unpublished PhD thesis.
European Union Agency for Fundamental Rights (FRA) (2014) *Violence Against Women: An EU-wide Survey – Main Results*, Luxembourg: Publications Office of the European Union.
Herman, J.L. (1981) *Father–Daughter Incest*, Cambridge, Massachusetts: Harvard University Press.
Hollaback (n.d.) 'Hollaback! You have the power to end street harassment', available at www.ihollaback.org/ (accessed 7 October 2014).
Kanyeredzi, A. (2014) 'Knowing what I know now. Black women talk about violence inside and outside of the home', unpublished PhD thesis, London: London Metropolitan University.
Kelly, L. (1988) *Surviving Sexual Violence*, Cambridge: Polity Press.
Kelly, L. (2013) 'Thinking in 10s: what we have learnt, what we need to know and do', inaugural lecture at the launch of the Durham Centre for Research into Violence and Abuse, 16 May 2013, Durham: Durham University.
Marolla, J. and Scully, D. (1979) 'Rape and psychiatric vocabularies of motive', in Gomber, E.S. and Franks, V. (eds), *Gender and Disordered Behavior: Sex Differences in Psychopathology*, New York: Brunner/Mazel, pp. 301–18.
Schneider, M. and Phillips, S. (1997) 'A qualitative study of sexual harassment of female doctors by patients', *Social Science and Medicine*, 45(5): 669–76.
Stanko, E.A. (1990) *Everyday Violence: How Women and Men Experience Sexual and Physical Danger*, London: Pandora.

12
STRANGER AND ACQUAINTANCE RAPE

Stranger rape is generally seen as having the greatest resonance with the 'real rape' stereotype, which feminist activists and researchers have spent much time and energy dismantling. Many feminist commentators have criticized the 'real rape stereotype', in which rapes that fall outside a narrow narrative (e.g. an 'innocent' victim, taken by surprise, who had neither been drinking nor taking drugs, is dressed modestly, has not been raped before and is generally seen as an 'upstanding' member of the community) are seen as something 'other than rape'.

This chapter starts by explaining why feminist researchers have tended to focus more on rape by known men than on rape by strangers. After this, some definitions of rape are considered in relation to perpetrators. Rape and the criminal justice system are then discussed, followed by Diana Scully's theory of why men rape. A selection of policy and practice responses are then outlined – namely Rape Crisis, sexual assault referral centres and specialist Police rape teams. As is the case for some of the other chapters, these responses to rape do not deal solely with stranger and acquaintance rape and can also be involved after rape by partners or family members.

Feminist research on rape

Most feminist attention has not focused specifically on stranger rape, but instead on rape by known men, or on rape and sexual violence more broadly rather than specifically on stranger rape. This probably for the following, overlapping reasons:

a   because stranger rape is and for some time has nearly always been taken more seriously at a criminal justice, media and societal level;
b   in line with this, the mythical excuses for raping women (she must have been 'asking for it', 'what was she wearing', etc.) are less prevalent because stranger rape conforms with the 'real rape' stereotype;

c because in many fields attention and resources have already been allocated to stranger rape (e.g. most police forces will openly say that they allocate significantly more resources to stranger than to acquaintance rape and some academics' work on rape purely or mainly looks at stranger rape without any real acknowledgement that other types exist – this is particularly common in the USA and in the fields of psychology and psychiatry);
d many of the investigative techniques used in stranger rape are based in forensic science, which is not the case for most crimes of violence against women; and
e stranger rape is sometimes seen as associated more with psychopathy than with social learning/feminist theories of violence against women more broadly.

Given this list, it may seem odd to include stranger rape, which I have argued is under-researched by feminists, in a chapter with acquaintance rape, which is an area that has been more subject to feminist scrutiny. This has been done for three reasons: first because this section of the book is on violence in public spaces, and also covers street harassment and workplace violence, meaning that both stranger and acquaintance rape seem to fit better conceptually in this Part of my book than elsewhere in it; second because the gap between what is a stranger and what is an acquaintance is in many cases a muddy one (overlapping with feminist critiques of the term 'date rape'), and there is some evidence to suggest that the more a stranger rapist makes himself an 'acquaintance' (however slight), the more he benefits from the myths and stereotypes associated with women and rape; and third because the police are beginning to recognize this and often now categorize these as two different types of 'stranger' ('stranger 1' – no previous contact and 'stranger 2' – very limited but some contact).

What is stranger and acquaintance rape?

Under the law in England and Wales, rape is rape – regardless of who the perpetrator is. Although the perpetrator's identity (a stranger, a person in a position of trust such as a teacher, a husband, etc.) may be taken into consideration when sentencing, the core definition of rape remains the same. Rape is defined legally as 'A' intentionally penetrating the vagina, anus or mouth of 'B' with his penis, where 'B' does not consent to the penetration and 'A' does not reasonably believe that 'B' consents (paraphrased from section 1 of the Sexual Offences Act 2003). Rape is therefore an act gendered in terms of who can perpetrate it (only men can rape since it requires a penis) but not in terms of who can be raped (since men also have an anus and a mouth).

An offence of similar gravity that is not gendered in this way was introduced in 2004 for the first time under the Sexual Offences Act 2003. 'Sexual assault by penetration', like rape, carries a maximum sentence of life imprisonment but does not require a penis and therefore gender-neutral (either perpetrator or victim could be male or female). This offence includes digital penetration and also penetration using objects such as bottles, etc.

The question of what is a 'stranger' and what is an 'acquaintance' is more complicated than would at first appear. What happens if a person has been texting or instant-messaging someone but they have never met in person? What if the two parties had been in the same nightclub (or festival, say), had made eye contact, had danced and even kissed during the evening but did not know each other's names or anything about the other? Does this make them strangers, acquaintances or even friends? What happens if all of the information a person gives about themselves over a period of time is false – are they a stranger again?

While underlining the fact that 'rape is rape' and there are no 'grades' of rape, the National Policing Improvement Agency (NPIA) (2010) – now the College of Policing – suggest that there are commonly used terms to describe different types of rape offence. They point out that these are not legal terms and are not mutually exclusive. They identify five types:

1   *acquaintance rapes* – where the victim can identify the suspect as someone they know (for example neighbour, friend, person known through dating);
2   *domestic or relationship rapes* – by intimate partner or family members such as siblings, parents or grandparents;
3   *drug-assisted rapes* – which involve the intentional administration of alcohol or drugs to the victim before committing rape;
4   *multiple offender rapes* – as the name suggests; and
5   *stranger rapes* – where the victim is unable either to name or to identify the rapist or where there was only a brief or single encounter so the victim would be able to identify them but would not call them an acquaintance.

Acquaintance rapes therefore occupy a space somewhere between 'stranger' and 'domestic/relationship' rape – depending on the context and the person. A recent inspection of policing found that these terms were being used inconsistently across and within forces, and as such it was impossible to know with any certainty what proportion of cases nationally represents stranger rape (HMIC/HMCPSI, 2012). The Crime Survey England and Wales (formerly the British Crime Survey) would be the obvious next place to look for these figures, but the Crime Survey does not ask about (or at least does not report on) the relationship between victim and perpetrator in sexual offences cases (though it does for non-sexual forms of violence).

Although exact figures are not known, many have emphasized the relative rarity of 'absolute stranger' rapes – in contrast to the media attention given to these crimes. This is backed up by smaller-scale/local research studies. For example, in her study of rapes reported to the police in North-East England, Hester (2013) found that few rapists (only 2) could be classed as 'absolute strangers', though 14 per cent (12 cases) had known the victim/survivor for less than 24 hours – often meeting at a bar or a party. She found that four main groups of cases could be identified, which had different victim and incident features and different patterns of progression through the criminal justice system – acquaintance, historical, domestic violence and 'recent family' (cousin and brother but not historic). The 'acquaintance' group, which she defined as where the perpetrator was known to the victim but was not a partner or a family member, was the biggest (37 per cent of her sample – 32 cases including the 2 strangers).

Rape and the criminal justice system

For all types of rape and other sexual offences, it is now acknowledged that most offences are not reported to the police. Many victims will not tell anyone about their experiences, while others might just anonymously talk about them with volunteers on Rape Crisis helplines. Research shows that a range of personal reasons are given by women for not reporting rape, some of which relate to the criminal justice system (shown in Table 12.1).

In 2012, with Jennifer Brown, I did a survey of 577 women in the general population about their likelihood to report different forms of violence to the police (Westmarland and Brown, 2012). Women in the four police areas we looked at – Northumbria, Cleveland, Durham and Cumbria – said that rape, domestic violence and stalking were extremely serious crimes, but many were reluctant to report these crimes to the police if they should experience them. This was lowest for domestic violence (only 49 per cent across the four areas said that they would definitely report domestic violence if it happened to them) but was also low for rape by someone known to them – 68 per cent said they would definitely report. The figure for rape by a stranger was higher – 89 per cent would definitely report – but this still means that one in ten women were reluctant to report even stranger rape.

When variables such as alcohol are included, or limited interaction with the stranger has happened, often women are even less likely to report. This is demonstrated in some of the most prolific serial rape cases that have come to light.

TABLE 12.1 Reasons for not reporting rape

Personal	Relatedness (loyalty to someone known to the victim)
	Feelings of shame/embarrassment
	Fear of further attack/retaliation
	Belief about own culpability
	Demographic vulnerability (age, class, education, ethnicity)
	Psychological vulnerability (mental health, learning difficulties)
Criminal Justice System	Beliefs about police ill-treatment of victims
	Expectation of ill-treatment
	Lack of confidence about being believed
	Fear of court proceedings

Source: Kelly, Lovett and Regan, 2005

The Savile case, discussed in Part 4 of this book, is one obvious example of how the power accorded to the perpetrator when he was an acquaintance (or maybe more accurately the 'stranger that everyone knew') operated to prevent many women, girls and boys from reporting his behaviour to the police.

Another prolific serial rape case, in which many rapes went unreported despite being by a 'stranger', is that of John Worboys. Worboys was a black-cab driver in London who would claim that he had just won some money and offer female customers a glass of champagne to celebrate with him. The champagne would be mixed with substances that would render the woman unconscious and Worboys would sexually assault or rape her. More than 60 of his 80+ victims did not make a police report at the time – because they were unsure what had happened to them during the journey and perhaps because they were unsure of how the police might respond. These cases show that, even when drug-assisted rape by a stranger is involved, it is still the case that the majority of women did not make a police report.

It is also now widely known that most rapes that are reported to the police do not result in a conviction for rape. This has been borne out by a number of studies since the mid-1990s, which all show the national rape conviction rate, from report to conviction, to hover between the 5 and 10 per cent mark (though with quite considerable variations between forces).

Hester's study (2013) is a useful one to return to because of the distinction she draws between types of rape in terms of relationship to perpetrator. As already mentioned, in her sample of rapes recorded by the police she found that acquaintance rape was the most frequent type. However, when she tracked these cases through the criminal justice system she found that acquaintance rapes were the mostly likely to 'drop out' of the criminal justice system at the police stage and therefore the least likely to lead to CPS charges being brought – with only 12 per cent of acquaintance cases getting as far as the charging stage. This compared with 20 per cent of domestic violence cases and 25 per cent of historical cases. There were not enough 'stranger' rapes recorded to draw useful comparisons.

This all throws doubt on the idea that there is any type of 'real rape' that exists in the stereotypical sense of the term – or that domestic violence rapes are more difficult to prosecute than those involving people not in a relationship.

Theorizing rape – Scully: rape as an act of 'normal deviance'

Diana Scully (1990) developed her theory of rape by interviewing 114 men convicted for rape and 75 men convicted for other offences in the USA. Although this is a very dated study, in a different cultural context and interviewed only convicted rapists, as far as I am aware it remains the largest qualitative study on sexual offence perpetrators that exists from a feminist/socio-cultural perspective (larger studies may exist from a psychological perspective). While not just stranger rapists formed Scully's sample, given that it was an incarcerated sample in the 1980s, the vast majority of them were stranger rapists. Scully's socio-cultural model of rape understands it as an acquired, learned, behaviour, supported by societies and cultural groups in which sexual violence is upheld and women are generally subordinated. She used Mills's (1940) concept of a 'vocabulary of motive' – where people attempt to explain an act in acceptable terms – as the basis of her theory, arguing that:

> [a]n important part of learning to rape includes the mastery of a vocabulary that can be used to explain sexual violence against women in socially acceptable terms.
>
> (p. 98)

Scully thus explains rape in terms of both individual and societal factors; men who rape do so as a low-risk, high-reward 'act of normal deviance' (p. 63) but the 'rewards' vary for different men in different situations.

One of the questions Scully was interested in was, since not all men growing up in rape-supportive cultures use sexual violence against women, whether there was any difference between the convicted rapists and the men convicted for other offences. This is an approach similar to that used in the 2000 Dobash *et al.* men and murder study discussed in Chapter 1 that looked at the differences between men who kill female intimate partners and ex-partners, and men who kill other men. When comparing the backgrounds of the two groups of men (rapists and other offenders), Scully found little difference in family, sexual, psychological and criminal histories. She then moved on to look at men's attitudes to women and was surprised to find how liberal some of the men were in their views on women and equality – again with few differences between the two groups of men. However, when looking more deeply at how this was measured she found that, while both groups of men were relatively liberal on questions relating to equality for women in terms of occupation, pay and education, they were slightly less so on equality in the domestic sphere such as equal rights to family property and income and men's involvement in housework and childcare. However, a third and final dimension revealed a less liberal mindset. Both the rapists and the other offenders tended to put women 'on a pedestal' – they thought that women should be more virtuous than men, need male protection, etc.. Even on the measure of acceptance of personal violence (Scully used Burt's 1980 scale), both groups showed similarly high scores – for example over three-quarters of both groups said that they believed a man should not 'give up' when a woman says no to sex. Similarly, 46 per cent of rapists and 40 per cent of other offenders said a man is justified in hitting his wife, and 45 per cent of the rapists and 40 per cent of the other men believed that some women like to be hit because it means the men care for them. Adding these results together, she found that men who held traditional or hostile attitudes to women, particularly in relation to 'pedestal' values, also tended to condone interpersonal violence in their relationships with women. This was the case for high proportions of both groups, but more so for the rapists. However, Scully does note that the differences were not as great as she expected, and puts some of this down to possible methodological issues. For example, she highlights that, although one group of men had not been convicted for rape, it is likely that a proportion were also sexually aggressive, if not unconvicted rapists.

Most of the stranger rapists were 'admitters' – men who understand the meaning of rape to women and enjoy the fear they cause. Scully found that most (58 per cent) said their original intent had been to commit rape. The others either said that their original intention had been a different crime on its own, e.g. robbery or burglary, or that they had originally intended something else – such as to help fix a car. She notes that in the cases where the original intent had been to rape, the men had spent time planning these offences in advance. These were not spontaneous attacks; there was a plan. When Scully asked the men how they decided who they were going to rape, the most striking commonality was that the victim was 'just there' – going about her day-to-day business, travelling to work, to college or at home. As one man put it: 'Didn't have to be her, she was just there at the wrong time' (p. 175). Some said that they did not even know what the woman looked like because it was dark. Scully concluded that:

> The answer to women who have wondered 'Why me?' is simple – randomness and convenience. For sexually violent men, women are interchangeable objects and one is as good as any other.
>
> *(p. 175)*

There were far fewer acquaintance rapes in Scully's sample because it was a prison sample and because, at the time when Scully was conducting her research in the 1980s, rapes by known men were under-represented in prison populations because women were less likely to report them and subsequently less likely to be believed. Amongst the 'admitters' group were ten men, all of whom were lone assailants. Scully found that the acquaintance rapes were more spontaneous than the stranger rapes – the men tended to start with a sexual interest but no specific intention to rape, then if the woman did not consent to use force. She found that these rapes were not 'gentle seductions' that then overstepped a thin line; one-third of acquaintance rapes involved weapons such as knives from the woman's kitchen. They were also associated with threats and injuries – half of the women sustained serious injuries and one was killed. However, this high incidence of weapon use and injury might be linked to it being a prison sample.

Responses to rape – Rape Crisis Centres

Rape Crisis Centres are the longest-running services for rape survivors in England and Wales, with more than 40 years' experience. They are part of a global movement that provides woman-centred support from a feminist perspective. Most local centres are members of Rape Crisis (England and Wales) and are woman-led, woman-centred, feminist organizations that provide support to women and girls by women. However, they are also part of a global Rape Crisis movement of practice and activism. As well as direct service provision (such as telephone helplines, advocacy, groupwork, counselling) they actively challenge the oppression of women in society, for example by supporting campaigns against the sexual objectification of women and girls (see Jones and Cook, 2008 for an excellent history of the Rape Crisis movement in England and Wales).

In the mid-2000s Rape Crisis Centres in England and Wales faced a major funding crisis. A joint report by the Women's Resource Centre and Rape Crisis in 2008 described one Rape Crisis Centre that receives its annual funding of £77,000 from a total of 14 separate sources. It also described centres with no or few sources of funding, for example one centre that had to close for part of the year because it had no income at all and another with an annual fund of just £306. Nearly seven in ten centres (69 per cent) described themselves as financially 'unsustainable', and nearly eight in ten grants (79 per cent) were for one year or less. Six centres reported situations in which they had not been able to pay their staff but where these staff had continued to work without pay during periods of financial crisis. However, despite this remarkably high level of staff dedication, nine Rape Crisis Centres had been forced to close in the five years between 2003 and 2008. The report concluded:

> While Rape Crisis centres have always been marginalized and suffered from underinvestment, the sector, en masse, is now at crisis point. Any further losses of centres, and their specialist expertise and experience, will, undoubtedly, impact heavily on survivors of sexual violence, their families and society as a whole.
> *(Women's Resource Centre/Rape Crisis England and Wales, 2008: 8)*

Since this crisis, and the media attention that was generated because of it (see for example the series of articles in *New Statesman*), Rape Crisis Centres have become more financially stable than before and more Centres have opened. However, without sustainable long-term funding, most centres' long-term futures remain uncertain.

Responses to rape – Sexual Assault Referral Centres

Sexual Assault Referral Centres (SARCs) are government-funded (and usually - led) centres at which a limited number of counselling sessions can usually be obtained and where forensic medical examinations can be conducted. Before SARCs were introduced, intrusive medical examinations took place in police stations or local hospitals – often in unsuitable rooms. Most SARCs focus more on recent rapes than on adult survivors of child rape/sexual offences and tend not to offer long-term support.

The first SARC in England and Wales was established in Manchester in 1986 within St Mary's Hospital. Known as St Marys SARC, it remains a leading SARC today and has played a key role in the training and development of SARCs in other areas as well as on the national agenda. Today, most police forces either have a SARC within their force area or have access to one in a neighbouring force.

The benefits of a SARC are said to extend to the victim, the health service and the criminal justice system and to include:

- a high standard of victim care, and high levels of victim satisfaction;
- an improved standard of forensic evidence;
- the provision of mental and sexual health services in the SARC increases the likelihood that the client will access the treatment they need and reduces the immediate and future burden on the health service;
- specialist staff, trained in caring for victims of sexual violence;
- the opportunity for victims, if they wish, to access these services as self-referrals, without any involvement from the police;
- the potential to bring more offenders to justice on the basis of better evidence, fewer withdrawals because of better victim care, increased reporting and access to intelligence from self-referrals;
- the development of a centre of excellence and expertise, providing advice, training and support to local health practitioners, police and CPS involved in this work and relieving pressure on police;
- strong links with the voluntary sector, enabling a seamless provision of care for victims and the sharing of information and good practice.

(DoH et al., 2005 and Lovett et al., 2004)

Specialist Police rape teams

Many police force areas have identified that benefits can be gained from having a team of specially trained officers and investigators who are dedicated to rape and serious sexual offences. A specialist team has been defined within a piece of work I did with colleagues as:

A specialist rape team has dedicated, trained staff working together in an integrated way to provide the highest quality victim care and investigative standards. It investigates rape and other serious sexual offences and may also take investigative oversight of other sexual offences. It should have access to an analyst and also play a role in education and prevention. Close partnership working with the Crown Prosecution Service, Sexual Assault Referral Centres, Independent Sexual Violence Advisors, Rape Crisis and other voluntary sector organisations is vital. The team should have strong leadership and coordination. It is not necessary for the team to be centrally located.

(Westmarland et al., 2012)

Based on this definition, in 2012, 44 per cent of forces were found to have a specialist rape team. Some of the benefits of specialist teams have been identified as:

- *improved victim care* – greater consistency, better keeping in touch, procedural justice, victims feeling that their case is a priority, wider understanding of what constitutes 'success';
- *improved investigations* – consistency and continuity, more experienced investigators, better audit and review mechanisms, improved case files for CPS;
- *improved criminal justice outcomes* – higher detection rates, improved rates of conviction on prosecuted cases, more ethical recording, decreased 'no-criming', faster progression through the criminal justice system;
- *improved strategic and operational partnerships* – more integrated working, improved liaison with the CPS, closer working with SARCs; and
- *improved trust in the police* – more rape reports (increased confidence to report).

Summary

This chapter has focused on some of the types of rape not covered earlier in Chapter 3 (sexual violence by intimate partners) and looked at rape by strangers and acquaintances. It has demonstrated how stranger rape has gained a reputation as being easier to report, prosecute and convict for. However, rapes where there has been no previous contact between victims and perpetrators are rare, and in most cases there is some level of acquaintance, however brief, even in rapes classed as stranger rapes. Nonetheless, and despite the additional resources often reserved for undetected stranger rapes, rather than getting a 'gold standard' treatment, still both police reports and responses often vary depending on the circumstances surrounding the rape – for example whether any alcohol or drugs were involved. This means that victim-blaming attitudes (including victim-survivors blaming themselves because of societal responses to women and sexual violence) are evident 'even' in cases of stranger rape.

References

Burt, M.R. (1980) 'Cultural myths and supports for rape', *Journal of Personality and Social Psychology*, 38(2): 217–30.

Dobash, R.E., Dobash, R.P., Cavanagh, K. and Lewis, R. (2000) *Changing Violent Men*, London: Sage Publications.

Department of Health, Home Office, Association of Chief Police Officers and National Institute for Mental Health in England (2005) *National Service Guidelines for Developing Sexual Assault Referral Centres (SARCs)*, London: HMSO.

Hester, M. (2013) *From Report to Court: Rape Cases and the Criminal Justice System in the North East*, Bristol: University of Bristol in association with the Northern Rock Foundation.

HM Inspectorate of Constabulary/HM Inspectorate for the Crown Prosecution Service (HMIC/HMCPSI) (2012) *Forging the Links: Rape Investigation and Prosecution – A Joint Review by HMIC and HMCPSI*, London: HMIC/HMSCPSI.

Jones, H. and Cook, K. (2008) *Rape Crisis: Responding to Sexual Violence*, Lyme Regis: Russell House Publishing Ltd.

Kelly, L., Lovett, J. and Regan, L. (2005) *A Gap or a Chasm? Attrition in Reported Rape Cases*, Home Office Research Study 293, London: Home Office.

Lovett, J., Regan, L. and Kelly, L. (2004) *Sexual Assault Referral Centres: Developing Good Practice and Maximising Potentials,* Home Office Research Study 285, London: Home Office.

Mills, C.W. (1940) 'Situated actions and vocabularies of motive', *American Sociological Review*, 5(6): 904–13.

National Policing Improvement Agency (2010) *Guidance on Investigating and Prosecuting Rape (abridged edition)*, Bedfordshire: NPIA.

Scully, D. (1990) *Understanding Sexual Violence: A Study of Convicted Rapists*, London: Unwin Hyman.

Sexual Offences Act 2003, London: HMSO.

Westmarland, N., Aznarez, M., Brown, J. and Kirkham, L. (2012) *The Benefits of Specialist Rape Teams*, A report commissioned and funded by the Association of Chief Police Officers, Durham: Durham University.

Westmarland, N. and Brown, J. (2012) 'Women's views on the policing of rape, domestic violence and stalking across the North East and Cumbria', Northern Rock Foundation, available from: www.nr-foundation.org.uk/downloads/women%E2%80%99s-views-on-the-policing-of-rape-domestic-violence-and-stalking-across-the-north-east-and-cumbria/ (accessed 7 October 2014).

Women's Resource Centre and Rape Crisis (England and Wales) (2008) *The Crisis in Rape Crisis*, London: Women's Resource Centre.

PART 4
Men's violences in institutions

There were many institutions that could have been the focus of chapters in this Part, and there exist overlaps with some of the other chapters in this book, particularly Chapters 10 (sexual harassment in the workplace) and Chapter 12 (the rape and sexual abuse of girls). Some institutions are intentionally absent because the sexual abuse was largely restricted to children and both boys and girls were abused in similar proportions. For example, in the case of the Catholic Church it is likely that more boys than girls were sexually abused. This is not to suggest that theories of gender, male entitlement and violence against women are irrelevant in these cases, but simply to say that this book is not about the sexual abuse of children nor that of men and boys – it is about men's violence against women. Chapter 13 looks at sexual violence that happens within celebrity culture and how public institutions have been implicated within this – with Jimmy Savile's sex offences being focused on in this chapter. The next chapter (Chapter 14) considers violence against women and girls in institutional care throughout the lifespan – from childhood to old age. Finally, violence against women in higher education institutions is discussed in the last chapter (Chapter 15), where levels of violence and the cultures that surround and support it are discussed.

Writing in 2000 in the *British Journal of Social Work*, Gallagher noted that, while the sexual abuse of children by people who work with them is a major concern among policy makers, practitioners and the public, the knowledge that exists about it is limited. He also noted that such cases were relatively uncommon and constituted a small proportion of all child protection referrals, though those cases that did exist tended to involve large numbers of victims and abusers. Writing today, nearly a decade and a half after that article was published, it is clear that there has been an explosion of disclosures about the sexual abuse of girls and boys in particular, but adults (particularly adult women) as well in some cases. The number of new cases being reported in the media almost on a daily basis feels overwhelming even to me, who has research, policy and practice knowledge of the extent of violence against women and girls.

A similar explosion in reported cases has happened in Australia, where a Royal Commission into Institutional Responses to Child Sexual Abuse was established in 2013. Its focus is on how institutions such as schools, churches, sports clubs and government organizations have responded to child sexual abuse. At the time of writing, the Commission had received over 16,000 telephone calls, over 7,000 letter and e-mails, and held 2,266 private sessions. Due originally to report in 2015, the overwhelming number of people coming forward to give evidence about the sexual abuse they experienced has required a two-year extension (the Commission is now due to report in December 2017). Numerous accounts have been taken of sexual and physical violence against children in children's homes, of boys openly using sexual violence against girls in children's homes but no action being taken by the adults whose job it was to keep them safe, of the Roman Catholic church too often siding with priests who were sex offenders and not taking allegations of abuse seriously. In some cases the institutional child abuse went on for decades. For example, the abuse by employees at the Retta Dixon home is said to have run over nearly four decades (between 1946 and 1980 when it closed). Many of the children abused were 'stolen generations' children who had been forcibly removed from their Australian Aboriginal and Torres Strait Islander families over an approximately 60-year period.

Naming the problem – problems with the term 'institutional child sexual abuse' in the UK context

The naming of acts has always been an important and powerful act within feminism, and it has been particularly important in the area of violence against women. However, naming has also served at times to obscure some forms. In this field, the term 'institutional child sexual abuse' – ICSA – has begun to be used as an umbrella term. This has the benefit of naming the problem, and naming is an important first step to doing something about it and creating change in society. It also has the benefit of recognizing that this form of abuse can and does take place against female and male children. However there are two main problems with this term. First, it hides the fact that most of those directly perpetrating these acts of violence are male – making the problem one with wider and more generic 'institutions' rather than individuals and groups of men using the cloak of organizations to hide and support their behaviour. Second, it obscures the fact that violence within institutions does not happen only to children, it happens to adults as well – overwhelmingly to women. For these reasons, I prefer to talk about men's violences against women and children within institutions. In bringing together the literature for these chapters, it is evident that much of the literature focuses on the sexual abuse of children within institutions. Part of the reason for this is the bias towards concern for children over concern for adult women – which shapes research funding and agendas. Part of this is because so much abuse does happen against children in institutions – with intersections of age, gender, disability, class, sexuality and ethnicity all playing a role in terms of power and inequalities.

There are many barriers to speaking up about violence generally – especially sexual violence – and when this violence takes place within an institution there may be different and/or additional barriers. These additional barriers are discussed in the chapters that follow, and include being afraid of speaking out against powerful men, a deep fear that the speaker will not be believed if the perpetrator is a well-liked figure and the power that perpetrators often have to make things worse for the victim.

A note on men's violences against boys in institutions

Men's violences against boys in institutions are no less horrific than men's violences against women and girls. The damage that one or two men can do to a large number of male children has been evidenced recently very close to me: the police force local to my university – Durham in the North-East of England – has recently been coordinating a large-scale investigation into male violence against boys.

Medomsley detention centre in County Durham has been subject to a major investigation into a group of sex offenders (newspaper reports and some police officers mistakenly call this a 'paedophile ring'), who were sexually abusing boys during the 1970s and 80s. The final number of victims is expected to be more than 500. An investigation by *The Guardian* newspaper found that the man who was probably the most prolific abuser – Neville Husband, who was in charge of Medomsley's kitchens – was raping boys on a daily basis for more than 15 years.

As with the other sections in this book, the focus in this section is on men's violences against women and girls. There is certainly enough violence against boys in institutions to justify a book on that subject alone, and it is a topic that is worthy of more research and academic literature. However, as an academic who specializes in men's violences against women, this endeavour will be left to others who specialize in violence against children and/or violence against men and boys.

Sexual abuse 'scandals'

Greer and McLaughlin (2013) argue that 'scandal news' is important in the UK for a range of reasons. Given the succession of scandals since the 1980s that have exposed the prevalence of sexual violence in care homes, private schools and religious institutions, they argue that it is not possible for British society to deny knowledge of sexual violence against children within institutional settings. They propose a two-phase model of how an ICSA scandal progresses – the latent phase and the activated phase. They argue that the 'latent phase' is when the abuse is known or suspected but remains broadly concealed. While threats might be made to 'blow the whistle', the abuse is still regarded as gossip, rumour, hearsay or speculation. The move towards the 'activated phase' relies on a news organization both knowing about the allegations and making the decision to report them and to name the alleged perpetrator. However, they argue that there are a number of factors that influence this decision and that with modern society's 'data overload' it is by no means inevitable that all sexual abuse scandals will be 'activated'. This theory is considered further in the next chapter, in relation to sexual violence against women within 'celebrity' culture and public institutions.

References

Gallagher, B. (2000) 'The extent and nature of known cases of institutional child sexual abuse', *British Journal of Social Work*, 30(6): 795–817.

Greer, C. and McLaughlin, E. (2013) 'The Sir Jimmy Savile scandal: child sexual abuse and institutional denial at the BBC', *Crime, Media, Culture*, 9(3): 243–63.

13
SEXUAL VIOLENCE, CELEBRITY CULTURE AND PUBLIC INSTITUTIONS

This chapter looks at how celebrity culture and institutions (primarily the BBC and some hospitals) have acted as a protective 'bubble' around a number of very-high-profile male public figures. It is important to note that a chapter on this topic would not have been on anyone's radar just a few years ago, and this is an area of violence against women that is still being analysed and understood. As such, much of the information cited within this chapter has been sourced from official investigations rather than academic papers. Given the centrality of Jimmy Savile and the fact that he is the focal point in most of the official investigations, it is on Savile that most of the chapter focuses. There are a huge number of official reports and investigations that have reported or are ongoing – as of 2013 there were 14 major inquiries open and a large number of smaller reviews (Gray and Watt, 2013). Much of the knowledge about other offenders does not come from official investigations but only from media reports. At the time of writing, only one academic paper had been published (Greer and McLaughlin, 2013) – and this focused more on the theory of 'scandal' than on Savile's offending.

The sex offender Jimmy Savile

Children's entertainer, radio and television DJ, and charity fundraiser Jimmy Savile has emerged as one of the most prolific sex offenders known to the police. The news that he had sexually abused girls and young women first emerged when five women were interviewed in a documentary to be shown on ITV1 ('Exposure: The Other Side of Jimmy Savile'). As often happens when women speak out about sexual violence publicly, their accounts were immediately doubted and challenged by many – there was heavy media coverage on the day the story broke before the documentary, which all focused not on the abuse that was claimed but on the question 'Did it happen at all?' The backlash against the women was particularly strong, since Savile had died and therefore was not able to defend himself against the allegations. This added fuel to the 'Why didn't they say anything when he was alive?' line of questioning. However, these voices soon dissipated as more and more women, and men as well, came forward to testify to the abuse they too had endured from Savile. As with the rest of the book, this chapter mainly focuses on the sexual abuse of women and girls, though this is not meant to deny in any way the abuse by Savile faced by men and boys.

The investigations that have been published to date have found that Savile sexually assaulted people aged between 5 and 75 across 28 hospitals during decades of 'unrestricted access' – including staff and patients, adults and children. There is a high probability he also sexually assaulted corpses in the Leeds General Infirmary mortuary. Of the offences reported to the police, nearly three-quarters – 73 per cent – of Savile's victims were aged under 18 at the time of the offence – most were female (82 per cent) and most were aged between 13 and 16 (Gray and Watt, 2013).

In time, as the investigation widened its scope, others came forward to say that they too had been abused by celebrities – sometimes linked to Savile, sometimes with no link. At the time of writing, over 600 allegations have been made against Savile and other celebrities – many working for the BBC at various times. The Metropolitan Police set up a special investigation – Operation Yewtree – to look into the allegations. This wider investigation is discussed later in this chapter after I have looked at the specific Savile investigations. –Savile's abuse was subject to three NHS investigations – at Broadmoor Hospital, Leeds General Infirmary and Stoke Mandeville – in response to the ITV1 'Exposure' documentary (considered later in this chapter). This is not to suggest that offending was limited to these NHS sites (less formal investigations are taking place at 31 other hospitals), but rather that these were identified as locations where a long and sustained pattern of assaults seem to have been committed because of the odd and presumably unprecedented access that he was granted to these institutions. This chapter focuses on the investigation at Broadmoor, given the particularly unusual access he was given there and the links to government minister Edwina Currie.

Broadmoor Hospital

One of the highest-profile investigations has been the one into his activities within Broadmoor Hospital, which spanned almost four decades (1968–2004). His officially sanctioned access to this place seems to have been particularly odd given the high-security nature of the hospital. Broadmoor Hospital (previously Broadmoor Criminal Lunatic Asylum) is a high-security specialist psychiatric hospital – one of three in England – but probably the most publicly well-known owing to some of its notorious residents (including 'the Yorkshire Ripper' Peter Sutcliffe, Charles Bronson and Ronald Kray).

In November 2012 an independent investigation was commissioned by the West London Mental Health NHS Trust board and the Department of Health, to review and investigate a number of matters (including past and current complaints of sexual abuse but also Savile's fundraising activities, compliance with policies, access privileges, etc.). Dr Bill Kirkup was appointed as the lead investigator in the Broadmoor investigation and separate lead investigators were appointed for Leeds General Infirmary and Stoke Mandeville Hospital (these three independent investigations and 31 smaller investigations were all overseen by Kate Lampard). The official report (Kirkup and Marshall, 2014) found ten allegations of sexual assault and one of indecent exposure to a minor linked explicitly to staff and patients in Broadmoor. However, it is likely that other assaults also happened on Broadmoor premises as the report adds that Savile used his Broadmoor-provided accommodation and caravan to 'entertain' a regular stream of female visitors that were not patients. The report also notes that until the late 1980s female patients were required to strip completely to take baths and change into nightwear and they would be watched by staff. Savile would sometimes watch this and make 'inappropriate remarks' about the female patients, though no staff or patient made a complaint about this – understandable given his position of power within Broadmoor.

Of course, it is Savile who is responsible for his offending – he is the one who made the decisions to act in the ways that he did. For that there can be no excuses made. It is also true, though, that certain people and institutions did support and make easier his sexual offending over the years. For example, the official report found that the Hospital's culture played a significant role in supporting Savile's abuse: 'the institutional culture of Broadmoor at the time strongly discouraged both groups from reporting' (p. 4).

The official report seems to delineate other forms of sexual violence, sometimes using euphemisms such as 'flamboyantly inappropriate' in the following extract, to suggest that his behaviour was uncomfortable, though not 'sexual violence' in itself, as long as it was not linked to children:

> Savile's general behaviour toward women was often flamboyantly inappropriate, including extravagant forms of greeting, inappropriate remarks and physical contact. Many women were uncomfortable with this and found him objectionable, but they thought at the time that it was part of his public act, 'just Jimmy' ... Department of Health officials were aware of his general reputation for leading a promiscuous lifestyle, but there was no suggestion then that this involved anyone underage.
>
> (p. 4)

Likewise, while allegations of sexual assault (ten) and indecent exposure to a minor (one) are quantified and named using criminal law terms, the finding that Savile would watch female patients bathing and make inappropriate comments, while condemned in the report, was neither identified as sexual violence nor named using the appropriate criminal law term: voyeurism.

It is clear within the report that Savile had significant power in Broadmoor, including a direct managerial role, and was a leading member of the Broadmoor task force. However, knowledge of Savile's unusual position and power within Broadmoor was not kept within the walls of Broadmoor, and the government's ministerial lead Edwina Currie met Savile, at his request, when she visited another hospital. Savile reported to Currie that he had witnessed a range of cases of fraud within Broadmoor, and said that he intended to use this knowledge to gain union support. Although there is no evidence that this fraud took place or that the threats were taken to the union, it appears that his position within Broadmoor was not questioned. Indeed, in notes from a meeting between Savile and Currie dated 15 September 1988 (Appendix 2A (iv) of official report) paragraph 8 states:

> If you would like a purely personal point of view I would say that he was 100 per cent sincere and committed in his desire to improve the management of Broadmoor and the lives of its patients, and it is his burning ambition to do so.

The 9th, and final, paragraph simply states:

> You might have warned me of his penchant for kissing ladies full on the mouth ....

'Mistakes were made'

The HMIC also conducted a review into the allegations that were made against Savile during his lifetime. They boldly titled their report 'Mistakes were made' (HMIC, 2013) in recognition of the mistakes made by the police and their concern that so many victims felt unable to report their experiences to the police at the time. In particular, the HMIC review was tasked with looking explicitly at which police forces received reports at the time regarding Savile or other men investigated by Operation Yewtree, whether any such allegations were robustly investigated and whether police failings were evident.

The Inspectorate found that seven incidents involving Savile had been reported to police forces in his lifetime. Two of these were intelligence records (an entry on the Metropolitan Police Service Paedophile Unit and a computerized record of an anonymous letter received by the Metropolitan Police) and five victims complained to three separate police forces that they had been indecently assaulted by Savile. HMIC found that some of the intelligence and early reports were restricted because of Savile's celebrity status, and that meant that forces investigating later allegations were not able to 'join the dots' and realize the severity of the pattern of abuse. Because of this, HMIC concluded, 'the potential for further investigation and a prosecution of Savile was missed' (p. 7). Even where some of the dots were joined, for example when three women unknown to each other all made allegations against Savile to Surrey Police, the victims were not made aware that it was not just they who had been assaulted:

A recurring theme was the isolation that each victim felt as a result of believing that she was Savile's only victim. At the heart of the matter in these cases lies the decision of the police not to inform victims that others like them existed.

(p. 7)

One of the reasons why this was so important was that one of the previous victims, who reported in 2003 that she had been sexually assaulted in 1973 by Savile at the BBC TV programme *Top of the Pops*, had been happy to make a police statement but had indicated that she was not willing to support a prosecution unless other victims were subsequently identified.

Silencing of victims' voices at the time of the offences

In 2013 the NSPCC held a series of focus groups with victims who had since come forward and reported abuse from Savile. The groups focused on why they had not feel able to report the abuse at the time. In their report *Would they actually have believed me?* (NSPCC, 2013), the authors explain that while some of the children immediately recognized that what Savile had done to them was abuse, for others this was more unclear – sometimes owing to their age at the time of the abuse and their limited knowledge of sexual behaviours. Most had not told anyone at the time about the abuse they experienced, but where disclosures had been made at the time (to hospital staff, friends or family), some recalled their allegations being laughed off or minimized. The key reason for not telling anyone about the abuse was that they did not think they would be believed – hence the title of the report. The victims not surprisingly felt helpless and inferior to Savile, who was a powerful and influential adult known for his high-profile charity fundraising. Sometimes children felt guilty – as if the violence was 'their fault' – and some did not want to be labelled as an 'abused child'. None of the focus group participants who were abused as children said they had considered reporting to the police – as well as the feelings of blame, guilt and shame, they saw the police as part of the adult world and did not realize that as children they could report something to the police.

As well as looking at the factors that prevented victims from being able to report to the police, the NSPCC also looked at what enabled or encouraged them to make a police report to Operation Yewtree. While support from friends and family was important, none of the participants said they would have made a police report had they not seen the stories of Savile's other victims in the press. As well as wanting to receive some formal recognition of the abuse they had experienced from Savile, they also felt that it was important to speak out in order to support and corroborate the experiences of those who had already done so. In this sense, some felt they had a 'duty' to report. For example, where they had overheard people being made out to be 'liars' or 'out for money', they feared how they would in turn be treated but simultaneously wanted to speak out in support.

The participants' experiences of making police reports were largely positive, with many commenting that they had not expected the police to take their reports as seriously as they did. However, there was a high degree of inconsistency in the police responses. Some who reported were given crime reference numbers, others not, some were told how to re-contact officers, others were not, and some were invited into the police station or officers came to their home to give full and signed statements, while others just had their verbal accounts taken down over the phone. The NSPCC conclude that this made some participants question whether their experience was counted within the reported figures and whether the police 'cared' about the abuse that they had experienced, in comparison with how others had been treated.

Operation Yewtree

Operation Yewtree is the police investigation into sexual abuse by Jimmy Savile and others. At the time of writing, Operation Yewtree was ongoing. Allegations of sexual violence had been made against a number of male celebrities, including Freddie Star, Gary Glitter (real name Paul Gadd), Dave Lee Travis (former BBC Radio 1 DJ), Rolf Harris, Stuart Hall, Max Clifford, Jim Davidson, Jimmy Tarbuck, Paul Gambaccini (BBC broadcaster), Chris Denning (former BBC Radio 1 DJ) and, most recently at the time of writing, Cliff Richard.

Other forms of violence against women and girls within celebrity culture

Some forms of abuse were not directly sexual, but were probably sexually motivated. In her column in *The Observer*, Radio DJ, TV presenter and journalist Lauren Laverne wrote about her experience of being bitten by Rolf Harris. She explains that she was interviewing Rolf Harris for TV when instead of shaking her hand he pulled her towards him and 'grizzled' into the side of her neck. She recalls pushing him off, making light of it and continuing with the interview.

> I remember it as icky, nibbly. Very beardy. But mostly I remember it as unremarkable. And that's a problem – the problem when it comes to the media at that time. It's not just that he bit me – it's that neither I nor anyone else around me thought much of it when he did.
>
> *(Laverne, 2014)*

She goes on to write that this was far from the worst experience in her career, and she is not even sure whether that was her worst experience that week. This, of course, is characteristic of this level and nature of abuse – because it is happening so frequently in so many forms that makes it difficult to 'pin down', to complain about, to name. How do you start to report to the police something that is being done on such a regular basis by such a large number of men? Have the police on speed dial? Have a daily 'check-in' with them for any incidents that happened over the last 24 hours?

The role of the BBC

The BBC became implicated in the Savile sexual violence case when it was claimed by the *Sunday Mirror* that BBC *Newsnight* had recorded, then decided not to air, evidence that Savile had sexually assaulted girls and young women in the 1970s. The first media outlet to specifically run with detailed evidence of Savile's attacks was ITV, which broadcast a programme called 'Exposure – the Other Side of Jimmy Savile' in which they ran interviews with three women who detailed what Savile had done to them. However this programme also pointed the finger at the BBC. Greer and McLaughlin (2013) delineate the three main allegations against the BBC as:

> a) sexual assaults by Savile and other celebrities had taken place on BBC premises;
> b) Savile's sexual depredations were 'common knowledge' in the BBC, but nothing was done to protect teenage girls from victimization; and
> c) Newsnight had been blocked from broadcasting the allegations.
>
> *(p. 252)*

Based on their theory of how an institutional sex abuse scandal progresses, it was the viewing of the 'Exposure' documentary that Greer and McLaughlin define as progressing the situation from 'latent' to 'activated' (as explained in the introduction to this Part of this book) – since this brought the abuse out in the open and forced reactions from those surrounding the case.

The erasure of women and girls from narratives of Savile's offending

Two things are strikingly absent from much of the reporting of Savile's offending – adult women, and the gendering of children. This is consistent throughout the official reports, the media reports and the limited academic literature.

It is worth at this stage reminding ourselves who was abused – according to the Operation Yewtree report, 73 per cent of the 450 people who came forward specifically in relation to Savile were children aged under 18 at the time of the offence, and 27 per cent were adults. The oldest adult to report abuse by Savile to Yewtree was 47 at the time of the offence. At Leeds General Infirmary, his oldest living victim was 75 at the time of the offence (age of bodies in mortuary not known). The vast majority of the victims recorded in the Yewtree report were in the 13–16 age group, and 82 per cent were female. The Leeds report states that most of the victims were in their late teens and early 20s – and that more adults than children were abused (Proctor *et al.*, 2014). Despite these figures, the problem is consistently described as one of child sexual abuse. This is not just a linguistic issue – it is one that has potentially led to the silencing of adults, predominantly women, speaking out about the abuse they might have experienced. This is perhaps particularly ironic given that the joint Metropolitan Police and NSPCC report was entitled *Giving Victims a Voice*. Below are just a small number of examples of the erasing of adult women and the gendered pattern of Savile's offending from the media picture:

- Continued reference to the National Association for People Abused in Childhood (NAPAC) and the National Society for the Prevention of Cruelty to Children (NSPCC) as the sole referral routes for victims and witnesses of Savile's abuse. Women and girl's groups and specialist sexual violence services such as Rape Crisis Centres or Sexual Assault Referral Centres (SARC) were not mentioned in any of the reviews or press releases I read for this chapter.
- The Operation Yewtree Stakeholder group did not have any representatives from women's and girls' organizations or the specialist sexual violence services (instead, NSPCC and NAPAC were the two NGO members).
- The Yewtree report uses 7 of its 38 pages to outline advances made in child protection legislation and sexual offences against children. There is no similar outline of offences against women, or against adults generally. Even where the Sexual Offences Act 2003 is mentioned the report states that it was introduced to 'update the legislation relating to offences against children' (Gray and Watt, 2013: 33).
- Rape Crisis have received reports of sexual offending by Savile from women who had not felt able to make reports to Yewtree (personal communication with Rape Crisis (England and Wales).

In their academic analysis of 'scandal', Greer and McLaughlin label the Savile case an 'institutional child sexual abuse' (ICSA) scandal. Although they do name the victims as 'teenage girls', in repeatedly calling this 'child abuse' they make invisible the experiences of those over the age of 18.

Summary

Failing to situate the offending of Savile and those around him within a culture of male sexual entitlement and sexual violence more generally is to miss the wider implications of, and lessons that could be learnt from, that offending. Failing to align it with other offences against women and girls and to look at it through its links with violence against women as a cause and consequence of women's inequality is to fail to understand how institutional cultures are gendered. Labelling Savile and the other Yewtree offenders as institutional child abusers is to divorce sexist culture from sex offending, and to view the problem solely as one of child abuse rather than one of gender inequalities. Institutional sexism within large institutions, and the overlaps this has with sexual harassment, need to be brought back into the picture in order to understand sex offending within institutions.

References

Gray, D. and Watt, P. (2013) *Giving Victims a Voice – Joint Report into Sexual Allegations Made Against Jimmy Savile*, London: Metropolitan Police and NSPCC.

Greer, C. and McLaughlin, E. (2013) 'The Sir Jimmy Savile scandal: child sexual abuse and institutional denial at the BBC', *Crime, Media, Culture*, 9(3): 243–63.

HMIC (2013) *'Mistakes Were Made': Hmic's Review into Allegations and Intelligence Material Concerning Jimmy Savile between 1964 and 2012*, London: HMIC.

Kirkup, B. and Marshall, P. (2014) *Jimmy Savile Investigation: Broadmoor Hospital – Report to the West London Mental Health NHS Trust and the Department of Health*, London: West London Mental Health NHS Trust.

Laverne, L. (2014) 'How Rolf Harris bit me and got away with it', *The Observer*, 20 July 2014.

NSPCC (2013) *Would they Actually have Believed Me? A Focus Group Exploration of the Underreporting of Crimes by Jimmy Savile*, London: NSPCC.

Proctor, S., Galloway, R., Chaloner, R., Jones, C. and Thompson, D. (2014) *The Report of the Investigation into Matters Relating to Savile at Leeds Teaching Hospitals NHS Trust*, Leeds: Leeds Teaching Hospitals NHS Trust.

Sexual Offences Act 2003, London: HMSO.

14
INSTITUTIONAL ABUSE IN RESIDENTIAL CARE

This chapter considers some of the abuse that girls and women may face throughout their lifespan if receiving some form of residential care in homes or systems. There are a range of possible forms and institutions, and the focus here is restricted to girls in the looked-after system, adult women in mental health care and older women in residential care for the elderly. The reason for looking across the lifespan is that these forms of abuse are not usually considered together. Rather, the abuse of girls is named 'child abuse', and the abuse of older women is called 'elder abuse' – meaning that the gendered and institutional links throughout the lifespan are often rendered invisible.

Girls in the looked-after system – residential children's homes

Recent decades have seen a considerable decline in the use of children's residential care homes, with family placements (e.g. fostering and adoption) now seen as a more professional and appropriate way of providing state care for children (Berridge et al., 2012). However, in the 1970s residential children's homes were a common way for a local authority to look after children who could not be cared for by a parent – either on a short-term or long-term basis. Despite this decline, it remains the case that around 15 per cent of looked-after children have lived in a residential placement at some point (Department for Education, 2011), many of whom have been moved there from home or foster care because of challenging behaviour (Berridge et al., 2012). The Department for Education (2011) found that over 40 per cent of children enter care because of abuse and neglect – and note that this figure is likely in reality to be much higher because of the high likelihood of undisclosed abuse. It is, in part, the high levels of abuse already experienced by looked-after children that make the abuse they sometimes suffer in residential care homes of even more concern. One example of the way children in residential care homes have been targeted by predatory males is the recent revelations about sexual exploitation in Rotherham.

Sexual abuse of girls in Rotherham

In 2014 it was revealed that at least 1,400 children in Rotherham had been sexually abused, some had been raped repeatedly and many of those who spoke out about their abuse did not have their reports appropriately acted upon (Jay Report, 2014). The Jay Report into child sexual exploitation in Rotherham has a wider scope than just looked-after children, although it is clear that residential children's homes were one of the places being targeted for sexual exploitation of children. The report notes that from the mid-1990s onwards, staff in some residential units felt overwhelmed by the problem of sexual abuse of the young women in their care. Jay notes that while some children were exposed to sexual exploitation for the first time when they entered children's homes, in other cases the situation was more fluid, with children having been exploited beforehand and that exploitation continuing or even increasing once they went into children's homes. She is bold in her criticisms of the local authority's lack of responses at the time:

> There was no appropriate management response to the problem of children being exposed to exploitation whilst in the care of the Council. Nor did we find that elected members as corporate parents were advised of the scale and gravity of the problem.
>
> *(p. 53)*

Unfortunately, many have pointed out that Rotherham was not a unique situation, and that there were many locations where this level of abuse and agency inaction took place.

Sexual abuse in Nottingham Children's Services

In 2014, actor Samantha Morton spoke out about the sexual abuse she had experienced and been aware of more broadly when she was in residential care in Nottingham. In a newspaper report in *The Guardian*, she describes the abuse as 'rife' within Nottingham Children's Services (Hattenstone, 2014). She recounts one incident in which she was abused by two men when she was 13 years old, but her police records describe the abuse as 'frolicking' rather than detailing her allegations, and no formal investigation was undertaken at the time despite the reports she made both to the police and to social services. Morton was speaking out on the back of the news breaking about the levels of sexual exploitation in Rotherham and the publication of the Jay Report, in order to raise awareness that widespread sexual abuse was happening in other areas too, and further investigations might be needed. She estimates that around 90 per cent of her friends from children's homes were abused, though not all of this abuse was perpetrated by members of staff. In her *Guardian* interview she says 'a lot of people who abused my friends were people in very, very top jobs within the social services. Nottingham in the '80s was rife with that.'

Responses – public inquiries

In 2009, the Time to be Heard forum was established in Scotland to listen to survivors' experiences of abuse while they were in care. This forum heard from 98 adults about their experiences of abuse as children while in one children's home – known as The Orphan Homes of Scotland and later Quarrier's Homes. Following this, a National Confidential Forum was rolled out across the whole of Scotland. Northern Ireland has a similar process ongoing – the Historical Institutional Abuse (HIA) inquiry. In both Scotland and Northern Ireland, public apologies have been offered to victims.

Responses – mandatory reporting of abuse of children?

When cases such as those discussed above come to light, many suggest a shift towards mandatory reporting of the sexual abuse of children as a possible response. In the UK, with the exception of Northern Ireland, it is currently not a requirement to report crimes against children, even sexual abuse, to the police. However, there does exist in England a statutory requirement under the Children Act 2004 to work together to safeguard children in order to keep them safe. This requirement covers teachers, GPs, social workers, etc. The main way this safeguarding is meant to happen is through the effective sharing of information – between professionals and with the area's local safeguarding children board (LSCB). However, given that covering up sexual abuse has now been found to have been prolific in local authorities in the 1980s, calls have been made to strengthen this requirement, and even to introduce a specific criminal offence of covering up, concealing or ignoring known child abuse.

Although this sounds like a useful approach in theory, there exist concerns that in practice it would reduce reports because it could create a culture in which speaking out about violence and abuse was even more dissuaded than it is now, because of the actions that would follow disclosures.

Adult women in mental health care

In 2002 ReSisters – a women and mental health action group in Leeds – conducted research to find out about women's experience of using mental health services in Leeds. They interviewed 87 women and found high levels of domestic violence, sexual abuse and sexual assault. Around three-quarters of the women had experienced at least one of these, and most linked their mental distress to their experiences of violence. Many of the women identified other issues of oppression that had affected their access to services as well as gender, including race and culture, age, disability and sexuality. The women described feeling not properly listened-to, not being respected or worthy of self-determination, and not being given the dignity of someone trying to understand why she is/was experiencing mental distress.

The focus of this chapter is on sexual violence experienced *within* institutions, and the ReSisters research is one of the few studies to consider this. Seven of the women in their research talked about being raped and sexually assaulted within the mental health system – by male workers (including GPs and male nurses) and by other service users. One woman described how she was assaulted while at her most vulnerable. She had taken an overdose and her GP went to her home, where he asked her to get undressed and then sexually assaulted her and attempted to rape her. Another described how she feared she would not be believed and felt that she would not have been attacked if she were not mentally ill:

> I was so distraught. I didn't have the confidence to complain – I couldn't believe it, so who'd believe me? He was a nice, amiable nurse that everyone liked.
>
> *(Woman interviewed by ReSisters, 2002: 31)*

Another piece of research – this time a 1998 survey by the BBC in South-West England – found even higher levels of sexual violence against female psychiatric patients. They reported that 49 per cent of the women who replied to their survey had been sexually abused (it is unclear what definition was being used), 16 per cent had been touched inappropriately and 6 per cent said they had been forced to have sex. Sexual violence was more common from patients than from staff (40 per cent compared with 21 per cent). However, it is unclear what the overall sample size was in this research since the report states that 404 questionnaires were sent to women in psychiatric wards but not how many questionnaires were returned. There is very little research on this topic, and it is an area that would certainly warrant further investigation.

Older women in residential care homes for the elderly

There is very little knowledge about violence against older women in care homes, particularly in the UK. Most of what is known comes from media reports, documentaries or from international research. The most comprehensive research report was published in 2014 by researchers in Australia, and the project – 'Norma's project' – was started directly in response to the sexual assault of the mother of one of the authors while in respite care in an aged care facility (Mann et al., 2014). For the purposes of this chapter I am going to focus on the sections of their report that discuss sexual violence against women in institutional or organizational care (what they call the 'aged care sector', which includes residential aged care and hospitals), though their report considers sexual violence against older women more generally.

They found a range of examples in which women had been abused sexually in the aged care sector – on some occasions by women but most often by men. In one of the examples in their report they cite a woman whose 86 year old mother was being showered by a man who sexually assaulted her, made sexually offensive comments and asked 'vulgar' questions. When she went to the management of the residential aged care home they agreed not to allow a man to shower her again, but seemingly took no further action. No official report was ever taken, and the woman felt that she had let her mother down, saying 'I wish I could have protected her better from this horrible experience' (family member of woman abused in rehabilitation centre, in Mann et al., 2014: 29).

In another example, a sexual assault worker recounted how a woman in her nineties suddenly became very unwell and confused. She reported to the nursing home manager that a man had come into her room in the night and raped her. The woman was taken to hospital where it was found that she had a urinary tract infection, and it was while she was in hospital that a nurse rang the sexual assault service. When the sexual assault worker and their specialist doctor went to visit the woman they found she had factures of both hips, which was consistent with someone lying on top of her. The sexual assault worker concluded that, while there was no identification of an offender, the woman probably had been sexually assaulted. However, this was not a view that was shared:

> [The nursing home] didn't even think of it as a possibility; they only thought, 'Oh, she's confused'.
> *(Sexual assault service worker talking about woman abused in residential aged care, in Mann et al., 2014: 31)*

Mann *et al.* conclude that the social context and how ageing bodies are understood is central to understanding the limited or inappropriate responses from many service providers. If older bodies are seen as asexual or as censored this means that both people in the wider community and service providers can fail to connect older people with sexuality generally, let alone sexual assault. They found that respondents talked about a general reluctance from service providers to see older women as attractive or sexual, and that providers tended to link sexual assault with sex rather than with power. One participant who worked in an aged care service summed up this attitude as 'Well, you know, she's not a very attractive older woman, why would you, why would anyone want to do that to her?' (in Mann *et al.*, 2014: 32).

Remembering past abuse can be confused with dementia, and this was a major theme within this study by Mann *et al.* – a diagnosis of dementia was used by some as a way of avoiding and denying abuse. Reports of current abuse were explained away as the recollection of past abuse, for example in childhood. While it is of course possible that past trauma could and does resurface during later life, the fact that some were not even considering the possibility of current abuse was problematic.

Institutional structures and managerial cultures emerged as important in the research by Mann *et al.*, as has been found with other forms of institutional or organizationally supported abuse. In Australia as in the UK, there has been a move towards private, for-profit ownership of care organizations, and Mann et al. argue that this has contributed towards the vulnerability of older women. In their research some of the respondents from sexual assault services pointed to untrained staff being asked to carry out intimate work such as washing people, and of trying to cover up stories of sexual assault and other maltreatment in order to uphold the reputation of the facility. Rumours had been heard that sex offenders who were prevented from working with children because of child protection procedures had instead turned to working in aged care facilities. A culture was reported of poor organizational responses linked to people, but also a lack of protocols, policies and codes of conduct in relation to sexual violence and sexual expression more generally.

Rosen et al. (2010) have argued that it is fellow residents who present probably the greatest threat of sexual aggression against older people. They name this 'resident-to-resident sexual aggression', or 'RRSA' and define it as:

> sexual interactions between long-term residents that in a community setting would likely be constructed as unwelcome by at least one of the recipients and have high potential to cause physical or psychological distress in one or both of the involved.
>
> *(p. 1970)*

They point out that this form of abuse has the potential to cause great harm and is also potentially fairly common within nursing homes, yet there has been remarkably little research on it. They go so far as to describe it as 'virtually unstudied' (p. 1971), finding only eight research studies internationally that focus directly on this form of abuse.

Their research consisted of a review of these eight research studies. They offer some preliminary findings in terms of risk factors for 'resident-to-resident sexual aggression', though note again the limited number of studies and the fact that many are based on small numbers of case studies. As risk factors for perpetration, they list cognitive impairment (including dementia and hypersexuality), and sexual predators who may also be registered sex offenders. They cite a US government report (United States General Accounting Office, 2006) that found that a minority (3 per cent) of nursing homes that received Medicare and Medicare funds housed at least one registered sex offender in 2005, but note that this figure will certainly be higher given the variability of whether nursing homes are told about sex offenders and whether this information is shared by management with all staff. As risk factors for victimization, Rosen et al. list being female, having a physical impairment, and/or having a cognitive impairment such as dementia.

They conclude that research is needed to provide guidance for physicians, administrators and staff on how to prevent or manage resident-to-resident sexual abuse. They point to the gaps in research, and suggest that, although it is a challenging topic to study, the priorities should be around qualitative research to understand the full spectrum of this type of abuse, and on the development of measurement tools to identify incidence, prevalence and outcomes, and that can be used to identify risk factors.

Ramsey-Klawsnik et al. (2008) also provide evidence that there exists a group of sexual predators who target elderly individuals residing in care facilities. As part of a wider study into sexual abuse against adults over the age of 18 living in care facilities, they investigated sexual violence perpetrators who had targeted adults aged 60 or over living in elderly care facilities in five North American states over a five-month period in 2005. All of these states had policies around mandatory reporting of suspected abuse of older people in care facilities. Data collected included survey data on all cases completed by trained representatives in the five states, a random file review to check accuracy and follow-up qualitative telephone interviews with a sub-sample from each state.

Of the 119 alleged perpetrators identified, most were male (78 per cent), with a mean age of 56 but a broad range between 19 and 96 years old. In contrast to Rosen et al. (2010), Ramsey-Klawsnik et al. found that in the USA it is staff rather than other residents that constitute the largest group of abusers of older residents. Facility residents were the next largest group (a close second), with family members of the victim and other visitors to the facility also reported as perpetrating sexual abuse. Not surprisingly given the sample characteristics, the victims tended to be aged between 60 and 101 with a mean age of 79. Again, most were female (77 per cent). Nearly two-thirds of the victims had an Alzheimer's-type dementia, nearly half required assistance in all activities of daily living and a range of disabilities were listed (in descending order – cognitive, psychiatric, physical, developmental and sensory). The nature of the alleged acts of abuse varied, and those most frequently alleged were (in descending order) fondling/molestation, inappropriate interest in body, vaginal rape, sexualized kissing, unwelcome discussion of sex topics, attempted vaginal rape, digital penetration and harmful genital practice.

Interviews with the alleged perpetrators were conducted in nearly two-thirds of the cases (63 per cent), and three-quarters of those interviewed denied the allegations. Some offered explanations for the allegations while saying the act(s) had not been abusive, some admitted the sexual contact but said it was not abusive and one accused the alleged victim of 'improper behaviour'. Out of the whole sample of 119 alleged sex offenders, only 1 was arrested. In this one case, the perpetrator was a member of staff accused of anal rape with an object (which resulted in the tearing of the victim's rectum) and harmful genital practices. Although the perpetrator admitted bruising the victim's genitals, the case was substantiated only for physical and emotional – not sexual – abuse.

The researchers found widespread disbelief of victims from staff, and a failure to follow procedures and be respectful when investigating allegations of sexual violence. While many of the victims had significant disabilities including communication limitations that might have reduced the chances of a successful prosecution, they note that others did not, and could have been quite able to communicate with investigators. They also raise concerns about offenders with criminal records, including sometimes for sexual assault, receiving no additional supervision. They conclude 'When a sexual perpetrator with access to vulnerable elders in a care facility remains unidentified, the risk to all in the facility is very high' (Ramsey-Klawsnik *et al.*, 2008: 372). They also recommend that closer scrutiny of criminal records and employee references, and skilful interviewing should take place, both of potential staff and of residents.

Summary

This chapter has shown that, from birth until death, some girls and women who use residential state care of different types face sexual and physical abuse. Sometimes this is directly perpetrated by staff and volunteers within the care system and sometimes it is perpetrated by other residents. In some cases the perpetrators come from outside the care system, but the abuse is condoned, hidden, ignored or otherwise brushed under the carpet – for years or even decades. What makes this abuse particularly difficult is that is it often perpetrated against those who are at vulnerable stages in their lives, and may already have a history of sexual abuse being perpetrated against them by a partner or family member.

References

Berridge, D., Biehal, N. and Henry, L. (2012) *Living in Children's Residential Homes*, Bristol: University of Bristol.

BBC (1998) 'Abuse rife on mental health wards – claims survey', BBC News, 27 November 1998, available at http://news.bbc.co.uk/1/hi/health/223343.stm (accessed 19 December 2014).

Children Act 2004, London: HMSO.

Department for Education (2011) *Children in Children's Homes in England Data Pack*, London: Department for Education.

Hattenstone, S. (2014) 'Samantha Morton: Rotherham brought back memories of my own sexual abuse', *The Guardian*, 12 September 2014.

Jay, A. (2014) *Independent Inquiry into Child Sexual Exploitation in Rotherham 1997–2013 (The Jay Report)*, Rotherham: Rotherham Metropolitan Borough Council.

Mann, R., Horsley, P., Barett, C. and Tinney, J. (2014) *Norma's Project: A Research Study into the Sexual Assault of Older Women in Australia*, Melbourne, Australia: Australian Research Centre in Sex, Health and Society, La Trobe University.

Ramsey-Klawsnik, H., Teaster, P.B., Mendiondo, M.S., Marcum, J.L. and Abner, E. L. (2008) 'Sexual predators who target elders: findings from the first national study of sexual abuse in care facilities', *Journal of Elder Abuse and Neglect*, 20(4): 353–76.

ReSisters (2002) *Women Speak Out – Women's Experiences of Using Mental Health Services and Proposals for Change*, Leeds: ReSisters.

Rosen, T., Lachs, M.S. and Pillemer, K. (2010) 'Sexual aggression between residents in nursing homes: literature synthesis for an underrecognized issue', *Journal of the American Geriatrics Society*, 58(10): 1970–79.

United States General Accounting Office (2006) *Long Term Care Facilities: Information on Residents Who Are Registered Sex Offenders or Are Paroled for Other Crimes*, GAO Publication No: GAO-06-326.

15
VIOLENCE AGAINST WOMEN IN HIGHER EDUCATION INSTITUTIONS

Although a much debated topic for several decades in the USA and Canada, higher education establishments in the UK have been slow to recognize and act on violence and abuse on campus. This chapter sets out the available evidence – drawing heavily on the findings from the National Union of Students' (2010) *Hidden Marks* survey, and also Phipps and Young's (2012) work on 'lad culture'. Approaches to highlighting the problem and reducing violence on campus are then considered, focusing on the 'It Happens Here' campaigns and Bystander Intervention programmes.

The *Hidden Marks* survey – the nature and extent of violence against female students

In 2010 the *Hidden Marks* study into more than 2,000 female students' experiences of harassment, stalking, violence and sexual assault was published by the National Union of Students (NUS).[1] The authors concluded that violence in college and university settings is commonplace, with many women struggling to complete their studies without coming into contact with some form of violence or harassment. This is demonstrated in Table 15.1 which shows, for example, that one in four women had been sexually assaulted, and over two-thirds had experienced verbal or physical sexual harassment.

The form of violence that women students were most likely to experience therefore was verbal and physical harassment. The survey asked about experiences such as 'someone making sexual comments that made them feel uncomfortable' and 'someone wolf whistling, catcalling or making sexual noises at them'. Most often these acts occurred in social spaces around the university, but in a significant minority of cases (16 per cent) they had occurred in a learning environment including libraries and lecture theatres. More than one in ten students said they had

TABLE 15.1 Experience of harassment, stalking, violence and sexual assault by female students

Type of incident	% of respondents
Control over course choice	2
Control over finances	2
Serious sexual assault	7
Less serious physical violence	8
Serious physical violence	11
Stalking	12
Less serious sexual assault	16
All physical violence	21
All sexual assault	25
Verbal and physical harassment on campus (sexual harassment)	68

Source: (NUS, 2010: 11)

felt uncomfortable within a learning environment because of comments being made that had a sexual overtone, and this was even more common outside learning environments (one in five in student unions and one in three in the university and college environment more broadly). In some cases these sexual comments were made by staff as well as students. For example, one student told of a lecturer joking about how to cover up spiking a drink with a rape drug, and another who showed a picture of a former student and said he fantasized about what could have happened between them.

On a different but connected note, the US website 'Rate my Professor' has been criticized for putting a chilli pepper as a 'hotness' (previously called 'sexiness') rating and for allowing some sexualized comments about (predominantly) female professors. The UK version – 'Rate my lecturer' – does not offer the 'hotness' rating and has not yet come under fire for sexualized comments but has relatively small popularity compared to the US site. However, 'Rate my Professor' can and does show UK lecturers who have been allocated 'hotness' ratings.

Partner violence against students at university

Most of the attention on violence against women students tends to be focused on sexual assault and on violences in public spaces, but universities are also a place at which young women might be entering into their first serious long-term relationships and even moving in with partners. Where this is the case, female students tend to report more repeated forms of violence and abuse. One of the students that was quoted in the *Hidden Marks* survey said that during her first and second years at university she experienced a range of acts of physical violence, including being choked, by her now ex-partner.

Rape and other serious sexual offences

The *Hidden Marks* survey asked students 'Whilst you have been a student at your current institution, have you ever had sexual intercourse when you didn't want to because you were, or felt, unable to say no?' Among responses, 8 per cent of women said that they had, and a further 3 per cent said they were unsure. Many 'unsure' responses had links to alcohol, with comments such as the following being added:

> What if you were absolutely hammered, don't remember anything but when you 'come round' someone is having sex with you? What does that count as?!

Drugs and alcohol, administered in different ways, were a factor associated with many of the rapes and serious sexual assaults more generally. Nearly one in ten said that they had been given alcohol or drugs before an assault and another one in ten said they were not sure. Some of the women talked about confusion about what had happened and therefore being unclear what they would tell the police. For example, one woman who thought she had been raped after having her drink spiked with Rohypnol had not reported it to the police because she was not absolutely sure that her drink had been spiked. On reflection, she noted: 'In retrospect I know something was put in my drink but I now feel it to be too late to do anything. I wish I would have known how to react at the time' (student quoted in NUS, 2010: 18).

The role of 'lad culture'

Phipps and Young (2012) were commissioned by the NUS to look at campus culture and the experiences of female students – especially the role of 'lad culture'. They define 'lad culture' as a form of masculinity – a cultural or subcultural practice that can be engaged in by men and/or women. They describe its key characteristics as being young, hedonistic, objectifying women, holding 'politically incorrect' views and 'having a laugh'. Furthermore, they emphasize its links to 'raunch culture' – the hyper-sexualized culture that objectifies women (women themselves might do this) and is linked to the mainstreaming and normalizing of the sex industry and sexual violence. Phipps and Young highlight alcohol and sport as major threads that link 'lad culture' to universities – a prime example of this being initiation to sports teams that often require high levels of alcohol consumption to demonstrate one's ability to be 'one of the lads'. They also highlight, more broadly, that we have very little UK-based research on university culture, and much of our academic knowledge base comes from studies of campus culture in the USA.

Phipps and Young also found a lack of support for women following violence, with around a third telling no one about their experience – not even their friends. Even in the case of serious sexual assault, only one in ten reported the assault to the police and nearly half told no one.

Perpetrators of violence against female students

The *Hidden Marks* survey found that most of the perpetrators of stalking, sexual assault and physical violence were men already known to the women. Often these were students studying at the same institution as the woman – although physical violence was split more evenly (just 48 per cent of perpetrators were students).

Policy and practice responses

Despite the relative lack of research into violence against women in higher education institutions in the UK, there do exist some responses – though these are mainly at the stage of raising awareness of the problem and very early stages of policy development. It is true to say that the higher education sector in the UK is far behind the USA and Canada in this area, which countries have been forced to address sexual violence on campus (in particular) for several decades now.

'It Happens Here' campaigns

Before an institution can even begin to create changes in responses to violence against female students, it needs to acknowledge the scale of the problem within its facilities. This might sound obvious, but in higher education particularly there exist a lot of competitive league tables that universities take very seriously. As well as the 'best university' type of guides – which often comment on crime rates in the vicinity – there even exists a standalone 'safest university campuses' league table. These league tables affect student choices and hence university finances. It is partly because of this that many colleges and universities have been loath to admit the levels of violence (particularly sexual violence) that exist – preferring to ignore its existence as far as possible.

It is because of this refusal to take violence against women seriously that 'It Happens Here' campaigns have been established. The first was run at Oxford University.

The 'It Happens Here' campaign has three programmes of work: education, advocacy and outreach. One of its earliest and most visual education methods was the production of a short film (available from its website – see the box on the following page for URL) that has pictures of students holding up signs stating some facts about sexual violence, and pledging to end the silence and work together to have conversations that have been neglected in order to ensure that everyone in Oxford is safe and respected. One of the other powerful things the campaign does is to publish anonymous survivor stories on their website of sexual violence that has happened while at Oxford. These stories include examples of problematic police and college actions, of confusion about what counts as rape, of students being forced to have sex by partners and even of one young woman who was anally raped while in Oxford attending her interview for admission. When she was offered the place she turned it down. Following the launch at Oxford, students at

> **It Happens Here – About us**
>
> We are dedicated to raising awareness about sexual violence and working with members of the University of Oxford and the wider community to ensure that Oxford is a safe place for all people.
>
> Anyone can be a survivor or a perpetrator of sexual violence. People of all genders, sexual orientations, races, cultures, religions. Undergraduates, postgraduates, university staff. Anyone.
>
> We believe that it's time for all of us to join together and say that sexual violence will not be tolerated in our community. That we will support survivors. That we will educate ourselves about consent. That we will create a culture free from damaging myths. That we will make here a place where change happens.
>
> www.ithappenshereoxford.wordpress.com

Durham University have also established their own 'It Happens Here' campaign. On their website they reinforce the words of the Oxford University campaign, stating 'We experience the same problem. We feel the same pain. We are equally committed to fighting sexual violence and we are here to say that IT HAPPENS HERE, too' (http://ithappensheredurham.wordpress.com).

Improving policy and support

One of the key recommendations in the NUS *Hidden Marks* survey was that institutions should have an institution-wide policy to tackle violence against women, which would set out the measures the institution would undertake to tackle violence against female students. The survey's authors suggest that by working together in a coordinated way, institutions and students' unions could reduce levels of violence and harassment, ensure that women receive the support they need, and encourage higher reporting rates. The following list is what they suggest the policy should:

- set out how the institution and the students' union will develop and implement activities to change attitudes and raise awareness of violence
- enable students and staff to recognize and deal effectively with violence against and harassment of female students
- discuss how to best utilize peer support in tackling violence and harassment
- contain plans for improving campus design and security so as to help students feel safe
- outline how the institution will work with relevant agencies to ensure that students access the support services that they need
- contain steps explaining how reporting will be encouraged and

- set out how the institution will respond to violence against women perpetrated by its own students.

Four years on from the publication of *Hidden Marks*, however, it is unclear whether any university or college has actually written or adopted such a policy (although some are thought to be 'in development'). In their research on university responses to forced marriage and violence against women in the UK, Freeman and Klein (2012) also considered institutional responses to be lacking – finding that the 'institutional response' often boiled down to the expertise and commitment of individual staff members. They argue that there needs to be a shift in perspective and that higher education institutions need to be more than sympathetic to students disclosing violence against them – they need to go further than this and see a contribution to intervention as part of an institution's core responsibility. The first step, they argue, is for higher education institutions to recognize that violence against women is something that directly affects their own students. Just as fire, building safety and public health considerations are core responsibilities, the ability to provide a safe and supportive learning and teaching environment is reliant on being willing and able to recognize and intervene in cases of violence against women (Freeman and Klein, 2012).

While senior staff at higher education institutions have been slow to act, students have been organizing on a policy front, with many university student union bars passing motions to ban the playing of the Robin Thicke song 'Blurred Lines' (or showing of the video). As of late 2013, the *Guardian* newspaper reported that more than 20 student unions had banned the song, condemning it for its degrading lyrics such as the lines 'I know you want it' and 'I'll give you something big enough to tear your ass in two' (*Guardian Music*, 12 November 2013).

Bystander intervention programmes

Bystander intervention programmes were developed in the USA and are beginning to get more popular and widespread in the UK. At the time of writing, two universities in England (Oxford through its 'good lad' programme and the University of the West of England's Intervention Intitative) are known to have programmes running, though there may be more and the idea is far more widespread in Scotland, where Scottish Women's Aid have partnered with Scottish NUS to roll out a programme across Scottish universities and colleges.

The Intervention Initiative at the University of the West of England (UWE) consists of eight facilitated one-hour sessions. It aims to empower students to act as pro-social citizens, to prevent sexual coercion and domestic abuse in a university setting (Fenton *et al.*, 2014). It aims to take students from understanding what bystander intervention means in a general sense towards feeling confident about their ability to intervene in a range of different situations. The resource is free for anyone to use, and is currently being evaluated (see www1.uwe.ac.uk/bl/research/interventioninitiative.aspx).

Summary

This chapter has shown that a range of violences against women are prevalent on university campuses, from a range of perpetrators including other students. 'Lad culture', a subculture at best tolerant and at worst actively supportive of male violence against women, is common in universities, and particularly linked to sport and alcohol. However, student-led campaigns such as the 'It Happens Here' campaign, and staff, student and voluntary-sector bystander intervention collaborations are working to try to counteract some of this culture: both its denial (university level) and its acceptance/promotion (lad culture and rape culture) of violences against women on campus.

Note

1   Thanks to NUS for their kind permission to reproduce material for this chapter.

References

Fenton, R.A., Mott, H.L., McCartan, K. and Rumney, P. (2014) *The Intervention Initiative*, Bristol: UWE and Public Health England, available from: www1.uwe.ac.uk/bl/research/InterventionInitiative (accessed 7 October 2014).

Fisher, B.S., Cullen, F.T. and Turner, M.G. (2000) *The Sexual Victimization of College Women*, Washington, DC: US Department of Justice.

Freeman, M. and Klein, R.C.A. (2012) *University Responses to Forced Marriage and Violence Against Women in the UK: Report on a Pilot Study*, London: London Metropolitan University.

Guardian Music (2013) 'Robin Thicke's "Blurred Lines" gets banned at another university', *The Guardian*, 12 November 2013.

National Union of Students (NUS) (2010) *Hidden Marks – A Study of Women Students' Experiences of Harassment, Stalking, Violence and Sexual Assault*, London: NUS.

Phipps, A. and Young, I. (2012) *That's What She Said – Women Students' Experiences of 'Lad Culture' in Higher Education*, London: NUS.

AFTERWORD – ON OUTRAGE

The pages of this book are filled with the outrageous treatment of many women and girls at the hands of some men. Reading the inquiries that showed how many people looked away from Savile's sex offending, watching the film in which Banaz Mahmod begged the police to help her and then watching her body being pulled out of a shallow grave in a suitcase, reading the examples of sexism, violence and harassment that are posted to @everydaysexism on an hourly basis – it is easy to become all-consumed and overwhelmed by men's violences. I have been involved in research, policy, practice and activism in the area of men's violences against women for 15 years – not as long as some others in the field – but I have felt immersed in this outrage for much of that time. I feel outrage not just at the men who commit these acts against women, but also – sometimes actually more so – against those who have the power to intervene, to make a real difference, to do right, yet fail to do so. Those who watch and do nothing are condoning men's violences and upholding the structures that systematically discriminate against women.

It is important to hold onto outrage not only about men's violences but also about sexual discrimination. It is easy when reading about fatal violence against women, about rape by partners, about the sexual abuse of elderly women in care homes, to put issues like equal pay, access to childcare and an end to discrimination against lesbian women on the back burner – to deal with 'later'. But these issues and more, just as they were for the 1970s women's liberation movement conferences, remain the pillars of sexual discrimination against women, and the structures that condone and allow male violence against women to continue.

Globally powerful institutions have accepted the feminist understanding of men's violence against women as being explicitly linked to sexual discrimination against women and girls worldwide. The United Nations and the World Health Organization, for example, both now understand violence against women to be a cause and consequence of women's inequality. To increase women's equality and to empower women is to shake the groundworks of men's violences against women. This is why campaigns against sexism are as important in the quest to end men's violences against women as direct campaigns against violence.

I have always been an optimist. It is hard to stay optimistic when faced with this level of outrage, but I do believe that there is nothing about men as a group that makes them innately violent, apart from their male privilege. I believe men's violence is condoned on an individual and structural level and that gender inequality is too often dismissed as something that is not an issue for Western women in the 21st Century. And this does mean that I believe that men's violences are not inevitable, and can be challenged, and can be vastly reduced. I do not think that all violence, or even all partner violence, would be eliminated in a gender-equal world – I think both men and women would misuse other forms of power including ethnicity and class (though these are likely to look radically different without gender inequality), and would continue to use violence against others. But I do think that gender would not be an organizing and permissive structure for that violence, and that there would be a reduction of all forms and an elimination of some (such as female genital mutilation).

This book has focused on men's violences against women in England and Wales. Amplified to the global scale, there are even more violences happening against women and girls than have been covered in this book. Elsewhere in the world, there are even more reasons for outrage. As individuals – as women and as men – we have differing abilities to act on such outrage. We have different opportunities at different points in our lives to speak out about men's violences against women. We need to commit to doing what we can, when we can, to act on our outrage, to make visible the connections, and to refuse to see men's violences against women as inevitable.

INDEX

adolescent: violence to parent 52, 54, 57–9 *see also* parent abuse
alcohol 15, 32, 56, 77, 97, 133–4, 140, 166, 170; abuse 16
Anti-social Behaviour, Crime and Policing Act (2014) 66–7
arranged marriage 61–3, 72, 77

Bail Act, The 44
bail decisions 15, 36; Clough, Jane 29, 36–7
Banaz – a Love Story 77
BBC 147–8, 151–3, 159; Savile scandal xviii, 135, 143, 147–154, 171
behaviour patterns 2–3, 5, 12, 51, 63
Black and Minority Ethnic communities (BME) 2, 3, 5–6, 48–9, 68, 76, 99, 111, 134, 145, 158, 172; Asian xvii, 5–6, 49, 64, 76, 81, 91; South Asian 10, 23, 40, 49, 62; Black xvii, 2, 5, 6, 10, 48–9, 68, 70, 76, 91, 99, 122 *see also* refugee and asylum seeking women
bystander intervention programmes 164, 169

celebrity 147, 150–2
ChildLine 95, 98, 100
child safeguarding 16, 44, 65, 158
Children Act (2004) 158
children's homes 144, 156–8
Children's Services 16, 27, 157
Clare's Law 20; Wood, Clare 27; '*right to ask, right to know*' 27

coercion 39–40, 47, 62–3, 66, 69, 108, 169; behaviour 3–5, 15; internalising 34; reproductive 30, 34
coercive control 3–5, 15, 30, 39–42, 45
control xvi, 3, 5, 12, 23, 30, 34, 39–41, 43, 51–3, 55, 62, 68, 77, 86, 95, 100, 122, 165; lack of 12, 53; of clothing 23, 26; over parent 51
Counting Dead Women v–vi, 17–18, 55–6
Crime and Security Act (2010) 26
Crime Survey for England and Wales 21–2, 53–4, 94, 133
criminal charges, fear of 58, 65
Criminal Justice and Public Order Act (1994) 33
culture and tradition xviii, 47–9, 62, 68, 84, 86, 89, 168; 'death by' 48, 76; as oppression 49, 159; victims of 48, 78

disability xvi, xvii, 11, 23, 31, 53, 61, 99, 107, 111, 145, 159, 162
disbelief 31, 134, 151, 162
domestic homicide reviews (DHRs) 14–16, 18
domestic violence 134, 158, 169; awareness 15; term 2; definitions 2–5, 47, 52–3, 54; impact of 25; practitioners 27; services 30; *see* partner violence *and* parent abuse
Domestic Violence, Crime and Victims Act (2004) 14, 45
domestic violence disclosure scheme *see* 'Clare's Law'

domestic violence perpetrator programmes (DVPPs) 20, 24
domestic violence protection notice (DVPN) 26
domestic violence protection orders (DVPOs) 20, 26

elder abuse 53, 57–9, 156, 159–63
economic abuse *see* financial abuse
equality xiv, xvii, xviii, 40, 56, 110; gender xv, 118, 128–9, 154, 172
ethnicity 5–6, 145 *see also* BME communities
Everyday Sexism xviii, 129; campaign 117–18, 120, 122–4, 171
'everyday' violence 103, 107, 120

Family Law Act (1996) 45
family, prevention from contacting 22, 25, 40, 43
family violence xvii, 17, 21, 47, 49–50, 72–3; incest 58, 97–8; prevalence 54
Female Genital Mutilation Act (2003) 83, 87
female genital mutilation/cutting (FGM/C) xviii, 2–3, 5, 17, 47, 81–91; death by 82; perpetrators of 88–9; types 82
femicide 9, 103, Montréal massacre 9
feminist theories xv, 81, 89–90, 111, 120–1
financial abuse 3, 22, 26, 39–43, 45, 61
firearms 12, 13–14, 18
forced marriage xviii, 2–3, 5, 47, 61–70, 74, 85, 169
Forced Marriage (Civil Protection) Act (2007) 64, 66
Forced Marriage Protection Order (FMPO) 65–7
Forced Marriage Unit (FMU) 63–5
Foundation for Women's Health Research and Development (FORWARD) 82–4, 90

gender xv, xvii, xviii, 2–3, 5, 40, 47–9, 51–8, 63, 69, 73, 76, 89, 105, 107, 111, 116, 118, 120, 124, 128–9, 132, 143, 145, 153–4, 156–8
gender politics 49

harassment 25, 39, 40–5, 103, 108, 128–9, 154, 164, 168; 'everyday' 120; sexual, definition 108; sexual, effects 116; street 104, 124–7; workplace 107–118, 127
Hidden Marks survey 164–9

higher education establishments 32, 143, 164–70
Hollaback xviii, 129
homicide: domestic/partner 1, 9–18, 36, 42, 57, 72–4, 136; familial 55, 68–9 *see also* 'honour' killings
'honour' 61, 84; -based violence (HBV) xiv, xviii, 2–3, 17, 47–9, 68–9, 72–8; codes of 48
'honour' killings xviii, 72–8; Ahmed, Shafilea 69; Mahmod, Banaz 72, 76–8, 171 *see also* Banaz – a Love Story; Naz, Rukhsana 75–6; Yones, Heshu 75–6
human rights 61–2, 86–7, 89–90; Universal Declaration of Human Rights (1948) 61; Human Rights Act (1998) 68

Imkaan 68
immigration and controls 40, 61, 67–8, 70
indecent exposure 128–9, 149
Independent Domestic Violence Advisors (IDVAs) 39, 44–5, 65
Independent Police Complaints Commission (IPCC) 9, 13–14, 16, 77–8
Independent Sexual Violence Advisors (ISVAs) 65, 139
injunctions *see* restraining orders
International Day of Action to End Violence Against Women 26–7
'intersectionality' 49
Iranian and Kurdish Women's Rights Organisation (IKWRO) 72–5, 78
Istanbul Convention, The xvi
'It Happens Here' campaigns 164, 167, 170

'Justice for Jane' 36–7; Clough, Jane 29, 36–7

Karma Nirvana 66, 69
killing of women: *see* Counting Dead Women
Ki-moon, Ban xv

lad culture 164, 166, 170
Legal Aid, Sentencing and Punishment of Offenders Act (2012) 36
lesbian xiv, xv, 49, 111, 129, 168, 171
'life space' 39, 41

male violence: excusing 48, 72, 75; organised xiv
marriage: consent 62–3, 69; definition 61; love 62–3

mental health 15, 55–6, 156, 158–9;
  ReSisters 158–9
micro-regulation 40–2
Ministry of Defence 113–14
Mirabal, Project 24; six measures of success 24–5
misogyny 9, 56
multi-agency working 15, 44–5
Murder in Britain Survey 11

Napo 42–3
Nia 18
NSPCC 95, 99, 151–2, 154; 'underwear rule' 99

online threats 105
oppression xvi, xvii, 40, 49, 73, 90, 122, 138, 158
outrage 171

parent abuse 2, 47, 51–9, responses 56–7
partner violence 1, 3, 20, 53, 68, 165: criminal offences 22; physical forms 20; sexual 29–37, 68; statistics 20–2; under-reporting of 21
patriarchy 56, 73
police: College of Policing 133; failings xvii, 16, 72, 77–8, 90, 150, 167; poor responses 6; recording 94, 140; reporting to 27, 57, 74, 94, 116, 123, 125, 134, 150–2, 166; sexual harassment/violence 103, 108, 110, 112–18; specialist rape teams 131, 139; training 74–5, 78, 139
pornography 29, 35, 95, 109
probation 42, 44
prostitution xiv, xix, 30, 104; children abused through 95
Protective Orders 32–3
Public Order Act (1986) 22, 42

racism xvii, 6, 49, 76, 107, 113, 122 *see also* BME communities
rape xiv, 12, 23, 31, 117, 124, 128, 133, 143, 159, 166–7, 170; acquaintance xviii, 32, 35, 103, 132–3, 137; attempted 33–4, 111, 159, 162; child 30, 35, 93–6, 138, 157; date 132; definition 132; drug-assisted 133, 135, 165–6; familial xviii, 47, 57, 77, 93–101, 133; known men 32; linked to murder 36; 'perfect' 32; pregnancy 97; 'real' 31–2, 131; stranger xviii, 32, 35, 103, 131–7, 140; types of 31; within marriage 29–30, 32–3

Rape Crisis Centres 32, 35, 99–101, 131, 137–9, 154
refugees and asylum seeking women xvi, xvii, 5–6, 40, 49, 85
refuges xvii, 11, 13, 40, 86
religion 31, 48–9, 68–9, 76, 82, 84, 143–4, 168
residential care: institutional abuse in 156–163; Nottingham 157–8; Rotherham 157
restorative justice 100–1
restraining orders 39, 43, 45
Rights of Women (2010) 109–10

self-harm 78, 97
sentencing 4, 24, 31, 34, 36, 43–5, 66, 69, 77, 83, 97, 132
sexism 49, 55–6, 108–9, 112, 118; 'everyday' xviii, 117, 122–3
sexual abuse: child 94–7, 101, 143–4, 154, 156–8; in mental health care 158–9; Retta Dixon Home 144; 'scandals' 145, 147–50, 154; stolen generations 144
Sexual Assault Referral Centres (SARCs) 99, 131, 138–40, 154
Sex Discrimination Act (1975) 108–9
sexual harassment *see* harassment
Sexual Offences Act (2003) 30, 94–6, 132, 154
sexual violence 21, 72, 117, 125, 164–7; adult survivors of child 35, 94, 97, 99–101, 138; culture of 154; during pregnancy 36; marginalising 58–9; normalizing of 104; partner criminal offences 20, 22, 29–30, survivors of 26, 31–2, 35, 41, 133, 137–8, 140, 159, 167–8
sibling abuse 52–3, 96, 133
smartphone 'apps' 41
Southall Black Sisters 68, 70
'space for action' 25, 39–42, 45
Specialist Domestic Violence Courts (SDVCs) 39, 44
stalking 21, 39, 42–4, 134, 164–5, 167; Dando, Jill 42; legal reform 43–4
stereotyping 18, 31–2, 40, 49, 76, 131–2, 135
stranger homicide xix, 10, 17
substance (mis)use 12, 15, 32, 55–6, 97, 140, 166
suicide 10, 32, 69, 74, 83; fear of 57

taxi drivers 103, 108, 112, 116, 123
technology enabled abuse 39, 41

tradition *see* culture and tradition

United Nations Declaration on Violence against Women xv
United Nations Women 103

victim blaming xiv, 40, 75, 140
victimization 6, 11, 26, 30, 35, 48–9, 93–4, 116–7, 153, 161
video games 104
violence against men xvii, xviii, 1, 10, 73, 145
voyeurism 95, 129, 149

weapons 10, 12, 20, 22, 25, 41, 69, 137 *see also* firearms

Westminster Parliament 103, 108, 110, 112, 114–15
Women's Aid 2–3, 18, 41, 169
women of colour 49; marginalising of 49; *see also* racism *and* BME communities
workplace bullying xviii, 107, 110
World Health Organisation (WHO) 10, 82, 86, 171; guidelines on violence against women (2013) 29

Yewtree, Operation 148–54
Youth Rehabilitation Order (YRO) 57